WHOLEHEARTED
LIVING

Other Books by Jennifer Grant

Love You More: The Divine Surprise of Adopting My Daughter
(Thomas Nelson)

MOMumental: Adventures in the Messy Art of Raising a Family
(Worthy Publishing)

*Disquiet Time: Rants and Reflections on the Good Book by the
Skeptical, the Faithful, and a Few Scoundrels* with Cathleen Falsani
(Jericho Books)

WHOLEHEARTED LIVING

FIVE-MINUTE REFLECTIONS
FOR MODERN MOMS

Jennifer Grant

LOYOLAPRESS.
A JESUIT MINISTRY
Chicago

LOYOLA PRESS.
A JESUIT MINISTRY

3441 N. Ashland Avenue
Chicago, Illinois 60657
(800) 621-1008
www.loyolapress.com

Scripture quotations taken from various editions are indicated within the text as follows:

CEB, Common English Bible, http://www.commonenglishbible.com/home;

ESV, The Holy Bible, English Standard Version® (ESV®), copyright © 2001 by Crossway, a publishing minist_y of Good News Publishers;

GNT, Good News Translation in Today's English Version-Second Edition, copyright © 1992 by American Bible Society;

KJ21, 21st Century King James Version of the Holy Bible, http://www.kj21.com;

MSG, The Message, copyright © 1993, 1994, 1995, 1996, 2000, 2001, 2002, NavPress Publishing Group;

NASB, New American Standard Bible,® copyright © 1960, 1962, 1963, 1968, 1971, 1972, 1973, 1975, 1977, 1995 by The Lockman Foundation;

NCV, New Century Version®, copyright © 2005 by Thomas Nelson, Inc;

NET, New English Translation, NET Bible®, copyright © 1996–2006 by Biblical Studies Press, L.L.C.;

NIV, The Holy Bible, New International Version®, NIV®, copyright © 1973, 1978, 1984, 2011 by Biblica, Inc.®;

NLT, Holy Bible, New Living Translation, copyright © 1996, 2004, 2007 by Tyndale House Foundation;

NRSV, New Revised Standard Version Bible, copyright © 1989 National Council of the Churches of Christ in the United States of America;

RSV, Revised Standard Version of the Bible, copyright © 1946, 1952, and 1971 National Council of the Churches of Christ in the United States of America.

ISBN-13: 978-0-8294-4054-6
ISBN-10: 0-8294-4054-2
Library of Congress Control Number: 2014945678

Printed in the United States of America.

14 15 16 17 18 19 Bang 10 9 8 7 6 5 4 3 2 1

*For all the okay-enough, life-giving moms who need the chance,
every single day, to be honest about the abiding joys and the
little deaths
that attend adulthood, raising children, and finding our places
in the world.*

Deus nobiscum, quis contra?
God is with us, who can be against us?

A darting fear—a pomp—a tear—
A waking on a morn
To find that what one waked for,
Inhales the different dawn.
—Emily Dickinson

Contents

Introduction

Good Enough and Perfectly Okay

Years ago, I met an old friend for coffee. I was eager to see her, perhaps especially because she was not yet a mother, so I knew our conversation would not involve sippy cups, Barney the dinosaur, or preschool philosophies.

In short, I needed a break from thinking like a "mommy."

As we got settled in at a coffee shop, my friend began to tell me a story. In her acting workshop the night before, a student had done an impersonation of his mother that had everyone laughing.

The student was one of four brothers, he said, who were very close in age. His father traveled quite a lot for work, and his mother was often home alone with the boys. They lived in the Southwest, and she wore cowboy boots, "24/7."

His performance?

Well, apparently when his mother felt like she was being swallowed up in the quicksand of never-ending loads of laundry, or when the kids refused to eat the meal she'd prepared, or when the boys were fighting or running wild through the house, or when her mood darkened and she confronted some secret, soul-crushing anxiety, she turned on the heels of her cowboy boots, retreated into one particular corner of the kitchen, faced the wall, and then jumped up and down in place for a minute or two, shouting, "What am I going to do? What am I going to do? What am I going to do?"

This ritual seemed to help her regain her equilibrium; afterward, she'd return to the boys, calm again.

I didn't laugh at the story. I felt like I'd just swallowed a jagged chunk of concrete. Turning toward the window, I covered my face and tried to stifle the sobs that came echoing out of me. My friend sat in silence as I tried to compose myself.

How could I explain to her that I was that mother?

Not literally, of course, but I knew just how she felt. I, too, was the mother of four very young children. Like hers, my husband traveled frequently. I knew just what it felt like to be exhausted and teetering on the edge of an emotional precipice. I was haunted by my own faults, regrets, and memories, just as she was.

Just as every mother is.

I knew how days could abruptly change directions: one moment I could be singing "The Wheels on the Bus" and savoring the happy rhythm of life at home with my kids and then, in the next, I'd be blown off course by anything from a catastrophic diaper to any other perfectly ordinary disaster.

"What?" my friend asked, her voice tender. "What is it?"

"It's hard sometimes. Being a mom. Really, really, really hard," I whispered. "Or maybe it's me. Maybe it's just hard for me."

She leaned across the table and put her hand over mine. "You're doing a great job, Jenni-June," she said, using the nickname she'd given me many years before. "You really are. Your kids are open, so engaged. They know they're loved. Really, you're doing great."

You're doing great. Her words quieted me.

It was true: my kids were all right. I was doing a perfectly okay job as their mom. Sometimes I was patient, fun loving, and quick to go down to the park or bring out the finger paints. Other times, I felt tired and irritable, secretly counting down the minutes until it was time for them to go to bed. Much of the time, I was somewhere in between.

I wasn't any better or worse than the jumping-up-and-down mom or any other perfectly okay, good-enough parent. My children were clothed and fed, and they lived in a safe, reasonably clean and organized home—and they knew they were deeply loved.

And, that was enough.

Running my hands over my face, I had to smile at the thought of that poor mom jumping up and down in her cowboy boots. Obviously she wasn't an abusive parent. If she had been, her son would never have created the affectionate portrait of her that my friend watched in her acting class. His was a good-enough mom: loving, prone to exhaustion, perfectly and imperfectly human. Like me.

"I hope those boys call her and send her flowers—and not just on Mother's Day," I said. "No, I hope they do way more than that. They owe her much more than roses and phone calls."

"I bet they know that," my friend said. "He seemed to know that."

"Good," I said. "And you know what? I'm thinking maybe that little ritual was the only way she knew how to pray."

Five Good Minutes

Nobody recites the old "sticks and stones" nursery rhyme anymore. Today we are quite certain that words have the capacity to leave us scarred. But words can do other things, too. Well-chosen ones give us hope, create connections, and help us perceive our lives more clearly.

They can turn our attention toward what is good and what is true.

Wholehearted Living is a book of short, daily readings for women whose season in life affords only limited time for contemplation. It's a "pause" button for mothers who want to take a break from talk of juice boxes and snow pants in favor of confronting their fears or reconnecting with their dreams.

It's for moments when you feel drawn toward the divine, as well as for those times when you feel like your frailties are holding you captive and you really just want to stand in the corner, face the wall, and scream.

Readers can spend fewer than five minutes a day with *Wholehearted Living*—or a few more if you choose to journal, meditate, or pray after reading the day's reflection. But a good five minutes actually makes a difference, affecting how we relate with others and how we perceive our lives for the rest of the day.

Countless studies show that just a few minutes of mindfulness affect our brains in positive ways. When we are silent and remain present and unplugged, we are less anxious and more equipped to liberate ourselves from the barricades that confine our spirits, barricades we often create and maintain ourselves. Taking just a few minutes every day to read this book and to think about the questions on each page will help you establish a practice of nurturing your mind and heart. You will build compassion toward yourself and others and be more fully awake to the gifts you've been given.

Wholehearted Living

Some of the reflections in this book will stir your imagination, others address spirituality, and all are intended to help you to move through the coming year with creativity and intention.

Many share wisdom I've gleaned from women I admire, including ideas about how to be intentional parents without completely losing our minds. A few contain very practical advice and proposed tasks and to-do lists.

You'll discover that I'm fond of saints, perhaps especially some of the least known—and outrageously named—ones. I scattered in a few saint stories here. The saints' brave and often bizarre acts of faith capture my imagination. Like us, they didn't choose the times or places into which they were born, and like us, they had to learn, by trial and error, how to live authentic, faithful lives.

The title, *Wholehearted Living*, is a tidy synopsis of this book. It describes being truthful and present, and looking with gratitude and compassion on who we are and the lives we have been given.

In the first four months of the year, we'll take a deep breath and reflect.

In the middle of the year, when the weather is likely finer and our schedules might be switched up for summer, we'll take risks.

And as the planet moves away from the sun and the ground is prepared to lie fallow, we will focus on rest.

Every month has been assigned its own practice relating to reflection, risk, or rest; and I hope as the months pass, these practices will help you connect, more and more, with your deepest self and with God's lavish and unchanging love for you.

Now—let's begin.

Reflect

*And now let us believe in a long year that is
given to us, new, untouched,
full of things that have never been.*

—Rainer Maria Rilke

January

Practice Patience

Be Gentle with Yourself and Others as You
Enter the New Year

Ask for a Do-Over

Everything that has a beginning has an ending. Make your peace with that and all will be well.

—Jack Kornfield (often falsely attributed to Buddha)

Playing kickball on the blacktop in elementary school, my classmates and I would ask for do-overs if the wind blew the ball off course, if the pitch came before we were ready, or even if a fire truck went blaring by the playground and distracted us.

"Do-over!" one of us would shout, and it would be granted. No one complained because we all asked for do-overs, all the time. Children don't mind asking for do-overs, but as we grow older, the words can catch in our throats.

Consider this New Year's Day a do-over.

Stow last year away like a book on a shelf, and give yourself permission to create a new story. May this be the year when you'll be more true to yourself. May you connect with your family and friends in meaningful ways and use your gifts more fully. May this be the year when the jumbled pieces of your life come together and make better sense.

⌒

Today, give yourself permission to call "do-over" and ask for a new pitch, a second chance.

Compassion toward Your Whole Self

It is lack of love for ourselves that inhibits our compassion toward others. If we make friends with ourselves, then there is no obstacle to opening our hearts and minds to others.

—Unknown

What are your plans today? Will you drag the Christmas tree down to the curb? Transfer birthdays to your new calendar? Savor a day off from work? Take the kids sledding? Feel guilty for not getting out of your pajamas all day long?

However you spend the day, take a few minutes to reflect on who you are. Don't think about what you should be doing, or what you should look like, or what you should care about, but about who you really are. What are your gifts? What makes you special to the people who love you? What do you daydream about?

If you are tempted to list your faults—stop! Remember that, like every other person who has ever lived, you are wrought with contradiction. Usually you're generous, but sometimes you're tight-fisted. You are grateful, but not when you obsess over what you don't have. You're disciplined, except when you're not. You are hopeful, until discouragement pulls the rug out from under you.

Look with compassion on your whole, fascinating patchwork quilt of a self as you begin a new year.

January 3
Resolving Not to Resolve

New Year's Resolution: To tolerate fools more gladly, provided this
does not encourage them to take up more of my time.
—James Agate

This time of year, we're clobbered with messages that tell us to change. "New year—new you!" they shout. "Stop smoking! Lose weight! Do yoga! Volunteer! Keep a budget! Learn to knit!"

These frantic orders are quickly followed by another message, a more cynical one. "By the end of the month," it predicts with a reproachful sigh, "you will have failed to keep your resolutions." So not only are we made to feel guilty about our faults and vices; we're told in the next breath that there is no hope that we'll ever be rid of them, no matter how hard we try.

How about we resolve not to make any new resolutions this year? If you have chosen a resolution you are committed to, by all means keep it if you like. But if you haven't, this is permission for you to drop the whole idea into the disposal. You know, like a bad grape.

Instead of letting the drumbeat of anxiety lead us into self-loathing, let's keep our focus on looking at ourselves with compassion as we begin this new year.

In what ways are you too hard on yourself?

Being Friends with Ourselves

Friendship with oneself is all important, because without it, one cannot be friends with anyone else in the world.

—Eleanor Roosevelt

My friend Mary and I have nine children between us. When we talk on the phone, we're almost always doing other things, too: cooking a meal, throwing a load of laundry into the dryer, watching the kids play at the park. We've even had long, involved conversations while one of us was navigating the aisles of the grocery store.

These calls are lifelines; her friendship keeps me calibrated.

Over the past few decades, Mary has been my confidant when my marriage has been in rough patches, when false friends have evaporated from my life, when I've struggled to negotiate a peace treaty between my work and family life, and when I've experienced other "slings and arrows of outrageous fortune," to quote William Shakespeare.

She sees the best in me, teases me when I'm taking myself too seriously, and yanks me from the brink when I'm being too self-critical or when I loosen my grasp on faith.

Maybe being friends with ourselves means doing some of the same sort of things.

How can you be a friend to yourself today?

January 5
God Made Us to Be Whole

Compassion allows.
—Robert Gonzales

Years ago, I interviewed a spiritual director for a newspaper assignment. I'm embarrassed to admit that, before meeting her, I had a low view of spiritual direction. I thought of it as a kind of watered-down therapy for self-indulgent people—people whose problems were not significant enough for a psychologist.

(I know. Nice, right?)

That assignment transformed my attitude. The woman I interviewed—her name, aptly, was Grace—seemed deeply connected to the Divine. She told me that her favorite Scripture verse was "Be perfect, therefore, as your heavenly Father is perfect" (Matthew 5:48, NRSV), and I immediately recoiled. What an impossible task. Perfect like God?

But Grace explained that "perfect" didn't have anything to do with excellent behavior or character, but meant "whole."

"God made us to be whole," she said. She hadn't always felt whole, and had recently recovered after about a decade of debilitating illness. She told me that when she was sick, she sometimes doubted God's purpose and love for her. But suffering had taught her true compassion. It made her more whole.

God made us to be whole—what could that look like for you?

January 6
Epiphany

e·piph·a·ny noun, plural e·piph·a·nies
a Christian festival observed on January 6 to celebrate the
manifestation of Christ to the gentiles in the persons of the Magi;
a sudden insight that is often initiated by a commonplace
experience.
—*Merriam-Webster Dictionary*

A friend recently told me about a "sudden insight" she had in therapy. Week after week for more than a year, she'd found herself talking about a particular friendship, a challenging one. Finally, one afternoon, in the quiet, familiar therapist's office, a thought popped into her mind. It was a flash of insight. An epiphany.

This friend is toxic, she thought. *I shouldn't spend time with her anymore.*

When she told her therapist this, he smiled. This had been clear to him all along. He had nudged her a bit and suggested as much, but it took spending the time exploring her feelings for my friend to realize it herself. She ended the friendship and now is washed over in relief.

She says that this experience taught her something important about listening. Because she went through the journey of being listened to well, she was able to receive that epiphany when it finally arrived.

Epiphanies—whether received by stargazing kings or by you and me—sometimes take time to find us.

What worries or preoccupies you? Imagine that an epiphany is on its way to you.

Listen to Your Life

*Listen to your life. See it for the fathomless mystery it is. In the
boredom and pain of it, no less than in the excitement and
gladness: touch, taste, smell your way to the holy and hidden heart
of it, because in the last analysis all moments are key moments,
and life itself is grace.*
—Frederick Buechner

It was summer, our kids were out of school, and my friend and I
made what felt like a Herculean effort to meet for lunch. Without
kids. At the restaurant, however, our phones rang and chimed, and
we never got past disjointed small talk to real conversation. Later,
we both apologized for being so distracted, and we promised that
the next time we met, we'd savor our time together. And, since
then, we have.

How can we all "listen to our lives"? Turning off our phones is
a good start. We can also start to keep a journal. Even if the idea
seems daunting, consider beginning to keep a perfectly imperfect
journal this year.

My blank book is a smorgasbord of to-do lists, writing exercises,
funny things my kids say that I want to remember, shopping lists,
and bits of emails I've taped to its pages. Sometimes I just doodle
in it when I'm on the phone.

When I look through everything I've written over a given week,
I see my life from a different perspective. (Oh, I am actually getting
something done! Oh, I am grateful for this full life of mine! Oh,
remember how funny that was?)

What could "listening to your life" mean to you today?

January 8
Patience Is a Virtue

Patience is a virtue; possess it if you can.
Seldom found in woman, never found in man.
—Unknown

When I was growing up, my mother repeated that little patience rhyme whenever she thought I was being impatient. I didn't like it, of course. Who likes to be criticized—and anyway, the saying let boys (and men) off the hook. How sexist!

Whether it's the result of hearing those words a hundred times as a child or of my particular personality type, I grew up to be a patient person. I don't (usually) mind standing in line. I don't (usually) lose my temper. Unlike one of my best friends who often, in her words, "gets her Irish up"—a state that includes much cursing and hand waving—I'm pretty even tempered.

But I'm often exceptionally impatient with myself. Or, to be precise, impatient with all that is unfinished within myself, to paraphrase poet Rainer Maria Rilke.

He writes: "Be patient with all that is unfinished in your heart and try to love the questions themselves . . . Do not now seek the answers . . . Live the questions now. Perhaps you will then, gradually, without noticing it, live along some distant day into the answer."

Beautiful, no? And excruciatingly hard, at least for me.

How might we live and love the questions in our lives?

Building Endurance

We could never learn to be brave and patient, if there were only joy in the world.
—Helen Keller

Ask a group of women what, in a word, is the most difficult thing about being a mom, and you will hear the word *patience* over and over again. Motherhood makes us wait. Babies aren't born on their due dates. Adoptions are delayed, the timing unpredictable. Hours go by before the pediatrician returns our calls. Toddlers seem to take forever to be potty trained. We keep waiting to become the mothers we always hoped we would be.

Whenever we would pass by a construction site, one of my sons—then about four or five years old—would say, "I wish we could just snap our fingers and that building would be done. All at once."

He didn't like seeing the scaffolding, mounds of gravel, or the chain-link fence. He'd snap his fingers with great intention, but alas, it would be months before the building was finished.

Buildings aren't completed in a day, and nor is the attainment of wisdom—in our kids or in ourselves.

⌒

Take a deep breath and know that you are building strength and endurance, incrementally, year by year. (Try not to mind the scaffolding.)

January 10
Patience When We're Frustrated

*The word patience means the willingness to stay where we are and
live the situation out to the full in the belief that something
hidden there will manifest itself to us.*
—Henri Nouwen

I know a woman who puts a high value on being patient, especially
with her children. But like all of us, she has moments when her
kids' behavior and quirks make her feel as if she were coming apart
at the seams. It isn't when they suddenly believe themselves to be
superheroes and launch themselves off the back of the sofa. It isn't
the messes they make or even their bickering. It's their questions
that sometimes make her want to scream:

Do dolphins sleep with their eyes open?

How do I know that I'm real?

Where does the snow go when it's not winter?

Her job entails managing others, keeping track of complex budgets, and thinking on her feet all day. So when she arrives home,
she doesn't want to explain the sleep habits of marine animals
or precipitation and the water cycle. Only after admitting to this
nasty tangle of guilt, irritation, and momentary (but extreme) dislike of children to friends was she able to detach from these feelings
and laugh about the peculiar questions themselves. As her friends,
we assured her that we'd all been there.

The next time one of her kids came to her with a question, she
was able to take a deep breath and answer as best as she could.

Confide in a trusted friend about what pushes your buttons.

Stay Hydrated

Anyone who drinks the water I give will never thirst—not ever.
The water I give will be an artesian spring within, gushing
fountains of endless life.
—John 4:14 MSG

The walls in the fifth-grade classroom at my church are painted orange, almost blood orange. Coloring pages, images of Our Lady of Guadalupe, cover one wall. The children have used yellow and orange crayons to depict the ball of light behind her. The room vibrates with color.

Recently, I taught a lesson on "living water."

"What did Jesus mean?" I asked my students. "When he told the woman that the water he gives will be a fountain inside her?"

"She'll never have to drink water anymore?" "That nothing bad will happen to her ever again?"

I wish I could tell these children that nothing bad happens to those who love God.

"Have you ever met someone who seems dehydrated? I mean spiritually?" I asked. One girl describes the bitter expression that's locked on the face of her teacher at school. The other kids laugh.

"Can you think of people who aren't parched or sour faced like that?" I ask. A boy says the name of a woman at our church. A stroke has taken her husband, unexpectedly. But behind her tears, her eyes are bright; she seems almost lit from within.

"Don't you think she's hydrated with God's love?" I asked. They nod.

"I want to be like that," one of the girls said.

When have you felt spiritually parched?

Aelred on Friendship

*We call friends only those to whom we have no qualm about
entrusting our heart and all its contents.*
—Aelred, Abbot of Rievaulx

January 12 is the feast day of Aelred, Abbot of Rievaulx, a monk, writer, and twelfth-century "spiritual director." He wrote about the "sacramental essence" of friendship—or, more simply, his conviction that our human friendships reflect the relationship between God and each one of us.

The four qualities of a true friend, according to Aelred, are loyalty, right intention, discretion, and patience. He defines a friend as "another self" whom you trust with your weaknesses and failings and "to whom you can entrust all the secrets of your heart."

My youngest child was a toddler when we adopted her. Before she was placed with us, I read that if a child in foster care bonds with a loving caregiver—as I'd later find that my daughter had—she will likely bond with her new parents as well.

She had a loving caregiver and indeed quickly came to trust us. I think Aelred would understand why that happened. Smaller loves open our hearts to bigger ones. Human love reflects the love of God.

*What are some ways you can mirror God's love to the people in
your life?*

Be Patient with Yourself When You Grieve

There is sacredness in tears. . . . They speak more eloquently than ten thousand tongues. They are the messengers of overwhelming grief, of deep contrition, and of unspeakable love.
—Washington Irving

A few years ago, on the first day of January, I learned that a friend of mine had died. We'd first met in high school, and he is scattered throughout my memories of college. After graduation, we'd run into each other at friends' holiday parties, and one summer we attended a weeklong wedding celebration in the Oregon Cascades. I treasured him. Although we'd been out of touch for a few years, I always expected to see him again.

On learning of his death, I felt compelled to go outside and walk. A layer of ice glistened over the snow that morning; it shattered under my feet.

I took a number of icy walks that month, but more often, I hid. After getting the children off to school, I retreated back under the covers. That January and the months that followed were full of tears. My heart felt battered, and other griefs were awoken inside of me.

Looking back, I can see that I did what I could. I walked, read, lay in my bed, and stared at the ceiling. But after a time, and little by little, I felt myself healing.

Spring came.

Be patient with yourself when you grieve. The heart takes time to heal.

January 14
The Tyranny of the Urgent

Never confuse motion with action.
—Benjamin Franklin

In his book *The Time Trap*, author and time-management expert Alec Mackenzie coined the phrase "the tyranny of the urgent." Mackenzie reminds us that the most urgent task may not be the most important one.

Comforting a crying baby, letting the dog out when he whines at the door, and meeting a work deadline are all urgent and important tasks. Planning for retirement, researching brands of washing machines for an upcoming purchase, and reading to your children are important but usually not urgent.

Chimes of email notifications, a ringing home phone, and requests from the kids' schools can feel urgent. Sometimes we ignore important things in favor of responding to what only feels urgent. When I respond quickly to things that can wait, I feel frustrated and spent.

I get more done—and enjoy my life much more—when I am strategic and turn off notifications. I set aside an hour or two every week to sign permission slips, skim school newsletters, and update my family's calendar instead of letting such tasks splinter every day into shards.

How do you manage the onslaught of information and news that comes into your home? How do you try to stay focused on what is truly important?

Journal Keepers

*By three methods we may learn wisdom: first, by reflection, which
is the noblest; second, by imitation, which is the easiest; and third,
by experience, which is the bitterest.*

—Confucius

Last week, we talked about keeping a journal in order "to listen to
our lives" with more intention. The people I know seem to fall into
one of three categories when it comes to journaling:

1. The joyful journal writer has kept a diary since about the
    second grade. She has a record of girlhood crushes, favorite
    rides at amusement parks, and books she's read. As a parent,
    she carefully records every insight she has about mother-
    hood and each adorable thing her children say. Her journals
    are her treasures.

2. The wistful, would-be journal keeper owns a journal but
    only infrequently cracks it open. The pressure to write
    something eloquent and even to write neatly hinders her
    from putting pen to paper. Her (mostly blank) journals
    make her feel guilty.

3. The contrary journal avoider knows, in theory, that keeping
    a journal helps us clarify our thoughts, but she is loath to
    hop on any kind of bandwagon. So, like avoiding exercise,
    eschewing trendy social media, or skipping her doctor's
    advice to take a multivitamin, she usually refuses to do it.
    The idea of journaling irritates her.

(Full disclosure: I connect most with this last type.)

*Do you recognize yourself in any of these journalers? If journaling isn't
for you, how else can you begin to pay closer attention to your
thoughts and feelings?*

Breathe

I took a deep breath and listened to the old brag of my heart.
I am, I am, I am.
—Sylvia Plath

Sometimes when I'm anxious or very focused, I hold my breath. I can be watching a thriller, waiting in line at the grocery store, or just sitting in traffic when I realize that my body is very still, my shoulders are locked and tense, and I'm taking in only tiny sips of air.

At those moments, I often gulp in a huge mouthful of air and end up in a coughing fit or with a bad case of the hiccups. Other times, I relax my shoulders and take at least three big, whole-body breaths.

"Take three cleansing breaths," I used to say to my kids when they seemed perched on the precipice of a temper tantrum. It often worked to calm them down. I knew it would because breathing helps me release tension, too. It recalibrates me.

Breathing does so much for us: helps our bodies release toxins, improves posture and mood, reduces our experience of pain, and relaxes us.

Don't forget to breathe.

Take three "cleansing breaths." Inhale through your nose, slowly fill your lungs, and then exhale through your mouth. Imagine that you are inhaling peace and exhaling negative thoughts.

January 17
Praying for Patience

*Let me ask you something. If someone prays for patience, you think
God gives them patience? Or does he give them the opportunity to
be patient?*

—God, as played by Morgan Freeman, in the movie
Evan Almighty

Often when I pray for patience, I really want something else: a problem to be resolved, a child to mature out of a difficult phase, or an end to my discouragement.

I prayed for patience when I was pregnant with my second child and heard the doctor assess the ultrasound images; she saw what she thought might be cysts on the baby's brain. "We'll keep an eye on this," she said. "It could be that they'll be absorbed by the body. We'll look again in a few weeks."

I prayed for patience, but what I really wanted was for my baby to be all right.

I prayed for patience when I was awaiting the completion of a court case that would finalize my daughter's adoption and bring her home. Paperwork was lost or judged incomplete. Holiday schedules further slowed down the process.

I prayed for patience, but what I really wanted was for her to be able to come home.

Ultimately, those cysts disappeared; my son was born without complications. My daughter's adoption was finally completed and she came home.

My real prayers, as obscured as they were, were answered.

When you pray for patience, is it something else that you really want?

21

January 18
Flawed St. Peter

*We all are fragile, we all have limits. Do not be afraid. We all
have them. Even in these difficult moments, it is necessary to trust
in the help of God, through filial prayer and, at the same time, it
is important to find the courage and the humility to open ourselves
to others and ask for help.*

—Pope Francis

Today is one of the days in the church year that celebrates the life
of St. Peter. Peter is one of my favorites from the biblical narrative.
The story of his walking on water to Jesus makes me laugh with
recognition; I see myself in his burst of optimism and his frailty.
But most of all, I love that despite all of Peter's faults, Jesus was
very fond of him and even said that Peter was the rock on which
the church would be built.

This "rock" was the one who denied Christ (three times!) after
swearing he would never betray him. Faithful Peter was quick
to doubt and nearly drowned during that little walking-on-water
exercise. Peter was always trying to linger in the good times and
slip away from the difficult ones.

I'm like that, too. But if God loved Peter and was able to use his
efforts to bring love and light to the world, maybe God can also
use my life—mercurial, fearful, and fickle as I can be—for good.

Maybe God can use you, too.

*In what ways are you like St. Peter? Do you believe that God delights
in you, faults and all?*

Valuable Gifts

Cleanliness is not next to godliness. It isn't even in the same neighborhood. No one has ever gotten a religious experience out of removing burned-on cheese from the grill of the toaster oven.
—Erma Bombeck

My mothers' group met in the church library every few weeks. We were a diverse group, ever trying to keep our heads above water and maintain our senses of humor as we cared for our young children.

One woman was an artist whose canvases were filled with painted handprints. She said these were meant to express the joy and mess of family life. Another mother was sort of a domestic goddess and knitted her children's hats and mittens, baked bread, and kept a large vegetable garden. Still another, a social worker, took her kids on regular trips to the arboretum, teaching them to identify trees, birds, and types of clouds.

I can't tell whether a cloud is a cumulus or a nimbus. I'm not a professional artist. And my efforts to sew have been disastrous. Sometimes I felt a little "less than" among the talented women in my mothers' group. But I came to see that I, too, had valuable gifts to offer my children. I loved doing watercolors with them, delighted in their almost-surreal knock-knock jokes, was very organized, and I truly loved reading picture books as much as they did.

Your natural gifts and interests are just what your children need.

January 20
Make Time to Be Still

I go amongst the buildings of a city and I see a Man hurrying
along—to what?
—John Keats

For the past several years, in early December, I have traveled alone to New York City. I sequester myself in a friend's brownstone and savor four or five days of solitude and writing.

Before I leave for the city, I keep an allegro tempo, to use the musical term. I speed through long to-do lists, filling my basement freezer with meals for my family and scheduling car pools and appointments. I even try to get most of my Christmas shopping done.

But in New York, the rhythm of my day is slowed to adagio. I look out the window, drinking in scenery, the lively corner with taxis and people speeding by so different from what I am accustomed to in my suburban neighborhood.

I feel like a person in a glass snow globe, except I'm the one who is still and everything outside is in motion. Snow falls. I hear jackhammers and the blare of car horns. I watch people enter and exit the café across the street. Unlike so many days at home, I give myself the gift of doing nothing, just watching the world go by outside.

Spend time today being still and doing nothing at all.

Perform Small Acts of Love

Accustom yourself continually to make many acts of love, for they enkindle and melt the soul.

—St. Teresa of Ávila

On school mornings, I'm in the kitchen just after 6:00 to make my children breakfast. When they come downstairs and sit at the counter, I like to have music playing, coffee brewing, and breakfast laid out.

Although my children are old enough to get their own breakfast and might prefer Honey Nut Cheerios to whatever attempt at healthier food I've made, giving them breakfast is a way I try to connect with them. It's a ritual, a practice, a way I express my love.

I know that the halls of middle and high school can be treacherous places for kids. Will one of my kids have to navigate unkind classmates, burned-out teachers, or a disappointment of some kind? I likely won't know much of what is going on in their school days, their minds, or their hearts. But I can extend myself to them in the morning.

I hope that my small acts of kindness, whether in the form of burned-at-the-edges cinnamon toast, a mug of hot chocolate, or a bowl of granola, will sustain my children as they go into the world and do the hard work of growing up.

What are the small acts of love that help you to connect with your family?

It Is Enough

There are two ways to get enough. One is to continue to
accumulate more and more. The other is to desire less.
—G. K. Chesterton

Years ago, my husband's first boss in the software industry took
him aside to tell him that he would be given a raise. I was pregnant
with our first child and working only part-time. The additional
income was welcome.

I'm sure my husband did some kind of happy dance. His boss,
a kind, grandfatherly man, had started the business from scratch
and was successful. He issued a word of caution to my husband,
saying that many people never feel they are making enough, whatever their salary. They continually change their definition of what
is "enough"—enough square feet, enough special features in a car,
nice-enough countertops, and so on.

When I feel impatient about what I don't have, I try to remember that I do have enough: I have enough to eat, a safe place to live,
and the gift of my family.

It is enough.

What might "enough" look and feel like to you?

Be Patient with Others' Failings

You must be kind toward all, a good and patient teacher.
—2 Timothy 2:24 GNT

For *years*, as she tells it, my friend was impatient with one of her children. His schoolwork was messy and incomplete. He was forever losing things. Teachers said he wasn't working up to his potential. It was frustrating—embarrassing even. My friend and her husband lectured their son about "applying" himself. They took away privileges and monitored his work. But still, year after year, their bright boy barely squeezed by.

When her son was in middle school, however, my friend came across an article on a cluster of learning disabilities not widely known or diagnosed. Every description of children with these issues matched her son. Neurological testing confirmed it, and soon the boy's parents and teachers understood that there was a better way for him to learn. He began to shine.

Not every person's poor performance or difficult behavior has to do with atypical brain function, but when I find myself locked in a holding pattern of impatience with someone I love, I remember this story.

And sometimes, when I patiently watch and wait, a new solution or perspective presents itself.

Which person tends to try your patience? Is there a new way to understand his or her behavior?

January 24
Know You Are Loved

What if Jesus really wanted us to know, in our very deepest places,
that we were entirely and irrevocably accepted as we are and not as
we should be?
—Margot Starbuck

What goes through your mind when you're standing in line at the grocery store and you skim the magazine covers? Maybe you're frustrated that they compel you to explain to your six-year-old what "drug overdose" and "polygamy" mean. But how do those magazine covers make you feel?

Dr. Mia Sypeck, a psychologist at American University, examined the depictions of women on magazine covers over a fifty-year period. She found—no big surprise—that women's ideal body size has drastically shrunk. She and many other psychologists chart a direct relationship between women's exposure to images of a "thin ideal" and disordered eating and dissatisfaction with our bodies and lives.

The more we see and internalize these ideals, the unhappier we are.

The thin ideal doesn't help us recognize what we mean to the people who love us, doesn't nudge us toward engaging more fully with our community, and doesn't help us use our gifts. It only focuses our attention on what we look like, on the outside.

Today, remember that your body is a temple, a home for your soul.
Feel God's loving acceptance of who you are, just as you are.

St. Dwynwen's Day

Nothing wins hearts like cheerfulness.
—St. Dwynwen

Today is St. Dwynwen's Day. Dwynwen, who died in AD 460, is known in Wales as the patron saint of lovers. Her name means "she who leads a blessed life." The many versions of Dwynwen's story read like fairy tales.

The most beautiful of twenty-four sisters, Dwynwen was in love but had been promised in marriage by her father to a different man. In some stories, an angel gave Dwynwen a potion that erased her memories of the man she loved. Dwynwen asked the angel that she never be forced to marry and that God forever answer her prayers on behalf of true lovers. Her wishes were granted.

Dwynwen became a nun and built a church on Ynys Llanddwyn (which means "Church of St. Dwynwen Island"), off the coast of Wales. St. Dwynwen's Church can be visited today, as can nearby Dwynwen's Well, the subject of more legends. Tradition claims that a sacred fish swims in the well, its movements predicting the fortunes of couples that visit. If the water in the well boils while couples visit, they will experience good fortune and lasting love.

January 25 is Welsh Valentine's Day, and lovers in Wales exchange cards and gifts.

If God promised to grant your wish, what would you ask for?

Patience with Our Growth

Rivers know this: there is no hurry. We shall get there some day.
—A. A. Milne (from *Winnie-the-Pooh*)

One of my sons has wanted, since he was very young, to be tall. Very tall, like one of his uncles, who towers above many of us at six foot four. When, as a sixth grader, my son's shoe size shot up to a men's size eleven, he asked me if that meant he'd be tall. I told him I didn't know.

Sometimes, when I'm impatient with my own growth, spiritually or otherwise, I think of my son's desire for height.

"Grow!" I want to shout. If only I could will myself to be wiser, to keep a looser grip on my desires, to be more sure of myself.

Occasionally when I check my son's height against the most recent line we've drawn on the wall, we see that he has indeed grown. An inch, a few centimeters—any change delights him.

Sometimes I realize that I'm calm in a situation that used to throw me. I discover myself listening better to a friend or remembering to breathe. And I mark it, glad to know I'm continuing to grow.

In what areas do you will yourself to grow? In what ways can you be more patient with yourself?

A Porous Ego

Make your ego porous. Will is of little importance, complaining is
nothing, fame is nothing. Openness, patience, receptivity, solitude
is everything.
—Rainer Maria Rilke

In his book *The Freedom of Self-Forgetfulness*, Timothy Keller encourages readers to think neither too highly of themselves nor too poorly of themselves, but to think of themselves . . . less often.

How do we break a habit of being preoccupied with ourselves and how others see us? Keller, a pastor, says that we must remain mindful that Christ has already "justified" us by his death and resurrection. As children of God, we have nothing to prove. Any good works we do are done in gratitude for the gifts we have been given, not to earn approval from others (or from God).

This is a hard one, isn't it? When we've spent our lives trying to please parents, teachers, and employers, resting in who we are as loved children of God might feel unnatural. We want to work for it, prove that we are worthy, and show that we are enough.

How do we begin to break this habit of proving ourselves? I find that when I unplug from situations (or social media platforms) that cause me to compare myself with others, I'm more self-forgetful. When I focus on my breathing, take myself less seriously, and find ways to serve those in need, I am better able to experience that freedom.

What are some ways you practice self-forgetfulness?

Faith That Now Isn't Forever

Faith is what makes life bearable, with all its tragedies and
ambiguities and sudden, startling joys.
—Madeleine L'Engle

So much happens in a year. We complete countless ordinary tasks: scrambling eggs, unloading the dishwasher, tying shoes.

And we experience extraordinary moments of joy and fear and awe and sadness. In the past year, I've attended funerals and baptisms, kayaked through a mangrove forest, spent occasional mornings lying in bed feeling paralyzed by discouragement, eaten fish and chips doused in malt vinegar, pulled my robe closed before walking down the hall to a mammogram, and have been awed by the sweep of pastels in the sky—skies painted by Monet and by the Creator.

Mostly, though, I have lived many, many perfectly ordinary days. The same will be true this year. There will be ups, downs, highs, and lows. And a whole lot of everyday, ordinary stuff.

Faith that these things have meaning, that I have a place in the world, and that I'm not locked in this or that moment permanently, is a gift. "Now isn't forever" is a phrase I say to myself when I'm struggling. Faith is trusting that time does heal wounds, storms do pass, and all the tiny moments of my life are adding up to something.

Graciously, now isn't forever.

Remember that "now isn't forever" and that whether you are in a difficult or more ordinary moment, your life will change course and startle you again.

Wait It Out

It is far better to endure patiently a smart which nobody feels but yourself, than to commit a hasty action whose evil consequences will extend to all connected with you.
—Charlotte Brontë

My friends, a married couple and the parents of five children, knew better than to hit "send" on the angry email they had written to the school. Instead, they asked my husband and me for advice about how to handle the very insulting comments their daughter said her teacher had made in class.

"What a terrible person this teacher must be," my friend said. "I'd love to show up and tell her exactly what I think of her."

"Wait," I said. "Remember that sometimes things are lost in translation. Talk to the teacher. Tell her what your daughter took from what she said. Puzzle it out together. But wait a few days before you contact her."

After their anger had cooled, my friends spoke with the teacher. Afterward, they told me that they found her well intentioned and intelligent. She had, however, failed to communicate the lesson clearly and had confused some of the students, including their daughter.

The teacher apologized to the class, clarified what she had meant, and vowed to be more precise when she talked about complicated issues in the future.

Practice patience, and take your time in deciding how to respond when you've been hurt or offended.

Safely in His Hands

Restlessness and impatience change nothing except our peace and joy. Peace does not dwell in outward things, but in the heart prepared to wait trustfully and quietly on Him who has all things safely in His hands.
—Elisabeth Elliot

These words—about waiting "trustfully and quietly"—might sound simplistic at first glance. You might imagine their speaker comfortably tucked away in a cul-de-sac, perhaps sipping chamomile tea and knitting a sweater.

But Elisabeth Elliot was never a prim, small-town optimist. Her life was full of adventure, and of loss. Elliot studied Greek in college and hoped to develop written language for people whose cultures didn't yet have it.

After moving to Ecuador in her early twenties to do mission work, she married Jim Elliot, a college classmate and also a missionary. When their daughter was just ten months old, Jim Elliot was murdered while visiting a remote tribe. After his death, Elisabeth remained in Ecuador with their daughter. She later lived with and served the same people, the Huaorani (then called the Auca), who had killed her husband.

How can someone like Elisabeth Elliot say that God has everything "safely in His hands"? How did she have the fortitude to stay in Ecuador with her baby on her own?

That kind of faith stuns me.

Who is someone who has experienced great loss whose faith, courage, and hope inspire you?

Living Forward

*Life can only be understood backwards—but it must be
lived forwards.*
—Søren Kierkegaard

We're waiting in line at the post office when I whisper to my daughter that the man mailing the huge package is sending a surfboard to his ninety-year-old father. He knows he won't use it but hopes that it will make him laugh, remembering an afternoon on the beach, decades ago, when he watched his son learn to surf.

"Really?" my daughter asks. "How did you know all that?"

I laugh and confess that I've made it up. Not only do I make up stories about strangers, but often I find myself taking stray memories and observations from my own life and crafting them into narratives. Some of the stories are positive. Remembering challenges I've overcome, I am reminded that I'm strong. Revisiting other stories leaves me feeling defeated or alone.

As we put January behind us, let us be mindful of the stories we tell ourselves and the way we tell them.

⌒

*What are some stories you can reframe or let go of in order to start
living forward?*

February

Practice Connection

Nurture Your Relationships, Reach Out,
Become More Aware of God's Presence

February 1

The Cruelest Month?

April is the cruellest month, breeding
Lilacs out of the dead land, mixing
Memory and desire, stirring
Dull roots with spring rain.
—T. S. Eliot

The first line of "The Waste Land" is unsettling. April is the cruelest month, declares T. S. Eliot's poem, because it paves the way for lilacs and stirs "dull roots" with rain.

Wait—what? Who doesn't like lilacs?

Perhaps it's that the promise of spring feels sinister to Eliot because it makes him more aware of how long the winter has been. Sadness is funny like that, right?

In my experience, February is usually the harshest month. If you're in a northern climate, by February you've already lived through three or four months of cold. Twinkling lights have been pulled down from the trees. Streets are icy, skies are often gray, and winter coats are smudged with road salt. Worse, February's omnipresent candy hearts and teddy bears can feel like an insult when you're feeling lonely or unloved.

This month we look at relationships from a different angle. Instead of relying on them to make us "happy," maybe our relationships are meant to transform us into the people we were created to be.

Whether it means lamenting a loss, celebrating new or renewed love, or simply finding a way to show kindness to someone in need, set your intention on being authentic with your feelings this month.

Types of Love

And now these three remain: faith, hope and love. But the greatest of these is love.

—1 Corinthians 13:13 NIV

My dog loves to lie under the window where sun shines in. My daughter loves the lead singer of a certain British boy band. I love crème brûlée, Gene Kelly movies, and Lavonda roses. Clearly, not all of these "loves" are equal.

In his book *The Four Loves*, C. S. Lewis explores four Greek words for love: *storge*, *philia*, *eros*, and *agape*.

I have affection (*storge*) for my dog; my daughter's big gaggle of friends; and, yes, for Gene Kelly.

I love my family and friends (*philia*). I miss them when we're apart; our common interests connect us; and I know, and am truly known by, them.

Eros is the love I felt as a twenty-year-old when I wanted to marry the man who is now my husband. It was about much more than romance or sexual attraction; I wanted to make a life with him.

The last type of love Lewis describes is *agape*, or unconditional love. This is God's love for us, a love that is given with no strings attached.

St. Paul wrote, "Neither death, nor life, nor angels, nor principalities, nor things present, nor things to come, nor powers, nor height, nor depth, nor any other creature, shall be able to separate us from the [*agape*] love of God" (Romans 8:38–39, RSV).

When have you experienced each of these four types of love?

Acts of Love

You have not lived today until you have done something for someone who can never repay you.
—John Bunyan

As we drove through town, my daughter pointed at a man who was sitting on a park bench. He wore layers of shirts and overcoats. A black garbage bag containing his belongings sat on the sidewalk beside him.

"Oh, there's John," my daughter said.

"You know him?" I asked.

"My friends and I buy him sandwiches sometimes when we go to Starbucks after school," she said with a shrug.

Pope Francis has said that we must make our love concrete: "love with actions, not with words. The wind whisks words away. Today they're here, tomorrow they're not." In other words, talking about having a "heart for the poor" is useless. Instead, we must find ways to help raise people out of poverty and address their needs.

We can support organizations that provide housing assistance and job training to those who need it. We can help fill the shelves at food pantries. We can also reach out to individuals, as my daughter and her friends have to John.

Has anyone ever reached out to you when you were in need? Is there anyone you might be overlooking who needs you today?

The Best Strawberries

A friend is someone who knows all about you and still loves you.
—Elbert Hubbard

In an essay about the crushing loss of a friendship, novelist Jacquelyn Mitchard crafted a brilliant phrase. To describe how she'd neglected other relationships during the ill-fated friendship, Mitchard wrote that she had given "the very best strawberries" of her personal life only to that one particular friend.

I was skimming a magazine in the waiting room at my kids' orthodontist when I first read those words: *the very best strawberries.* The phrase ran through me like a chill; I didn't want to forget it. It made me consider my own relationships. Was I hanging onto any friendships that were lopsided or unhealthy, as Mitchard later discerned that one to be? Were there any friends I was taking for granted?

What were my "best strawberries," anyway? Listening well? Surprising a friend with a meal? Sending an encouraging note? The gift of my time?

After reading the essay, I resolved to make sure to nurture my healthy friendships and to share more of myself with the people I love.

What are your "best strawberries"?

Love Story

Love means never having to say you're sorry.
—Erich Segal, from the movie *Love Story*

One evening, my daughter and I happened on the trailer for *Love Story*, the 1970 tearjerker, starring Ryan O'Neal and Ali MacGraw. It ends with a photo of the ill-fated couple and the words "Love Means Never Having to Say You're Sorry."

"What?" my thirteen-year-old shouted, seeing the movie's tag line. "That is the stupidest thing I've ever heard!" I burst out laughing—she was absolutely right. Of course love requires that we say we're sorry, as awkward or difficult as it can be.

A few years ago, an apology saved one of my most cherished friendships. It had been months since my friend and I had talked. I'd chalked it up to our schedules and living in different time zones. But when I called her, I heard a sting in her voice. After a few minutes, she said she'd seen pictures online of a recent trip I'd taken and wondered why I hadn't made the effort to visit her.

I was able to explain that my travel had been work related and my expenses paid, but I had to admit that I hadn't done enough to take care of our friendship. I apologized, she forgave me, and we talked about how to stay in better touch. (And we have.) That difficult conversation kept a door from closing between us and pushed it open wide again.

Is there someone you need to call?

February 6

Open Arms

God gives nothing to those who keep their arms crossed.
—West African proverb

Every parish seems to have one: a cantankerous person who finds fault with everything from the homily to the way the coffee is brewed at coffee hour. Many years ago, ours was a woman I'll call Beverly.

One weekend, the women at my church came together for a retreat. Older women were paired with younger ones to be "retreat buddies." We'd sit together at meals, take walks, and debrief with each other over the course of the weekend. When I entered the church, a friend pulled me aside and said, "I put you with Beverly. I hope you don't mind."

My heart sank, but very soon, my attitude changed. During our time together, Beverly opened up to me about the abuse she had suffered in her marriage, her interest in crime novels, and her affection for Siamese cats.

Beverly was no longer a caricature to me ("the grumpy old parishioner") but a person who had valuable wisdom to offer and funny stories to tell. I came to see her sharp comments about church details as her way of remaining involved in the life of the parish in her older age.

At the end of the weekend, I thanked my friend for pairing us. I'd received so much from Beverly.

Whom do you find difficult? Is there a way you can better know that person's story?

Stories We Tell

*Much of the work of midlife is to tell the difference between people
who are still dealing with their issues through you and those who
are really dealing with you as you really are.*
—Richard Rohr

Not long after I turned forty, someone I trusted ended our friendship abruptly. Reeling, I told a friend, and instead of uttering the
kind of sympathetic words I'd expected, he told me a story. A man,
fed up with his life, decided to leave town and start over. Arriving
at a new place, he called out to a local.

"Tell me," he said. "What are the people like around here?"

The man answered with a question: "What are the people like
where you used to live?"

"Awful," called the man. "Selfish. Mean-spirited. They
failed me."

"I'm sorry, friend," the other man said, "But you are going to
find that people here are exactly the same."

The point is, of course, that our attitudes and expectations drive
our experiences. My (erstwhile) friend was simply acting out a
story she'd told herself many times. No one understands me. Life
lets me down. She'll likely keep repeating it until deep wounds are
addressed and healed.

The experience made me take a hard look at the stories I tell
myself.

*What stories do you tell yourself about how you've been treated? Are
they coloring your perception of others?*

February 8
Miraculously into Place

*You have given me the desire to be a builder; make up for my lack
of skill, and bring the work of building this holy house to
its completion.*
—St. Cuthman

I'd say that St. Cuthman was a quirky, unlikely saint, but aren't so
many of them? Cuthman was an Anglo-Saxon hermit born in 681.
He is remembered as a church builder and for the stunning ways
he interacted with the Divine.

Cuthman spent his childhood tending his father's sheep. Once,
weak with hunger, he left his flock to return home. To keep the
sheep from wandering, he drew an invisible circle around them
with a stick. When he returned, he found them waiting within that
boundary.

Sometime later, Cuthman's father died, leaving both the boy
and his mother destitute. Cuthman built a wooden cart, tied it to
his shoulders with ropes and willow branches, and transported his
elderly mother to another part of the country, certain that God had
directed him to do so. He walked until the cords broke, and at that
very spot, he began to build a church.

When the church was nearly completed, Cuthman was unable
to raise the crucial supporting beam, or "king's pole." Christ
appeared to him and moved the beam miraculously into place.

Fascinated by Cuthman's story, playwright Christopher Fry
wrote a play about the saint, called *The Boy with a Cart.* Fry wrote
of Cuthman's discouragement during the church building: "when
I prayed my voice crashed to the ground." But then Christ appears
to him and the church is completed.

⌒

*Have you ever felt something move "miraculously into place" in your
own life?*

Regaining Perspective

*The beginning of this love is the will to let those we love be
perfectly themselves, the resolution not to twist them to fit our
own image.*
—Thomas Merton

Sometimes I don't like being married, and I know there are times my husband doesn't like being married either. One of us, by turns, can be aloof, selfish, petty, demanding, or some combination of unattractive traits.

At those moments—and, honestly, those "moments" can stretch into hours, days, and even weeks—my single friends' lives appear blissful and uncomplicated. Other people's marriages seem bathed in a golden light. Everyone else seems happier, better adjusted, and better off than me.

It's as if I'm standing on an observation deck at the Empire State Building, my forehead pressed up against the viewfinder. But I've forgotten to put in a quarter and the machine is out of focus and pointed straight down at my feet. All I can see is black.

When I can summon the resolve, I've found that taking a breath, quieting my ego, and reminding myself that feelings are temporary helps me. I regain focus and remember that the purpose of marriage isn't to make me "happy" but, I believe, to transform me into a mature person who reaches out and makes this a more just world.

Remembering that now is not forever puts a coin in the machine, changes my point of view, and helps me see the big picture again.

What helps you regain perspective when you are feeling discouraged?

February 10
Loneliness

*The trouble is not that I am single and likely to stay single, but
that I am lonely and likely to stay lonely.*
—Charlotte Brontë

Every few months, my friend and I used to drive from the suburbs
of Chicago to a homeless shelter for women in one of the roughest
parts of the city. We led writing workshops for residents, who
wrote of childhood abuse, the desperation and indignity of selling
their bodies, and the pull of drug addiction. I would listen and
nod, my hands knotted into fists in my lap. Each story was complex, disturbing, heartfelt. It hurt to hear them.

One night, a woman new to the shelter offered to share what
she'd written. I took a deep breath.

"All my life," she began slowly, her head bent over the page. She
was quiet for a moment and then continued, "All my life I've suffered from . . ." She fell silent again before reading the last word.

"Loneliness." *All my life I've suffered from loneliness.* Those were
the only words she had written, words that made as powerful an
impression on me as had the intricate stories the other women had
shared.

Her confession still haunts me, underscoring the terrible pain
of loneliness.

*What do you do when you feel lonely? Can you think of someone in
your community who suffers from loneliness, someone to whom you
could reach out?*

A Time for Everything

*To every thing there is a season . . . a time to be born, and a time
to die; a time to plant, and a time to pluck up that which is
planted; a time to kill, and a time to heal; a time to break down,
and a time to build up; a time to weep, and a time to laugh; a
time to mourn, and a time to dance . . . a time to embrace, and a
time to refrain from embracing; a time to get, and a time to lose; a
time to keep, and a time to cast away; a time to rend, and a time
to sew; a time to keep silence, and a time to speak; a time to love,
and a time to hate; a time of war, and a time of peace.*
—Ecclesiastes 3:1–8 KJ21

There may be a time for everything, but when you are grieving
and everyone around you seems to be dancing, it can feel very,
very bad.

The wife whose husband has just left her might experience the
hearts and cupids of Valentine's Day as a slap in the face. A woman
who longs for a child wishes she could fast-forward over commer-
cials that show misty-eyed moms and newborns around Mother's
Day. After the pain of foreclosing on their home, your friends
might not be up for your housewarming party.

Ecclesiastes, though, reminds us that things change. Our feelings change. Now isn't forever. If you are lonely and heartbroken
this year, you might feel differently next time the stores are hung
with red and pink hearts.

The best you can do this year might be just to take a deep
breath, direct your focus elsewhere—perhaps into a good book or
toward gratitude for what you have been given, if you can summon
the resolve—and know that this, too, shall pass.

Sometimes the best you can do is get through today.

*Is there someone you can confide in about feelings of pain
or loneliness?*

February 12
Believing the Best

The better part of one's life consists of his friendships.
—Abraham Lincoln

About a decade ago, my friend Tricia and I made a pact. We had seen other people's friendships die of preventable causes: misunderstandings, crossed signals, and perceived slights.

"Let's make a deal that we'll always assume the best of each other," I suggested. And, simple as that, we did. Of course, by the time we made this agreement, we'd been through a lot of life together; I knew she was a friend I didn't want to do without.

Because of that promise, I never worry over our friendship. When one of us is busy and has been out of touch, the other doesn't take offense or assume that there's anything wrong. I know that if she has a problem with me, I'll be the first to know about it. If she already has plans with another friend when I call her, I don't get jealous or paranoid. Most of all, when one of us confides in the other, we never doubt that our secrets will be kept.

This sort of freedom allows me to open up with her in ways I rarely do with other people.

Who are your most trusted friends? How can you protect those friendships?

Tangible Love

Darkness cannot drive out darkness; only light can do that. Hate cannot drive out hate; only love can do that.
—Martin Luther King Jr.

Last Christmas, my mother gave me half a dozen soccer balls. The year before, my husband and son bought me a bike built for desert conditions. And a few Decembers ago, my friend Elizabeth gave me a live chicken.

As you might have guessed, these gifts were in the form of donations, made in my name, to humanitarian organizations I love: World Vision, World Bicycle Relief, and Heifer International, to be precise.

Cards telling me that a donation has been made in my name are among my favorite gifts to receive. Well, those and gifts of cheese. I'm actually not kidding about the cheese: a few of our best friends send artisan cheeses to my husband and me around the holidays or for our birthdays. Smoked gouda, truffle and salt cheddar, brie with apricots. Lovely luxuries, but I digress.

To honor the ones you love this Valentine's Day, think outside of the heart-shaped box.

If your daughter is an animal lover, consider expressing your love for her by donating pet food or money to a shelter. If your father has a heart for the hungry, shop for a local food pantry, take a picture of the boxes and bags of items you're donating, and create a card telling him that his life makes others better.

Or, you could just give your loved ones cheese.

What is the best gift you have ever given or received?

Love and Vacuuming

I don't know if I am vexed or not. I know I care very much about you!
—Thomas Hardy, *Jude the Obscure*

I first heard Billy Bragg's song "The Short Answer" when I was a newlywed. I'm happy to report that, unlike the couple in Bragg's exquisite lyrics, my husband and I never split up. But still, their story and the playful way he tells it has always resonated with me.

Early in our marriage, in the tender time after my husband and I had argued, I often thought of "Mary" in Bragg's song; she says that "no amount of poetry" would mend her broken heart. But, she suggests helpfully to her love, he can begin to make her feel a teeny-tiny bit better by . . . vacuuming the apartment.

There is pain and disappointment in every single marriage, even solid, generally happy ones. Excruciating conversations. Moments when we misunderstand each other. Times when we speak too roughly, explode with impatience, or are unsure of each other.

Isn't it true, though, that when your husband helps around the house, suddenly it's much easier to forgive him his failings?

Is there a simple task you could do today to show love to your partner?

Teaching Trust

I love these little people; and it is not a slight thing when they, who are so fresh from God, love us.
—Charles Dickens

My kids are all tweens and teens now. And much as I loved making up songs or silly stories with my children, watching them on the swings, or engaging in all manner of other sweet activities we no longer do, I also remember the downside to having young children.

Exhaustion and disrupted sleep. The tedium of potty training. Seeing them run toward the street, oblivious to traffic. Wondering if that rash or fever is a sign of something life threatening. Fearing that they'll never be able to tie their shoes, refrain from flinging food off of the highchair tray, sleep through the night, or learn those darn math facts.

But then these things pass.

The truth is, your children won't remember how many times you showed them how to write their names or how many books you read to them or how patiently you answered their questions or tended to their scraped knees. But that doesn't mean that those acts of love don't matter. Each kind word and act helps create and strengthen the bond you will share for a lifetime.

Remember that the work you do—even the most tedious tasks—teaches your children to trust, to know that you "have their backs."

Your People, My People

You and I are created for transcendence, laughter, caring. God deliberately did not make the world perfect, for God is looking for you and me to be fellow workers with God.
—Desmond Tutu

My friends Mark and Mary have five daughters, all of whom were adopted. Mark tells the story of once connecting in a special way with one of his daughters by echoing the verse "Where you go I will go, and where you stay I will stay. Your people will be my people and your God my God" (Ruth 1:16, NIV).

"You go, I go," he said. "Your people, my people." It's a mantra of love and connection that they have shared since then.

It's from the story of Ruth and Naomi. Naomi, widowed and crushed by the death of her sons, is stranded in a foreign land. She's so deeply unhappy that she threatens to change her name to Mara, meaning "bitter" (Ruth 1:20, NIV).

I don't know how you were brought up to think about God, but I didn't often get the message that we could be quite so, um, expressive to God when we were angry or resentful. God, though, proves in this story (and all through the Psalms, among other places) that we can be completely honest in our prayers.

One way God actively loves Naomi is through her daughter-in-law's devotion and kindness. At the beginning of the book, Naomi tells Ruth to go to her own mother's house, but Ruth says: "Whither thou goest, I will go."

Ruth's choice to stay with Naomi is a beautiful gift, but it is not the only gift she gives Naomi. When Ruth has a son, it is Naomi who nurses and cares for him, bringing her joy and hope for the future.

Talk honestly to God, make your thoughts into prayers, and know that you are loved.

Random Acts of Kindness Day

What wisdom can you find that is greater than kindness?
—Jean-Jacques Rousseau

My mother has a great habit. Whenever she's asked to do a favor, she says, "Yes!" with great glee even before knowing what she's being asked to do.

I'll begin: "Mom, I'm calling to ask you a really big—"

"I'll do it!" she interrupts. You'd think it was me doing her a favor. And the more I read about altruism, I think there's some truth to that.

Psychologist Jonathan Haidt has said that when we witness someone extending kindness to someone else—or when we perform a kind act ourselves—we experience a kind of "elation." It's what we sometimes call the warm fuzzies, when your heart feels expansive and open, suddenly connected to all of humankind. It's the Grinch's heart growing three sizes when he realizes that the folks down in Whoville have joined hands and are singing their "Welcome Christmas" song, even after he stole all their presents. They share love, connection, community.

Today is Random Acts of Kindness Day, an opportunity to experience (and spread) this elation and to feel a happy connection with humanity. We can pay for the person behind us in line at the drive-through. We can shovel our neighbors' driveway. We can send flowers, anonymously, to our children's teachers. We can stock up on gift cards from the grocery store and hand them to people in need.

Kindness is contagious. How can you help spread it today?

Love in Community

We have all known the long loneliness and we have learned that the only solution is love and that love comes with community.
—Dorothy Day

When I met Amy Hilbrich Davis, she lived in my neighborhood. I'd often see her on the school playground or run into her at Target, our carts loaded with toddlers and diapers and juice boxes.

Once, on leaving a store, I found her standing in the middle of the parking lot, laughing at herself for having forgotten where she parked. As is inexplicably true of many women I've met who have several children—she has seven!—Amy always seemed ready to laugh.

Life sort of kept putting us in the same room together, until she moved away several years ago. Since then, I've watched her become a nationally recognized parenting expert and grow her company, Family Life Success.

One of Amy's mantras for parents is that they do not isolate themselves but seek out and develop support networks, places where they can raise their hands when they're drowning and be rescued. I know she practices what she preaches because I have sat at her kitchen counter with other moms when she lived near me, talking about the pressures, disappointments, and small triumphs we'd all had that week. Being together, saying it all out loud, helped.

Are there groups at your workplace, place of worship, or community center that you can join? How can you build your support network?

Reaching Down and Lifting Up

There is no exercise better for the heart than reaching down and lifting people up.
—John Holmes

My friend's sister died after a prolonged battle with cancer, and I knew his grief was crushing. "I don't know what I can do," I told my friend Katie.

"First of all, send a card," Katie said. "People sometimes think it won't make much of a difference—and the sentiments on so many sympathy cards seem too flowery and trivial—but receiving cards actually helps."

She speaks from experience; her brother was killed in a car accident when she was a child. "If nothing else, opening the mail every day is a distraction," Katie said. "And seeing the cards pile up is a kind of comfort. Just knowing that other people are thinking of you."

Sometimes it's even harder to reach out to the dying. Should we enter into such a vulnerable moment? Is our friendship close enough to merit making contact? I wrangled with those questions recently when I learned that a friend was dying; I finally wrote a note thanking him for his friendship and humor and brilliant life, and expressing hope that we'd see each another again "on the other side."

His response was as warm and witty as I could have hoped for, and two days later, he was gone.

What have the losses you've experienced taught you about offering condolences? What helps you get through terrible times?

Showing Up

There is nothing I would not do for those who are really my friends. I have no notion of loving people by halves, it is not my nature.

—Jane Austen, *Northanger Abbey*

As the train pulled into the station, a young man approached me, a kind smile on his heavily pierced face. "Where you going?" he asked.

I handed him my ticket, avoiding eye contact with the screeching hawk that was tattooed on his neck.

"Oh, this train goes inland," he said. "Yours is the next one."

So, as he (and everyone else) boarded, I stood back and let the train go. The station was beautiful, with a grand façade and ornate ironwork. There were towering palms on the roadway. Ah, California. I sighed.

And then all the lights slammed off, and I was standing with a dead phone on an empty train platform. I found a schedule; no trains would come until the following morning. I wandered the streets near the station but saw no one. Finally, I found a security guard who let me into his office. I phoned the one person I knew who lived in that part of the state.

"Keiko," I said. "I'm in Glendale. I'm stranded."

In a half hour my friend was there, her white SUV a knight's steed coming to my rescue. She took me home, gave me something to eat, and tucked me into one of her children's beds.

I don't remember ever being so grateful to see someone in my life, and her kindness has marked me, revealing who she is to me, and models for me what it means to be a true friend.

Who are the friends who have shown up for you?

February 21
Self-Love?

Every child comes with the message that God is not yet
discouraged of man.
—Rabindranath Tagore

A friend posted a question as his status update on Facebook: "Do you think that, sometimes, our love for our children is actually a kind of self-love? And, if so, is that good or bad?"

The responses begin to come in, fast and furious:

"Yes, and that's good."

"Our spirit is in them, so we love ourselves in them."

"Yes and yes."

"Without a doubt. I love seeing the best parts of me come out in my kids. On bad days, it makes me feel like I did something right."

"Hardest challenge as a parent is our kids aren't 'ours.' They've been entrusted to us by God. We nurture and lead for a season. Then the roles change."

"From doing something for ulterior motives, we cultivate the impulse to do the same from more refined motives."

I like these answers, perhaps especially the last. It reminds me that serving others—actively loving others, including our children—awakens real love and depth in us.

What do you think? Is love for our children tainted by our own selfishness or self-absorption? Does it matter?

February 22
Hospitality

What is there more kindly than the feeling between host and guest?
—Aeschylus

One of my assignments for the local paper was to write restaurant profiles. Not reviews, but short pieces for which I interviewed chefs and owners and ate at their restaurants. It was not fancy: I was paid, but my expenses weren't covered. Usually, I broke even.

At the time, I discovered Ruth Reichl's book *Garlic and Sapphires: The Secret Life of a Critic in Disguise*. Reichl is a distinguished food writer and former editor in chief of *Gourmet* magazine. I subscribed to *Gourmet* for years, really just so I could read her delectable editor's letter every month.

Although I wasn't a real food critic like Reichl, I did learn a few things about restaurants.

And what I concluded, over and over again, was that hospitality was almost always just as important as the food at restaurants. A rude waiter could expunge the delight of perfectly cooked risotto. When, an hour before closing, chairs were loudly stacked on the table beside us or the odor of bleach solution filled the space, the vegetarian tasting menu was wrecked.

What mattered most was how welcome we felt.

∽

What makes you feel most welcome at a restaurant or when you get together with friends? What sort of hospitality do you practice at home?

February 23
Stages of Life

Growing up is such a barbarous business, full of inconvenience . . .
and pimples.
—J. M. Barrie

The sixth graders are the first to perform at the middle school orchestra concert. They are short and sweet faced, and they play haltingly. They seek out their parents on the bleachers and wave unabashedly when they see them.

The seventh graders are next. They are outgrowing their black concert uniforms. Acne has started to appear on their faces, and they look around nervously at one another as their conductor walks to the podium.

The eighth graders are tall. Many of the girls wear makeup and look poised as they await their turn to play. They sit up straight and listen quietly. And when they perform? It's music!

Parents of middle schoolers are thrown into a kind of strange time machine. We remember how excruciating that time can be. Suddenly our children have friends whose parents we don't know. Schoolwork is harder. One mom I know says kids this age are "self-interested monsters."

So, as our kids navigate this hard time, we do, too, ever looking back on our own awkward dances into adolescence, sometimes stepping on our kids' feet as we mature along with them.

In time, however, we adjust and start to make beautiful music again.

Look back on when you were in transition as a child. What made you feel most loved?

The Logs and Splinter

There is nothing noble in being superior to your fellow man; true nobility is being superior to your former self.
—Ernest Hemingway

The police blotter opposite my family life column was always more or less the same: DUIs, retail theft, property damage. And after the newspaper staff was cut, there was no one to do the "cops report," so I was asked to step in.

Every week for more than a year, I paged through dozens of reports at the police station and chose ten or twelve to recap in the paper. For me, it was not only an extra fifty bucks a week but also entertaining. Sitting in the inner sanctum of the police department with the reports of our town's dirty little secrets, I felt morally superior to these people with their embarrassing DUIs and domestic disputes.

It all went well until I included news of the arrest of two young men for drug possession. What I didn't know was that one lived in my neighborhood and had been quite troubled, much to his parents' despair, for years. The blurb in the paper hurt them badly.

Not long afterward, a new reporter was hired, and my editor asked if I wanted to continue with the blotter or be done with the assignment; I happily let it go. The novelty had worn off, and I'd lost my taste for other people's bad news.

When do you feel summed up or judged? Is there someone you can look on with more love?

February 25
Take Turns

Don't let the sun go down on your anger. Tell your wife she is
beautiful every day. Give him space at the end of the day to
transition out of his work mode. Set a budget and stick to it.
Take ballroom dance.
—Common bits of advice

Often, advice given to newlyweds strikes me as not only sexist, but
hopelessly unproductive.

My husband and I have gone to bed angry. He doesn't tell me
I'm beautiful every day. We've never been any good at making or
keeping budgets. And I'm too clumsy even to consider taking ballroom dance. But all the same, we've created a solid and happy
marriage.

I think, more than any of the above platitudes, one of the best
pieces of advice I'd give young marrieds is, "When possible, take
turns." If he cooks, you clean up. If you load the dishwasher, he
should empty it. And taking turns goes further than household
chores. If he's talking, listen. And he needs to listen when you have
something to say, too.

Think of your vows: if he's sick, try to be a healer. If you are
poor of spirit, let him find ways to remind you of how fortunate
you are.

Take turns leading, whether or not you're on the dance floor.

In what ways do you take turns with your spouse?

February 26
The Web of Family

In time of test, family is best.
—Burmese proverb

It was a long drive from Chicago to Charlotte, North Carolina. And I don't just mean the distance. My husband and I had argued about his driving; he took issue with the way I slammed my right foot down on an invisible brake pedal when he came up too close on another car. The kids' tempers flared over musical preferences and boundary issues.

I texted my sister-in-law as we sped down some unfamiliar highway in Tennessee. "Fantasizing about being anywhere but here."

"Long road trips = brutal," she responded. "Got a good Chardonnay chilling. See you in a few hours."

"If I'm not in the car with them, don't come looking for me."

On arrival, we plunged into the fray of in-laws and cousins. I secretly counted the minutes until I could be alone. But after dinner, my father-in-law announced that he and my mother-in-law had made a slideshow of family photos, spanning the fifty years of their marriage. Inwardly, I crumbled.

Scores of black-and-white wedding pictures were followed by baby pictures of my husband and his brother. Somewhere in the 1970s, my husband and his brother sporting heavy bangs and plaid suits with bell-bottoms, my heart began to soften. And by the time my wedding and the faces of my children flashed on the screen, I was wishing the slideshow wouldn't end.

The pictures calmed me, reminded me that my life was beautifully and inexorably bound together with the people around me by our choices, our shared history, and love.

What makes you feel closer to your extended family? When do you feel most connected to them?

Messes People Leave Behind

A good head and a good heart are always a formidable combination.
—Nelson Mandela

I was talking with a group of parents about our biggest "fails."

A young man raised his hand. One glance at his beard, retro eyeglasses, and flannel shirt made me picture the homemade granola he probably ate that morning—with rice milk. In college, we called his type "earthy-crunchy." Now they're called hipsters.

Anyway, Hipster Dad said he had always imagined that he and his wife would use cloth diapers and make their own baby food when they had a child, but as the first year of his son's life progressed, they began lowering their standards. Cloth was replaced by plastic. The pureed sweet potatoes came from a jar.

"You know when you're in a parking lot and you see a big, messy diaper on the ground and you wonder what sort of awful person would have done that?" he asked. "Well, that was me. I did that."

He told the story of a feverish baby; an explosive diaper; the eye-watering stench; and how, in utter despair, he had stripped his son, bathed him with baby wipes, folded the whole mess all together into a destroyed onesie, tossed it under his car, and driven off.

Now when he sees the messes people leave behind, he feels empathy, not scorn.

Can you think of something you did that you thought you'd never do? Look on yourself with love; we all are doing the best we can.

Time to Reflect

Let yourself be silently drawn by the strange pull of what you really love. It will not lead you astray.

—Rumi

As February comes to a close, think back over the month. Look over the February entries in your journal (if you keep one), the events you jotted on your calendar, and the reflections you read this month.

Look at all the ways you have loved and been loved this month.

What did Valentine's Day mean to you this year? Was it a day when you felt loved, showed love, or felt more alone?

What was the best gift of love that you received this month? The best one you gave?

Do you have any unfinished business this month: cards to send, or apologies to make?

How are you defining love in new ways?

Have there been times this month when you felt aware of God's presence and love for you?

Take time to reflect on the people you love.

Leap Ahead, or Don't

Just don't give up what you're trying to do. Where there is love and inspiration, I don't think you can go wrong.
—Ella Fitzgerald

As a child, I found the concept of "leap year" disturbing. An extra day every four years? Whenever February 29 appeared on the year's calendar, I'd dread landing on it all month long. Did I think we might accidentally get stuck there, in some strange temporal loop? What a relief to wake up on March first and turn the calendar page.

All over the world, leap year is steeped in superstition. In Greece, couples avoid getting married during a leap year, thinking it bad luck. The Italian proverb *anno bisesto, anno funesto* means "leap year, doom year." Yikes!

Do you pick up pennies from the sidewalk? Avoid walking under ladders or letting black cats cross your path? Do you knock on wood or cross your fingers for good luck?

We all wish we had some dependable way of controlling our fortunes. We wish we had some magic trick to keep our children safe and healthy, make our investments succeed, and prolong good weather.

But, of course, we can't. If you are reading this on February 29, consider it an extra opportunity to look at your life with acceptance for all of its uncertainty, magic, and heartache.

Today, embrace the whole mix of your life.

March

Practice Presence

Be Here Now

March 1

New Habits

We are what we repeatedly do. Excellence, then, is not an act,
but a habit.

—Will Durant

I hear it all the time, and often say it myself: "I want to be more present." But then I go back to rushing through making dinner, listening to music, checking email, helping my kids with their homework, and chatting online with a friend. All. At. Once.

Some of it can't be helped, but some can. And I know this kind of multitasking comes at a cost. I lose my grip on gratitude. I overlook beauty and the ordinary blessings around me. I skim over the surface of my life. My relationships suffer.

This month, join me in practicing presence.

Sit still and take several deep breaths. Close your eyes. What do you hear? The refrigerator's hum? The ticking of a clock? A bird outside? Listen for a few moments. Open your eyes. What do you see? The wisp of cloud that is smeared across on an otherwise clear, blue sky? Your daughter's smile?

Slow down your mind today and notice something you've been missing. Maybe it's the way carrots bleed orange on the cutting board when you chop them. Or maybe it's the flecks of gold in your son's brown eyes.

Maybe it's a desire for more stillness that gently tugs at your sleeve.

How can you be less scattered and more present today?

Showing Up

March came in that winter like the meekest and mildest of lambs,
bringing days that were crisp and golden and tingling, each
followed by a frosty pink twilight which gradually lost itself in an
elfland of moonshine.
—L. M. Montgomery, *Anne of the Island*

Before the play begins, the director gives the curtain speech. In closing, he says, "Now please turn off your devices. Cut yourself off from the outside world for the next ninety minutes. Be with us."

People pull out their cell phones, and there is a little symphony of beeps as they power off.

Understand that the finest gift you can give to another person is your presence. The people who are in the room with you deserve to come first. When your child approaches your workspace, close your laptop. Drop the cell phone into your pocket and greet the person bagging your groceries.

Remember that each person's life tells a rich story, including yours. Today, set your to-do list aside, breathe, and be present in your life in a deliberate way.

What might it mean for you to "show up" today?

Be Present with Difficult Feelings

*Compassion isn't some kind of self-improvement project or ideal
that we're trying to live up to. Having compassion starts and ends
with having compassion for all those unwanted parts of ourselves,
all those imperfections that we don't even want to look at.*

—Pema Chödrön

After church, my children and I stop for bagels. Three of my four
are taller than me. In our puffy winter coats, we take up a lot of
space in the small shop. It's hot, it's crowded, and we are taking too
much time figuring out our orders.

One of my children has recently announced she's vegan. "I
guess there's nothing I can have," she says, somewhat despondently.
She stares at the menu.

"Plain bagel with honey?" I ask. Did someone behind me just
clear his throat?

"Oh, so you consume insect products?" one of my sons says.
"Do real vegans eat honey? You don't care about bees?"

She glowers at her brother. Another one of my kids makes a case
for getting a Coke after I've said no to fountain drinks. The bell
above the door jingles and more people join the line. I start feeling
irritable.

I often stop being present in these kinds of everyday, fleeting,
frustrating moments. There's a traffic jam of thoughts in my head,
mostly imaginary complaints hissing from those behind me in line.

But, like every moment, this one passes and soon we're making
our way out of the shop, stepping over piles of slush, and getting
into the car for home.

*What makes your thoughts get knotted in your head? Does it help to
remember how fleeting our feelings can be?*

The Joy of Doing Nothing

Be happy in the moment, that's enough. Each moment is all we need, not more.

—Mother Teresa

The two hundred mothers in the audience drew back and stared at me as if I'd suddenly been transformed into a wildebeest. No, I hadn't told them to leave their marriages, beat their children, or get face tattoos.

All I'd said was that we all should take at least ten minutes every day to do nothing.

"Why is that important?" I asked. "Doing nothing?"

Someone raised her hand. "To pray?"

I shook my head. "Nope. Prayer isn't 'nothing.'"

"To meditate?" someone suggested.

"Not that either. We need to just sit. Daydream," I said. "I like to stand at the kitchen window, watch the birds on my feeder, and just sort of space out."

Most of the day, we're bombarded with information, news, music, sounds, and thoughts that spray graffiti on all the white spaces in our minds. Being silent and still—and doing nothing—quiets and centers us. It allows us to relax, to hear God's voice, and to be present.

Someone raised her hand. "My kids stare off into space a lot," she said. "I'm always jealous of that."

"So now's your chance to schedule some daydreaming time. Ten minutes of nothing. Every day."

~

Turn off your phone and set a timer for ten minutes. Take a deep breath and let out a big, heavy sigh. Stare out the window, at your hands, or at a picture on the wall. When the timer goes off, pay attention to how you feel.

March 5
Be Still

Be still, and know that I am God.
—Psalm 46:10 NIV

At the height of my multitasking addiction, I felt as if I was pulling one over on the space-time continuum. I had four young children! My work was published in the newspaper every week! I kept in close touch with faraway friends! I volunteered at church and at my kids' schools!

I used every little slice of time the day afforded me to do everything from pitching a story idea to an editor to cleaning out the refrigerator to teaching my son the names of the planets.

I said I didn't believe in the notion of supermoms, but let's be honest, I thought I just might be able to become one.

The problem was, little by little, my joy was slipping away.

There are certainly seasons in life that require some multitasking. But then we grow addicted to living that way and can't easily see our way back to a quieter, more balanced way of life. We load up on tasks, even when we don't need to.

When we're doing, doing, doing, it's difficult to remember how to just sit still. It's hard to be still or quiet enough to be aware of God's presence.

It's hard to feel whole.

Are you a multitasker? Can you imagine trying to do one thing at a time? What would be the costs of slowing down? Can you afford to give it a try?

The Painful Present

You must live in the present, launch yourself on every wave, find your eternity in each moment. Fools stand on their island of opportunities and look toward another land. There is no other land; there is no other life but this.

—Henry David Thoreau

For thousands of years, humans have been told that the key to happiness is avoiding pain and seeking pleasure (hat tip to the philosopher Epicurus).

As much as many of us like to wax eloquent about the benefits of being "mindful," mindfulness's dirty little secret is that being present can be much more painful than keeping busy and distracted and skimming over the surface of life.

If I distance myself from feelings of grief or disappointment by watching television, drinking a few glasses of wine, playing a game on my phone—or, as is so often depicted in "chick flicks"—downing a pint of good ice cream—I don't have to experience those feelings.

Problem is, they'll be back.

When I'm present with uncomfortable feelings, either by journaling, talking about them to a therapist or a friend, or praying about them, I revisit old wounds. I experience my losses again, viscerally. And in time, it will be the wounds that I've exposed, and for which I've sought care, that will heal.

When do you distract yourself from the present and from your feelings? Can you think of a way to be more present even with the difficult parts of yourself?

A Friend's Presence

*Life is a gift we're given every day. That's why it's called
the Present.*
—Unknown

My friend Caryn and I were just beginning to forge a friendship
when my sister died. Caryn had written a book about motherhood
and identity, and I'd interviewed her for my parenting column. I
so enjoyed our conversation about writing and faith and parenting
(and trying to balance all the above) that I asked her to lunch.

We met once or twice more at my favorite Thai restaurant, but
unlike most of the friends who would be at my sister's funeral,
Caryn had not yet experienced much of my real life. We'd not been
to each other's homes, confided in each other about the tricky parts
of our marriages, or had occasion to come together and solve a
problem. These things would come, but at that point, she and I
were more like acquaintances.

That is, until she showed up for my sister's funeral. I'll always
remember that day not only as the end of something but as the
start of a friendship I treasure.

And it was all because she showed up.

*Who has been present for you when you are grieving? How can you
show up for a friend?*

TMI?

Brevity is the soul of wit.
—Shakespeare, *Hamlet*

Sandwiches, the puddle she almost stepped in, a phrase she some-how found "tweet-worthy"—a former colleague of mine compul-sively recorded (by snapping pictures with her phone and posting them online) ordinary moments that didn't merit much attention. These were captured and captioned, rapid fire.

Do you know anyone like this?

It was extreme. As soon as the waiter brought us our meals, a picture of my beet salad would be broadcast on three different sites. She'd then look at her phone over and over, updating me on who said what in response to her post.

"Maggie says she hates the goat cheese here." "Bill says to try the sweet potato fries."

"Wait—don't drink that yet. Let me get a picture of it." And then my cappuccino would have its fifteen minutes of fame. Of course, the irony was that with all of that "capturing of the moment," she was never really there.

Later, I might be able to see exactly what I ate for lunch, but I never felt that we had real conversation or connection. She was always talking to someone else, someone who wasn't in the room with us.

Be with the people in the room with you rather than broadcasting snippets of your experience to people who aren't.

Alone Time

*The mind is sharper and keener in seclusion and uninterrupted
solitude. . . . That is the key to invention. Be alone; that is when
new ideas are born.*
—Nikola Tesla

I can't think of one mother who hasn't admitted to having the occasional escape fantasy.

A friend of mine recently wrote a rant to our group of friends about what a rough week she was having with her kids. She announced that she was not going to "see the good" and would not "be the change" she wished to see. She said it was all she could do just to keep from abandoning them all for a desert island somewhere.

Of course we all understood. In response, another friend wrote: "I just want to go where all the missing socks go."

When parenting feels too demanding and my husband seems distant or unappreciative, I indulge in a fantasy of taking a Greyhound bus to some remote town out west. I see myself working at a diner and living alone in a small, sparsely furnished apartment over a hardware store.

When I start imagining my gray polyester uniform, the smell of coffee left too long in the pot, and the semitrucks whizzing by on the highway, I know it's time for some alone time.

When I'm wise, I make sure that I get some.

When were you last all by yourself? Is it time for some time alone?

79

Waiting Places

I'd like to interrupt this sassy winter to say that spring will come.
—Eileen Button

My friend Eileen wrote the wonderful sentence I've quoted above as a status update on Facebook. Can you tell she's a writer?

It's such an "Eileen" thing to say—not only because, like her, it's charming and optimistic, but also because while it declares hope for the future, the coming of spring, it also shows an attitude of acceptance for the present, not-so-glorious moment.

By directly addressing winter, personifying, and throwing her arm around it, she befriends a season that has been long and frozen with arctic blasts. Or "vortexes" as they keep calling them on the news.

On the same day as Eileen's post, other friends of mine had lamented over school being canceled (again!), worries that the pipes would freeze, and the injustice of the unrelenting winter.

In her memoir *The Waiting Place*, Eileen underscored the fact that "to wait is human." We wait in traffic jams, in checkout lines, to grow up, to get well. And, of course, we wait for spring.

But, Eileen says, what matters is that we know that God is with us in all of our "waiting places."

Take that, sassy winter!

Instead of wishing away winter or other times that feel like "waiting places," how can we be present in them and trust that God is with us?

Right Now

The ability to be in the present moment is a major component of mental wellness.
—Abraham Maslow

What are you aware of right now? What are you feeling right now?

These common prompts, asked by yoga instructors, spiritual directors, and others, ask us not only to "be in the present moment" but also to acknowledge our feelings without judging them.

The questions are not, What *nice* things are you aware of right now? Or, What *happy* feelings are you feeling right now? They aren't about what you *should* feel, but about what you really and truly *do* feel.

Your child's teacher calls and asks that you come in for a conference. Before your mind starts its anxious origami—folding itself up into tiny triangles of worry—stop. Sit quietly for a few minutes. Relax your jaw and your shoulders. Breathe.

Then ask yourself, maybe more than once: What am I feeling right now? Dread? Worry? Fear? Anger at this child, or at the teacher? By taking a moment to clarify what you feel, you will be better equipped to have the conversation.

What makes your heart suddenly race? A forgotten appointment? A critical word? Seeing a certain name pop into your inbox? Relax your body. Stop and breathe.

Ask yourself: "What am I feeling right now?"

Make a habit of being more present with your real feelings.

The Flowers of St. Fina

Rejoice in hope, be patient in suffering, persevere in prayer.
Contribute to the needs of the saints; extend hospitality
to strangers.
—Romans 12:12–13 NRSV

Today is the feast day of Seraphina, who was born in Tuscany in 1238 and known in her lifetime as "Fina." Hers was a poor family, but Fina was admired for kindness and beauty.

At age ten, however, sometime after the death of her father, she contracted a disease that left her disfigured, paralyzed, and in constant pain. Wishing to imitate Christ's suffering, Fina asked that she be placed on a wooden pallet and not in bed. Her only possession was a crucifix, and she spent her days in prayer.

When her mother died, Fina was left destitute. In some stories, she then had only one visitor because her stench and ugliness repelled most people. But despite her suffering, Fina had unbending faith in God's goodness.

Fina died when she was fifteen years old, and it is said that white violets blossomed on her pallet. Since 1481, the town of San Gimignano has celebrated Fina's life on March 12, the day she died. She is credited with ending the plague there in the fifteenth and seventeenth centuries after the townspeople prayed for her to intercede on their behalf.

Every March, violets bloom in San Gimignano. They are called *fiori di Santa Fina*, "the flowers of St. Fina."

⌣

Despite her suffering, Fina was sure that God was good. What causes
you to doubt God's love for you?

Acknowledging Our Imperfections

No one is without difficulties, whether in high or low life, and
every person knows best where their own shoe pinches.
—Abigail Adams

A friend of mine is a college theater professor. Every year, he does a clowning exercise with his students, but not the kind that will bother you if you are not so very fond of clowns.

(Fun fact: Coulrophobia is the fear of clowns, and I admit to suffering from it.)

Anyway, for this exercise, my friend has his students identify a physical trait that they don't like about themselves. They write a short scene for a character that has an exaggerated version of the trait. The character has to somehow acknowledge and overcome whatever obstacles the imperfection generates. When they perform their scenes, the students must wear red clown noses.

One of his former students was extremely large breasted. She made her character even bustier by stuffing pillows under her shirt. Another student had bad acne and used makeup to draw huge red spots all over his face.

The busty woman's scene was about her character struggling to stand up straight, given her outsized pillow breasts. She overcame this by putting on a backpack, filled with heavy objects, to create counterbalance.

After acknowledging and poking fun at what they fear is the only thing people see when they look at them, the students are freed up from self-consciousness. Then they can create characters on stage that shine.

What do you fear is your worst physical trait? Can you acknowledge
your imperfections and take them more lightly today?

Real Life

*All things are literally better, lovelier, and more beloved for the
imperfections which have been divinely appointed.*
—John Ruskin

True confession: Sometimes I wish I were Jamie Lee Curtis.

It's not her movie career, whimsical (and best-selling) children's
books, or general effervescence that I most admire but, rather, the
stellar way she keeps organized. I read about it in a magazine a few
years ago.

Jamie Lee's home is a wonder. She stores everything from brown
sugar to cereal to DVDs in neatly labeled containers and binders.
All original packaging is tossed out. Her Christmas shopping is
done six months in advance. There is so much white space in her
house that you'd think she was just moving in.

And then there's me.

Although I love my label maker and my kids allege I'm a "neat
freak," I'm no Jamie Lee. I unload the groceries (packaging intact)
as fast as I can onto the jumbled shelves of my pantry. I'm years
behind on my photo albums. Instead of modern art, my daughter's dried-bean art and my son's childhood paintings hang in the
kitchen.

But to be present in my own, real life means I can't be Jamie Lee
Curtis, and my house won't look as sleek and pristine as hers.

And, honestly, when I stop and look at it, really look at it, I see
that this one, imperfect life I've been given is pretty sweet.

*What does your life look like in your fantasies? Today, try to be present
with your home, just as it is, and see the imperfect beauty of it.*

Releasing Worry

Beware the Ides of March.
—Shakespeare (spoken by a fortune-teller to Caesar in
Julius Caesar)

Today is the day known as the "Ides of March," the day—in Shakespeare's play—on which Julius Caesar was killed after being forewarned by a soothsayer. Although no mysterious stranger is alerting you of your impending death, I bet you have worries that haunt you and sometimes disturb your sleep.

When I find myself wide awake at 3 a.m., it's as if all my worries have been huddling together, biding their time in some shadowy corner of my mind until I awaken. And when I do, they all begin making noise, bumping up against one another, and clambering for my attention.

Unfinished tasks. Concerns over one child's grades or another's group of friends. Upcoming deadlines. Worse, as the minutes slog on, I'm subjected to a greatest-hits montage of my failures and regrets.

When I'm wise, I practice mindfulness to quiet those worries and shut off that ominous reel that shows all my faults.

I breathe deeply. I silently repeat a phrase such as "I am grateful" or "I breathe in, and I breathe out." I tell myself that I'm doing my best. I thank God for all the good that is in my life.

And, then, usually, I can sleep.

What worries keep you up at night? Can you acknowledge them during the day by talking to a therapist or a friend or by journaling about them?

Culling Clutter

Our life is frittered away by detail. . . . Simplicity,
simplicity, simplicity!
—Henry David Thoreau

At coffee hour after church, a woman I barely know plopped down next to me. "You know the rummage sale?" she said. "Well I, for one, don't have anything to bring to it."

A strange conversation starter, but I was game. "Oh, no?" I asked. "Why's that?"

"I finally did it! I got a Dumpster. It's in my driveway right now. This was me all weekend." She made a tossing motion, her arms arcing over her head. "It's such a relief. I've lived in clutter for too long."

"You're telling the right person," my husband said. "Jen hates clutter."

I do, but clutter happens.

I have four children who seem always to be carrying extra stuff when they come home. Goody bags. Bottles of blue sports drinks. Endless hairbands. And they keep leaving mounds of shoes and shirts and jeans in the wake of their growth spurts.

When I regularly do a "slash and burn," clutter is kept to a minimum. "Can we give this to someone who needs it?" I ask, holding up a trinket or sweatshirt or toy. (I feel it's a softer question than "Can I pitch this?") Usually, they consent.

Maybe they know that when the house is uncluttered, their mother is able to be more peaceful and present with them.

What helps you feel at peace in your home environment?

Liminal Places

No one ever told me that grief felt so like fear. . . . The same
fluttering in the stomach, the same restlessness, the yawning. . . .
There is a sort of invisible blanket between the world and me.

—C. S. Lewis

The first weeks at a new job or first trip to the grocery store with a new baby. Meeting the neighbors. Standing awkwardly at coffee hour after Mass on your first visit to a church. In times of transition, I feel uncertain, judged, and sure that everyone knows I'm floundering. These are "liminal places."

Grief can also put us in a liminal place.

My sister was my first family member to die, and her death was complicated. She had been out of touch with our family for years and had led a troubled, difficult life. But a few weeks before cancer took her life, she contacted us to say she was sick. Mercifully, she came home to us, and my brother and I were at her bedside when she died.

Afterward, I was in a liminal place. I didn't know this agonizing experience would change me. I knew that others saw me as fragile. I had to jump into taking on new, unexpected responsibilities with my sister's child. I felt emotionally exhausted and out of sorts.

And there was no way around my grief except through it.

⌒

Are you crossing over a threshold in your life? Be present with your
feelings, and walk through them, knowing that liminal places help us
become stronger and better able to love others.

Lent's Forty Days

No one but Night, with tears on her dark face, Watches beside me in this windy place.
—Edna St. Vincent Millay

Crosses are veiled. The word *Alleluia* is not spoken or sung. Flowers have disappeared from altars, and religious art is draped in cloth. Lent's forty days walk us slowly through the darkness to Easter.

The number forty echoes through the Bible. Moses spent forty days with God on Mount Sinai. The Hebrew people wandered for forty years in the wilderness on their way to the Promised Land. Christ was tempted for forty days in the desert.

And during Lent, many Christians endeavor to shift the focus of their lives to spiritual matters. We pray, practice self-denial, and give money to the poor.

A friend of mine once nicknamed Lent an "unwelcome visitor." We know it's on its way, year after year, and we anticipate the sacrifices we'll make—giving up sweets perhaps, or taking on a more difficult spiritual discipline. Which one of us, truly, looks forward to denying our ever-hungry, ever-egotistical selves?

But, after forty days of walking with our sober friend Lent, we are all the more ready to embrace the bright colors and Alleluias and indulgences of Easter.

⌒

Do you have a usual Lenten practice? How does focusing on Lent help you celebrate Easter more fully?

March 19

Presence in Nature

*Every day that dawns is a gift to me and I take it in that way. I
accept it gratefully without looking beyond it.*
—Henri Matisse

The wildlife refuge my family and I visit every summer in Florida
is an otherworldly place. Mangrove trees grow out of shallow salt-
water. Tiny fiddler crabs swarm on their branches and scurry along
the shore.

As we kayak through the refuge, we watch for egrets and herons.
I scan the bay for manatees. The air is warm, the sky a blue ceiling
above us. It is deeply quiet.

No phones ring; nothing calls my attention away from the
moment and place where I am. I *am* in the splash of water, the
tingle of the sun's rays, my arms rising and falling as the oars slice
through the watery path.

It's hard to imagine, on an icy March day in Chicago, that the
mangrove forest even exists. Was I ever really there? The low rumble of the snowplow passes outside my window. I pull a blanket
around my shoulders and reach for a mug of tea.

I can almost taste the salty water of Tarpon Bay.

*Where do you feel most present? Take a moment to remember what it
feels like to be there. What does it smell like? Look like? Feel like?
Taste like?*

Connections to Those Who Suffer

No one has ever become poor by giving.
—Anne Frank

Presence isn't just about savoring the sights, smells, and tastes we encounter every day. Nor is it only about taking time to appreciate and connect with our family and true friends. It's also about being authentic in this world and creating connections between ourselves and those who suffer.

Half the world's children are born into poverty. Take a moment to think about that. *Half.* That's hard to imagine if you live in a home where your children go to sleep every night, fed and warm and cuddled up with cozy blankets and pillows, stuffed animals and iPods.

Meanwhile so many other children live in places where violence and scarcity are the rule. Others are yanked from security and comfort when illness or random acts of unspeakable hate disturb the rhythm of their lives. Cancer diagnoses, school shootings, terrorist acts.

There is so much pain in the world.

A healthy mindfulness must include asking ourselves how we can accompany those who are hurting and how we can use our resources and gifts to alleviate hunger, suffering, and pain.

How can you address the needs of those who suffer?

March 21

Posture Telegrams

A good stance and posture reflect a proper state of mind.
—Morihei Ueshiba

I could blame my tendency to have bad posture on the years I spent pushing strollers around. Or I could explain it by telling you how many hours I spend at my computer every day, my shoulders hunched over my desk.

But honestly, I think I've always been a sloucher. Introverted, taller than my peers, and a little bit clumsy, when I was growing up I felt more comfortable slipping into the back of a room, shoulders stooped, and just watching what was going on. (I suppose that's the very definition of a wallflower, isn't it?)

But as I've grown older, I've worked at standing up straight, walking confidently into a room, and engaging with others. I am drawn to positive, outward-looking, secure people—and I want to project and embody those traits myself. Embody them.

But even now, when I feel intimidated or shy, my body reveals it. In fact, that's one thing I know about posture: it telegraphs how we feel about ourselves to anyone who's paying attention.

~

What are you telling others about yourself by your posture? Take a deep breath, drop your shoulders, and raise your chin. Does it make you feel different?

March 22

Focus

All in the wild March-morning I heard the angels call,—
It was when the moon was setting, and the dark was over all;
The trees began to whisper, and the wind began to roll,
And in the wild March-morning I heard them call my soul.
—Alfred, Lord Tennyson, "May Queen"

"Oh, sorry. I was somewhere else."

Have you ever said that? Although you were sitting right there, you weren't really there? You lost focus.

There are some things you absolutely cannot do unless you're focused. Deep reading, real listening, and prayer are among them. *Focus*, of course, has a few meanings. It can be a verb meaning "to make something clear." It's also a synonym for words such as *lucidity*. It can also refer to devoting oneself to a task.

We often use *focus* in that last way when we are trying to resolve a problem or deal with the aftermath of a crisis. Someone who's been very ill says, "I'm focusing on my health." Spouses whose relationship feels rocky might say, "We're focusing on our marriage." A person with a new or flailing company says, "I need to focus on my business."

But what about choosing to devote ourselves to a task *before* a crisis comes? What if we focus on presence before we lose touch with our kids, our spouses, our faith, or our dreams?

Is there anything in your life that needs better focus?

Just You and Me

"Doesn't it seem to you," asked Madame Bovary, "that the mind moves more freely in the presence of that boundless expanse, that the sight of it elevates the soul and gives rise to thoughts of the infinite and the ideal?"
—Gustave Flaubert, *Madame Bovary*

Our young children say, "Watch this!" twenty times a day, pull our faces toward theirs, ever demanding our undivided attention. Then years pass, and they start to play it cool.

On a recent vacation, I realized that it had been a while since one of my daughters and I had spent time alone together. We were jangly and out of sync. One rainy morning, I whispered in her ear, "Hey, let's get out of here. Just you and me." As soon as we were outside, she slipped her arm through mine.

The beach was empty, the water as steely gray as the heavy sky that hung just above it. We stepped over broken horseshoe crabs and mussel and oyster shells. I found a broken whelk, traced its spiral end, and dropped it into my pocket.

"Hey, look at this!" we shouted over the noisy waves. When we returned, our jackets sagged with shells and our shoes and clothes were soaked by waves and drizzle. And things felt right again.

I remembered then what I have learned so many times: when things feel skewed between one of my kids and me, spending time together is the solution. Just the two of us.

Is one of your children longing for your undivided attention? Can you give that today?

March 24

A Voice for the Voiceless

We must not seek the child Jesus in the pretty figures of our
Christmas cribs. We must seek him among the undernourished
children who have gone to bed tonight without eating, among the
poor newsboys who will sleep covered with newspapers
in doorways.

—Archbishop Óscar Romero

Archbishop Óscar Romero was assassinated on this day in 1980 while celebrating Mass in his native El Salvador. He had finished his sermon, walked to the altar, and was elevating the chalice when he was shot.

Romero was a controversial figure in El Salvador because he denounced human rights abuses by the government. His sermons were often broadcast on the radio, and Romero had a listening audience larger than any other Salvadoran radio program at the time.

He boldly cited cases of torture and repression, news that the government did not want him to spread. The day before he died, he implored Salvadoran soldiers not to violate the human rights of others, even when the state directed them to do so.

Romero is remembered as a twentieth-century martyr and a "voice for the voiceless poor."

In what ways can you speak out against injustice?

What We Don't Know

When the well's dry, we know the worth of water.
—Benjamin Franklin

My friend had his ups and downs.

When he was up, he'd grab my hand and insist we escape from campus for ice cream or to walk, tightrope-style, along the edge of the fountain in town. On parting, he'd pull me close, give me a hug, and spin himself out of my arms. "See you when I see you!" he'd call.

Then there were the downs. Groggy and out of sorts, he'd crash; stay in bed for days; and miss meals, classes, and work. But it always passed, and he'd be back to his happy self.

When, on a sunny March morning, I learned that my friend had taken his life, I was stunned. Only the day before, we'd been together, silly and laughing. "See you when I see you," he'd said.

After his death, a time of grief, anger, and confusion sent me into life-giving therapy and inspired me to learn much more about mental illness. I've long since stopped condemning myself about what I didn't know as a twenty-year-old, that I didn't recognize his illness or prod him toward help. I just didn't know.

Can you forgive yourself for mistakes you made out of immaturity or ignorance? Try to let go of judgment and remember that you did the best you could with what you knew.

What Makes You Cry

*Whenever you find tears in your eyes, especially unexpected tears, it
is well to pay the closest attention. . . . [M]ore often than not God
is speaking to you through them of the mystery of where you have
come from and is summoning you to where . . . you should go next.*

—Frederick Buechner

I see it over and over again. Often when women approach forty,
they get new clarity about their gifts and how they want to engage
with the world. Maybe it's because their kids tend to be older; no
longer caring for infants or sleep deprived, mothers have the ability
to take a broader view of their lives.

They begin to prune their relationships. They are bolder in
articulating what they want. They feel a restless and growing desire
to bring something new into the world, and that something usually
doesn't require a diaper bag. The idea of starting in a new direction
energizes and frightens them.

Some women I know have started nonprofit organizations or
small businesses, have attended college or nursing school, or have
become parents after they turned forty. They left comfortable,
familiar patterns behind and were willing to do so because making
a life change felt like a mandate.

The moment of decision often came when, surprised by the
tears that accompanied this vision, they saw the path where they
wanted to go. They knew that embarking on that path would be a
risk, but life had already taught them that every single act of love
is a risk.

*May we have clarity and faith as we pay attention to where God may
be directing us.*

Friends You Haven't Met

There are no strangers here; only friends you haven't yet met.
—William Butler Yeats

Speeding through the city, I stifle a sneeze. My taxi driver careens to the side of the street and turns around to look at me. "You have a cold!" he shouts.

"No, just sneezed," I say. (Did I miss some new legislation outlawing riding in cabs under the influence of a virus?)

He scowls at me and lunges back into traffic. I feel another sneeze coming.

"You have a cold," he says.

I look out the window as though I haven't heard.

"You know what to do?" he asks. He launches into a treatise on avoiding fruit, sugar, and raw food for five days. "And no dairy!" he shouts.

"But you know what's most important? Drink water. Room temperature. So much that you use the bathroom ten times a day."

"Okay," I say.

We arrive; I pay and open the cab door. As I step out, he shouts: "You!"

I lean back in.

"People drink orange juice," he says, grinning at me now. "They think it's going to help, but no. It gives them pneumonia. You remember the water?"

"Room temperature," I say. "And lots."

We both laugh. I watch him pull away, and he waves without looking around, as if he knows I'm still watching.

Be present with the odd and delightful not-yet friends you meet today.

Savoring Meals

When walking, walk. When eating, eat.
—Zen proverb

Nine years ago, after my husband and I relocated, one of our first house projects was to replace the kitchen countertop, widening it in one section so that it's more like an island. (It's actually a peninsula, if you're picky about your land formations.)

We planned to replace the cupboards whose doors hang slightly askew, switch out the floor for something more to our tastes, and do other fixes, but so far, we haven't.

Honestly, I don't mind. I'm just glad for that counter. On it we've dyed Easter eggs, done countless pages of homework, carved pumpkins, wrapped presents, and rolled out pizzas and piecrusts. The kids eat breakfast there every morning before school, facing me as I scramble eggs and make their lunches.

The one activity at the counter that I dislike with a fiery passion is when my husband grabs a plate of something and wolfs it down, standing at the counter, crumbs descending. It's like he's on autopilot.

It happens less and less, and not just because of my complaints. As the kids get older and we have less hands-on parenting to do, he takes time to taste the good gift in front of him.

Try to do only one thing when you are eating; sit and savor the meal, appreciating the way it looks, smells, and tastes.

How Close Is God?

Truth will not conform itself to our frantic avoidance of Reality.
—Adyashanti

One Ash Wednesday, I heard a homily that shook me. "Lent is not a self-improvement plan," the priest said. "It's not an opportunity to get rid of our vices, and it is most certainly not a time when you can get closer to God."

I flinched. It isn't? So what have I been doing all these years?

"God is as close to you as ever," he continued. "Close as the nose on your face."

Then we went forward to be marked with ashes, to remind us of our mortality, our smallness in the world. We're dust and will be again.

I had given a lot of thought to what I'd give up for Lent. I was not only going to practice self-denial, but was also going to take on a new spiritual practice. By Easter, I would be almost luminescent, holy and close to God. And now I was being told, quite clearly, that this was a silly, empty thing to imagine.

As the service continued, I realized that if I'm trying to "draw closer" to God, the God I'm picturing must be somewhere very far off, ever standing still, and out of reach.

Do you picture God as being close to you or far away? Where did you get this idea about God?

In Childhood

I cannot remember the books I've read any more than the meals I have eaten; even so, they have made me.
—Ralph Waldo Emerson

They started materializing around the house. Hardcovers with soft, yellowing pages. Paperbacks, their covers reinforced with cardboard. Thin, crinkly plastic taped over dust jackets.

When she was about eight, one of my daughters discovered Beverly Cleary, author of *Beezus and Ramona*, *The Mouse and the Motorcycle*, *Ramona the Brave*, and many others. I loved these books as a girl. I even wrote a fan letter to Beverly Cleary when I was in the second or third grade, and she wrote me back.

When asked in what year her books took place, Cleary always answered, "In childhood." And when I started seeing these old favorite novels of mine around the house, vivid snippets of my own childhood began returning to me.

Reading in my bed in summer, willow branches scratching across my window screen. Sitting in a classroom in winter, my socks wet in heavy boots. The cacophony of smells at the lunch table: sweet apple, pungent mayonnaise, and sour milk. Hearing the bells at the courthouse in town strike twelve.

I watched my daughter reading in bed, a stack of novels beside her, and wondered what details of her childhood she will remember when she's grown.

How can remembering fond details of your childhood help you connect and be present with your children?

Real and Ideal

The real enemies of our life are the "oughts" and the "ifs." They
pull us backward into the unalterable past and forward into the
unpredictable future. But real life takes place in the here and now.
—Henri Nouwen

I agreed to host several college students for dinner. A few days before they came, however, I was told—warned, really—that one of them came from an extremely affluent family and had a half dozen stunning homes all over the world.

Why was this worth mentioning? Was I supposed to serve caviar?

I hoped this young woman wouldn't be condescending. I hoped I wouldn't be distracted by knowing about the many spectacular homes she had and thus sour on my own house's imperfections: scratches and dings, the corner of the footstool the dog chewed when he was a puppy, and so on.

Finally, the students arrived and, on entering, the young woman whom I was concerned to meet almost burst into tears. "Your house!" she said, grabbing my arm. "I love it. It feels just like what a home is meant to feel like."

I would learn about the sorrow she'd grown up with and about her longing for a safe, comfortable place to call home. And again, I was reminded to be grateful—truly grateful—for the real, dented-up life I have.

Comparison is the enemy of joy; try to avoid it and to be grateful for
your life.

April

Practice Self-Care

Embrace Nurturing Habits and Rituals

April 1
April Fool's Day

Above all do not forget your duty to yourself.
—Søren Kierkegaard

April Fool's Day may be the perfect day to begin a month of reflections on self-care because most women I know (including myself) have an almost ridiculously complicated relationship with it.

Too many of us put ourselves at the bottom of a long to-do list. As mothers whose time is spent serving others—checking backpacks for permission slips, doing endless loads of laundry, quizzing kids on math and spelling words, clipping fingernails, buying groceries and making meals—we may think that taking time to care for ourselves is impossible.

Self-care can sound like a boring medical term or, worse, narcissistic. And yet we want to model good habits for our kids. We want to be healthy. We want to feel open and happy.

This month I'll share the ideas and perspectives of several different women on this topic, and I hope you will discover—as I have—that self-care is essential to our spiritual, emotional, and relational well-being.

Regardless of today's date, it's no joke.

What's your relationship with self-care?

April 2

Open to Nourishment

It is lack of love for ourselves that inhibits our compassion toward others. If we make friends with ourselves, then there is no obstacle to opening our hearts and minds to others.

—Unknown

The Romans named the fourth month of the year *Aprilis*, which is thought to be a derivation of the Latin verb for "to open." April is known as the month when buds open and bloom into flowers. Where I live, it's when we open windows; unzip our coats; and feel, finally, released from the confinement of winter.

It seems fitting to think about self-care in the context of opening. Taking care of ourselves isn't about self-improvement or "doing better." It's about being open—open to the unique and distinctive person you are, open to what makes you smile, open to putting yourself higher up on the priority list.

My friend Abby, a mother of three including one child with disabilities, puts it this way: "Rather than a point on my to-do list, I see self-care as a foundation, a grounding concept. It helps me to stay grounded in who I am and who I am becoming."

She continues, "Self-care relates to identity. I heard someone say recently that we must parent from our identity, not find our identity in parenting. Self-care supports this. Self-care is about the nourishment of you."

This April, pay attention to what helps you open up and what nourishes you.

True to Where You Are

We look before and after,
And pine for what is not,
Our sincerest laughter
With some pain is fraught:
Our sweetest songs are those that tell of saddest thought.
—Percy Bysshe Shelley, "To a Skylark"

My friend is struggling. She lives in a part of the country where winter loiters in April. The clouds have shrouded the sun for months. Mounds of gray snow resist melting, even on warmer days. She feels depression pull her up into its lap and hold her tight, refusing to let her go.

She sees a therapist, takes medication, and says she feels herself stabilizing. She doesn't feel happy or sad, just a low hum of detachment. In a recent email, she described trying to get well, and then said, "The worst thing is, I can't do anything for anyone outside my family. I can't volunteer or reach out."

She's a helper, ever ready to take on a neighbor's child for the afternoon or stand at the copier for hours volunteering at her kids' school. It feels unnatural for her to keep saying no, but she must. She needs to devote herself to getting well, not to being the person others might be accustomed to knowing, the person who brings cupcakes to the bake sale or volunteers at the food pantry.

It's not her turn to do these things. It's time for her to care for herself.

Self-care begins with paying attention to what you are feeling right now.

April 4

Courage to Say No

*In fact that is why the lives of most women are so vaguely
unsatisfactory. They are always doing secondary and menial things
(that do not require all their gifts and ability) for others and never
anything for themselves.*

—Brenda Ueland

Sometimes self-care means just saying no.

After directing the summer children's program at my church, I learned to fill positions by talking with each potential volunteer about what they most enjoy doing. You like cooking? Great—how would you like to be in the kitchen? Enjoy working with nonprofits? Okay—you're the liaison for the service project. And so on.

When asked about self-care, my friend McKenna said, "After making a few cross-country moves, I noticed that it began to be a relief to leave each place because I had so overcommitted myself. For the past two decades, I've practiced the best word ever: *no*."

McKenna said she's learned, from much trial and error, that "some things just don't have my name on it." These include "hosting loud boy sleepovers, mentoring young women, and agreeing to too many meetings or small groups."

"Saying no allows me to be able to say yes to the things that come my way that are cut out for me," she said. "It's a good way to live."

What tasks are you really cut out for?

Surprisingly Wonderful

Nourishing yourself in a way that helps you blossom in the direction you want to go is attainable, and you are worth the effort.

—Deborah Day

Margaret is a working mother of three who, after a difficult year, has renewed her commitment to self-care. After moving to a new part of the country with her husband and children, she had let self-care "fall by the wayside."

"Last year was a year of transition," Margaret said. "I yelled at the kids a lot, drank a lot of wine, and ate a lot of nachos. I gained almost ten pounds. I felt depressed."

When her kids were settled at their new schools and her work life had stabilized, Margaret stepped back and addressed her own needs more deliberately. She told me what she'd learned.

"What works best for me is paying for help with the things I care about the least, such as grocery shopping, errands, and household tasks. Being with my kids when they aren't in school is more important to me than being the one who picks out the oranges."

She began attending an exercise class twice a week, established a weekly date night with her husband, and keeps Sundays peaceful and unscheduled with her family. She describes her exercise class as "surprisingly wonderful." Her new practices aren't things she feels she "should do," but things that truly make her happy.

Is there any area of your life that feels out of balance?

My Favorite Things

Raindrops on roses and whiskers on kittens . . .
—Oscar Hammerstein (from *The Sound of Music*)

My daughter loves creating photo collages on her bedroom walls. The walls are covered with pictures: actors, singers, friends, her sister and me in black-and-white strips from photo booths.

One wall is decorated with every picture in a book of photos I bought for her at the Museum of Modern Art in New York. She opened the gift on Christmas morning, turned to me, and asked, "Can I put these up?" *Up* meaning that she would slice into the book and hang each one with sticky tack on her wall. (The effect, actually, is pretty remarkable.) Looking at the walls of her room is like looking into her heart.

Self-care is about knowing what your favorite things are, and celebrating them.

For my friend Margaret (the one who descended into a sea of wine and nachos in her bad year), favorite things include an entire day off on Sunday with her family. It's date night. It's her "surprisingly wonderful" early-morning exercise class.

My own favorite things include the tuna tartare at my favorite restaurant, my friend Keiko's homemade salted caramels, a hot bath with lavender bath salts, and playing Scrabble with my husband.

Self-care is about knowing what feeds you, what drains you, and what helps you not only persevere but even, sometimes, thrive.

What are some of your very favorite things?

April 7
Loving Ourselves

To love oneself is the beginning of a life-long romance.
—Oscar Wilde

When you were working on your favorite things list, were you tempted instead to craft a self-improvement plan? If you wrote "making healthy meals," "exercising every day," and "keeping an organized home," you might need a refresher course on what it means to be you.

Self-care isn't about being a supermom or having a perfect body-mass index. It's about being acquainted with—and loving—your real-life, imperfect, quirky, wonderful self.

Whenever I enter a friend's birthday into my calendar, I try to think of some of her favorite things so that when the date pops up again next year, I have a cheat sheet for buying her a gift. Under my friend Becky's name I have a list: Ben and Jerry's Chocolate Fudge Brownie, peaches, Johnny Depp. Under Elizabeth: gerbera daisies and chocolate-almond ice cream. I don't need to write it down, but my mom likes Vernors ginger ale and Canadian butter tarts.

What music do you like listening to? Which is your coziest pair of socks? Do you have a comfy blanket that you can't do without? A favorite pair of jeans? What smell always makes you linger? What brings you joy?

Embrace all the preferences and quirks that make you unique.

April 8

Free to Be

Man is free at the moment he wishes to be.
—Voltaire

A therapist friend told me, years ago, about a client who said to her, "I want to be all sparkly and spectacular again." She told me nothing else about the client—neither the issues she was dealing with nor anything about the woman's physical appearance. But I felt that I could pick her out of a line-up. I think I'd know her from her eyes.

I've had conversations with friends about that kind of wishing. I remember one woman telling our mother's group that she had a visceral memory of being a young girl and just pulling a dress on over her naked body and running around the yard in summer. "I wish I could be that free again," she said.

Another friend once spoke beautifully about how girls, a few years shy of their thirteenth birthdays, seemed so smart, buoyant, and full of possibility. "I want to be like that again," she said. "To believe in myself like that."

Is part of getting older losing that sense of expectation, that feeling of excitement about being alive, just as we are, in our own bodies? I don't think so. I know women in their nineties whose style, wit, and energy would charm you.

Maybe they even grin at themselves in the mirror, just for being so spectacular.

What makes you feel refreshed, special, even sparkly?

Loving Like We Love Ourselves

You shall love your neighbor as yourself.
—Mark 12:31 NRSV

What does it mean to love your neighbor? If you grew up in the church, chances are, you heard this verse many, many times.

My neighbor's life matters. I pay attention to its ups and downs, extend help when she's suffering, and laugh with her when she has good news. It's about being outward looking.

It's similar to the Golden Rule: treat others the way you would like to be treated. But I think it goes beyond that. If we love our neighbor "as ourselves," we perceive his or her life as meaningful and maybe even extraordinary.

So what does that have to do with self-care?

A friend put it this way, "Self-care is a biblical concept. God speaks to us about loving others based on the understanding that we value and love the individual life He has gifted us. Self-care is not self-absorption. It's the difference between seeing myself as an instrument versus an idol. I can be self-absorbed and egocentric, or I can see my life as an instrument God has given me to enjoy and to share with others."

How can you better enjoy the life, the body, and the personality that you have been given?

God Delights in You

*The lord your God is in your midst; he is a warrior who can
deliver. He takes great delight in you; he renews you by his love; he
shouts for joy over you.*
—Zephaniah 3:17 NET

Sometimes the church songs we learned as children haunt us. Their
lyrics may seem innocent enough, but for whatever reason, they
stick in our minds and make us feel ashamed. I have a friend who
calls these "toxic hymns."

When he was young, he was taught, "What a Wonderful Way
to Spell Joy," and every time he sang it, he felt a little bit more
diminished by its lyrics:

J is for Jesus for He has first place,

O is for others you meet face to face,

Y is for you, in whatever you do,

Put yourself third and spell JOY.

As a child, the message he heard from those lines was, "You don't
count. You come in dead last." As an adult, he's a devout, caring
person. But talking about what he likes and what refreshes him,
and making time for these things feels almost sinful to him.

Self-care is about taking care of your very human self. It's believ-
ing that God delights in us, made us just as we are for a reason, and
that just like everyone else, we deserve to love and be loved.

*Do any messages from childhood interfere with your notion
of self-care?*

Unsteady Balance

I know why families were created, with all their imperfections.
They humanize you. They are made to make you forget yourself
occasionally, so that the beautiful balance of life is not destroyed.

—Anaïs Nin

Last month we recognized that being present can be more painful (initially) than skimming over the tops of our lives, and that it's worth it. Self-care has a dirty little secret, too: when you commit to it, you'll probably have to let something else go.

Maybe dinner at your house will be later three nights a week, you'll have to resign from a volunteer position or two, or maybe—gasp—you'll have to reduce the amount of time you're online.

You'll have to make room for it.

My friend Joyce, a busy mother of three, says she "creates sanity in the midst of a full life" by staying up late. "I'm an introvert," she says. "After a full day, it renews me to spend some time alone. Even though I get less sleep, I find that my tomorrow begins on a good note when my today has ended with some time to process and regroup."

She continues: "One way that I deal with my frequent late nights is taking naps. When I can, I'll go back to bed for an hour or two after the kids are off to school. Even a catnap in the afternoon can be renewing."

How can you shuffle your priorities so that you can better care
for yourself?

April 12
Expose Your Wounds

Most things break, including hearts. The lessons of life amount not
to wisdom, but to scar tissue and callus.
—Wallace Stegner, *The Spectator Bird*

Abby tells a story: "A number of years ago, I had a miscarriage that devastated me. About a month afterward, I went to have a massage, which is something I love, but rarely do.

"The therapist, whom I knew, asked me about my physical health before beginning, and so I told her about my miscarriage. She wisely prepared me and said that sometimes people cry during a massage. She said that it was okay to do so.

"And cry I did, quietly and steadily, as my body released pain and as it received nurture. It was a bodily and spiritual healing and one of the best examples of self-care I have ever experienced."

Again, when we are present with our real feelings—rather than burying them under a busy schedule, endless texting, or some other way we check out from life—it can be painful. Only when we expose our wounds can they be healed.

Do you have wounds that you hold inside that need to be addressed?
How can you be kind to yourself about what you've suffered?

April 13

What You Say to Yourself

*The sick in mind and, perhaps, in body, are rendered more darkly
and hopelessly so, by the manifold reflection of their disease,
mirrored back from all quarters, in the deportment of those about
them; they are compelled to inhale the poison of their own breath,
in infinite repetition.*

—Nathaniel Hawthorne

Another way to care for yourself, to love yourself as you love
your neighbor, is to pay attention to what you say to yourself. If
you break a glass or thoughtlessly shout at your kids, what's your
response? *Nice one, klutz! I'm such an idiot!* or *Why am I such a bad
mother?*

One of my best friends called me, years ago, on a very bad
mothering day. She sounded hoarse and was whispering.

"You okay?" I asked. "You sound awful."

"I lost my voice," she said. "I've been yelling at the kids all afternoon. I am a terrible mother."

Of course she is not a terrible mother, but she was definitely
having a terrible day. I asked her what happened, and she croaked
out the whole long story. The bickering kids. Water streaming
out of the broken dishwasher. The important conference call she'd
missed.

Do you think I told her she was an idiot? Of course not. I
told her that it was completely understandable that she was coming apart at the seams, that no one should have so many rotten
things happen in a row, and that she is a wonderfully good-enough
mother (which she is).

We all are.

⌒

*Next time you mess up, pay attention to your self-talk. Can you speak
to yourself like a supportive friend?*

April 14

Always and Never

*Three things in human life are important: the first is to be kind;
the second is to be kind; and the third is to be kind.*
—Henry James

When we were engaged, my husband and I went through a pre-
marital counseling class at the church where we would be married.
It met every Saturday morning for a few months, and decades later,
it's funny how few things I can remember from the class.

First, I remember the leaders telling us that sex is the "oil that
keeps the lamp burning." Second, that we should never begin arguments with "You always" or "You never." And I think that is the
full collection of words of wisdom that I recall from eight weeks of
counseling.

My spotty memory aside, I'd say that the second piece of advice
applies beautifully to self-care. When we're angry and say "You
always" or "You never" to ourselves or someone else, we are summing up. You're not "always" or "never" anything.

You are ever in process, becoming.

⌒

*Don't sum yourself up negatively in your self-talk. Speak with
compassion and know that you are still in process, still growing, still
becoming the wonderful person you know that, deep down, you are.*

U.S. Tax Day

*In this world nothing can be said to be certain, except death
and taxes.*

—Benjamin Franklin

Every weekend, starting sometime in February, our dining room table, where homework is done, board games are played, and—yes—dinner is eaten, is transformed into Tax Preparation Central.

My husband peels back the tablecloth and plunks down accordion files, his laptop, and piles and piles of paper. I don't envy him. I mean, even Albert Einstein said, "The hardest thing in the world to understand is the income tax." Albert Einstein!

If you are bleary eyed after weeks of preparing your forms for the IRS, consider how you might indulge in self-care.

Whether we are feeling flush or not, I buy fresh flowers for our entryway almost every week. They are nothing extravagant, just a cheap grocery-store bouquet of tulips in the winter or sunflowers in the summer. I like the fragrance. I like walking past them several times a day on my way up and down the steps. I like that, when people come into our home, these flowers are the first things they see.

Flowers make the space feel inviting, hospitable. In cold winter months, they point confidently to spring, and in nice weather, they just sort of show off God's imagination.

What small, special things bring you pleasure?

April 16
"Whatever"

*One person with passion is better than forty people
merely interested.*
—E. M. Forster

Of all the bad words my kids have used—and I'm aware that I don't know every word they have uttered in lunchrooms or on lacrosse fields—the very worst, most objectionable one I've heard them say is "Whatever."

Whatever. When that word started popping up, I knew I had to take swift action to outlaw its use in our home. There's nothing helpful, nothing healthy about it.

Whatever, spoken with a great heaving sigh, means "I don't care" or "That's mind-numbingly dull" or "I knew I'd lost that battle" or "I refuse to engage with you." *Whatever* indicates there's no passion, commitment, or engagement. It's an insult. What-ever.

I hated the thought that my kids would make "whatever" a part of their vocabularies. I want them to be curious and engaged with the world. I want them to care.

As you look at your own passions, favorites, and interests, don't "whatever" yourself. Don't let the fact that you've been immersed in never-ending responsibilities as a parent make you lose the person you have always known yourself to be.

⌒

*Grown-ups have passions, too. What are yours? How can you begin to
jump back in to them with both feet?*

Daily Examen

He who carries God in his heart bears heaven with him
wherever he goes.
—St. Ignatius of Loyola

My friend Angie, mother of two daughters, is an author who, as she puts it, "goes in stages when it comes to self-care."

"Some seasons I'm rocking it; others I fail and burn myself out. The good news is that the good seasons are getting longer, and more frequent."

One of the ways she nurtures herself is to practice the Daily Examen every evening, an ancient prayer practice in which she reflects on the events of her day and discerns God's presence with her.

"I'm a night owl, so night works best for me," Angie said. "I tried the morning thing. Fail!

"One of the steps is to pay attention to your emotions. Since I'm such an emotional and intuitive person, this is the part where I really connect to God. I imagine myself nestled in God's lap while we share this time together."

The five steps of the Daily Examen are

Becoming aware of God's presence

Reviewing the day with gratitude

Paying attention to your emotions

Choosing one feature of the day and praying from it

Looking toward tomorrow.

Might making a daily time of prayer or meditation be an effective
way for you to practice self-care?

April 18
Baby Steps

Small steps lead to big change.
—Unknown

A decade ago, as the mother of four kids age seven and younger, I knew that I was falling behind in terms of taking good care of myself, but I didn't have the time or the mental space to give it much thought. My priority was the children, and looking back, I think I took on my responsibilities with a bit more—ahem—urgency than was required.

Note to younger self: parenting is a marathon, not a sprint.

After the birth of my first child, I aimed to be the quintessential Earth Mama with wooden toys, natural fibers, and organic foods. No grains of refined sugar would fall on my precious babies' lips. I started out strong, but the entrance of each subsequent child caused my impossibly high standards some wear and tear. And we are all the better for it.

I did notice that other moms took pottery classes or weekend trips with their friends. They wore workout clothes to preschool drop-off so they could go from there directly to the gym.

I was in process, just getting my footing as a mother, but if I could talk to my younger-mom self, I'd tell her to pay attention to those women. They were onto something.

Do you ever feel an internal nudge to take better care of yourself or take time for your own interests?

Say Good-bye to the Duke of Swirl

Insist on yourself; never imitate. Your own gift you can present every moment with the cumulative force of a whole life's cultivation.

—Ralph Waldo Emerson

A mom in my parenting support group admits that she hates board games. The way she says it, you'd think she was confessing to having murdered the postman with a dull kitchen knife.

"I hate it. I just hate it," she says. "But you're supposed to play with your kids so I sit there, by the hour, playing Candy Land."

Now I have to admit, I'm a Candy Land fan, but I don't love seeing mothers squeeze themselves into impossible molds that were made for someone else.

"What do you like to do?" I ask. "Like even before being a mom. What did you do with a free afternoon?"

"Oh," she says, relieved to be off the topic of Duke of Swirl and Gramma Nutt. "Let me think. You mean what I really like to do?"

I nod.

"I loved to bake. I mean, I *love* to bake."

"So, what if you didn't play Candy Land anymore but started teaching your daughter to bake?"

Her relief was palpable, and I could almost see that game as it flew into the recycling bin. And I could also see a mom who would have much more fun with her child and feel more authentic and happy.

⌒

Self-care is about being authentic with your kids. What activities can you share that nurture you, too?

Staying Awake

Compared to what we ought to be, we are half awake.
—William James

Sometimes self-care is about staying awake.

For most of us, staying awake isn't merely about the hours we keep, but about not sedating ourselves with distractions.

One friend admits, "Sometimes, it's tempting to default to something that anesthetizes me when I have a free hour instead of choosing something that truly nurtures me. Self-care can mean saying no to myself when I am tempted by things I know are not good for me, even though I don't like hearing myself say it."

It's hard, isn't it? Self-care isn't about eating your vegetables and taking your vitamins but about doing what leaves you refreshed.

But we know that sometimes the things that bring us momentary pleasure aren't best for us. We eat too much, spend too much, drink too much—all in the name of "indulging ourselves" after spending too much time serving others or working hard at some task. These indulgences can make us feel more hollowed out, more in need of the refreshment we crave.

Choose what truly sustains you.

It's no fun to take a hard look at our vices, but breaking our unhealthy, default patterns can be the most loving choice we can make for ourselves.

Rejuvenate

I don't want to be alone. I want to be left alone.
—Audrey Hepburn

Maeve is an at-home mother of five. Her youngest is an infant, and her four older children attend three different schools. She and the baby, she says, "live in the car."

Asking her what she does to refresh her spirit is like asking if she's ever been to outer space. She looks dumbstruck at the suggestion. Her older children are swamped with homework, four of the kids play instruments, and she's committed to ensuring that all her kids have unscheduled time to just roam the neighborhood and play with friends. She knows it's essential for their emotional health just "to play."

But how does Maeve "play"?

"Hmm," she says, "aside from the occasional movie with friends, I find it a struggle to find any time for myself these days."

She's not alone, of course. Many mothers, especially mothers of infants, can barely find time to shower. But is it hopeless?

Maybe Maeve can refresh herself by taking small steps, such as praying the Examen, using time in the car to listen to music she truly likes, and letting the laundry go unfolded so she can take a bath or read a novel.

Would any of these things rejuvenate you?

~

Even if you're in a season of life that affords little time for yourself, pay attention to what feeds you. Now isn't forever; a time will come when you have more space to tend to your own needs. Try not to forget what they are.

Deep Breathing

When you arise in the morning, think of what a precious privilege it is to be alive—to breathe, to think, to enjoy, to love.
—Marcus Aurelius

One of my first jobs was as an administrative assistant in Manhattan. I had a cubicle in a maze of cubicles, a computer with two big floppy-disk drives, and a swiveling chair. I learned to master the Telex machine, did filing, made spreadsheets and slideshows, and ordered lunch for my boss.

Although I didn't smoke, I looked forward to when, one by one, the smokers would stand up and touch two pointed fingers to their lips in a quick motion. *Time for a smoke.*

I took the elevator down with them, and we stood outside, rain or shine, chatting and laughing for the few minutes it took them to finish their "cancer sticks," as they called them. I had the best of all worlds: a break from the fluorescent lights and recycled air; the easy camaraderie of the smokers; and pink, happy lungs.

One day, I had a flash of insight. Sure, my colleagues were addicted to nicotine, but they were getting something else from smoking: deep breathing. I began taking long, deliberate breaths, too; it relaxed me.

Take three "cleansing breaths." Inhale through your nose, slowly fill your lungs, and then exhale through your mouth. How does that make you feel?

St. George's Day

It does not do to leave a live dragon out of your calculations, if you live near him.
—J. R. R. Tolkien, *The Hobbit*

Today is St. George's Day. George is not only the patron saint of England and several other nations; he is also the subject of more legends than perhaps any other saint. And, from Raphael to Kandinsky, artists have illustrated him slaying that fierce dragon.

But honestly, not much is known about the historical St. George. Some stories say he was born in the third century in what is modern-day Turkey, that he was a Roman soldier, or that he resigned from his high-ranking position in protest over Emperor Diocletian's persecution of Christians. He was then punished for his faith; he was force-fed poison, boiled in molten lead, and tortured in many other ways. Finally, he was beheaded.

It's a strange paradox that the most recognizable image of the man who was so horribly persecuted and murdered is that of a winsome knight slaying a vicious dragon.

But in countless paintings and works of literature, that is the St. George we remember: the heroic dragon slayer on his white horse, saving the life of a fair maiden.

When have you been bravest? What do you want to be remembered for?

New Normal

Hold fast to dreams
For if dreams die
Life is a broken-winged bird
That cannot fly.
—Langston Hughes

Sometimes the monsters we battle are invisible to others and locked deep within us. Depression. Sickness. Grief. Self-doubt. When we are mired in a dark place or when the very best efforts we can muster are anemic, it's hard to imagine ever feeling like ourselves again. What was it like to feel alive and happy and free?

And we realize—and most of the time we're spot-on—that no matter how well we heal, we won't ever be the person we were before. Things have changed; there's a new normal.

A breast cancer survivor and mother of three, one of my friends is in the habit of identifying herself as a runner: among many other races, she's completed three marathons. But now, after treatment, she says, "I couldn't run a mile if I tried."

"I couldn't run for several months, simply due to recovering from surgery. And that got me out of the habit," she said. "I found myself weepy and solidly depressed for about six months."

She wants to begin again but is aware that it might be a different experience for her now. But she hopes she can find the courage to give it a try.

Have you lost touch with any of your passions? Can you reengage with them, knowing that the way you do them now might be different from before?

Have Fun Out There

Laughter is the closest thing to the grace of God.
—Karl Barth

My husband coached both of our daughters' softball teams when they were younger. I admit that I signed him up every year without asking, because I knew that, given our busy lives, he might hesitate to volunteer. It wasn't a burden but a chance for him to spend focused time with our girls. Coaching made him happy.

One of my favorite things about the way he coached was that, several times a game, he called out: "Hey, girls! Are you having fun out there?"

They'd wave at him, grin, and give a thumb's-up.

He retired as a coach when they reached fourth grade. "It gets too cutthroat for me," he said. And he was right. As the girls got older, tensions ran higher during games. I've seen parents storm out onto the field, shout obscenities at the high school boy who was umping, and glower at their kids after they played poorly. That, I'm glad to say, is not my husband's style.

When he coached, my husband cared about the girls growing as players, coming together as a team, and learning the fundamentals of the game. But most of all, he wanted them "to have fun out there."

⌒

How do you coach yourself? Do you shout at yourself for every dropped catch and bad throw, or do you, several times a day, remind yourself to "have a little fun"?

April 26
Counting Our Blessings

Hold hard then, heart. This way at least you live.
—Derek Walcott

My friend Angie realized she wasn't "having fun out there" as a mom. She thought it might have to do with how often she judged herself, silently scolding herself for something she should be doing as a mom but wasn't.

One morning, she decided to count how many times that day the word *should* crossed her mind. She lost count well before noon. "I realized that in each instance I was disparaging myself for not measuring up," Angie said. "I was expecting something of myself that is utterly impossible, and getting mad at myself for failing. I was my own worst enemy, and I knew something had to change."

She continued: "I started by accepting God's grace into my mothering world, and by praying that God would help me be graceful toward myself. I asked and continue to ask daily for a sense of humor, a playful spirit, and a willingness to experience adventure and laughter."

She said that it has taken years to release herself from that disparaging voice, but now she takes herself much less seriously. "I work to count blessings instead of chide myself."

Ask God for a playful spirit in your mothering today.

Find Refreshment

True silence is the rest of the mind, and is to the spirit what sleep is to the body, nourishment and refreshment.
—William Penn

Hazel is ninety something, my only nonagenarian friend. We met about a dozen years ago when she cared for the preschoolers at our church. My youngest, Mia, was three and had a serious speech impediment, but whenever we arrived at church, there was no second-guessing what Mia was saying. "Where's my classmate?" she'd call. "Where's my Hazel?"

And Hazel loved their friendship as much as Mia did.

A few years ago, Hazel stopped coming to church because her husband, also in his nineties, became too fragile to make the trip. Now a lay minister brings the Eucharist to them at the "senior citizen storage facility," as some of its residents playfully call it.

Hazel told me recently that she sometimes feels burned out by the full-time job of caring for her husband at the home. When her need to be alone is dire, she prolongs trips to the pharmacy or grocery store by stopping in at a coffee shop, just to sit in the corner, sip a warm cup of tea, and be all by herself. These times refresh her, and when she returns home, she is eager to be with her husband again and ready to take on the day's challenges.

She ended the conversation the way she always does: "Now, enough about that. Tell me how my classmate's doing these days."

What can you do to refresh yourself when you are feeling spent?

Nails, Nails, Nails

Do something every day that is loving toward your body and gives
you the opportunity to enjoy the sensations of your body.
—Golda Poretsky

I've never been a "girlie girl."

As a child, I liked kicking through the woods by myself, reading books, and playing basketball with my brothers. I never understood the girls whose hair was shellacked into place, whose use of cosmetics went beyond Bonne Bell Lip Smackers, or who spent their free time at the shopping mall solemnly considering the fashions displayed on faceless mannequins.

But in my twenties, I discovered the joy of lipstick. A little dot of plum on my lips and I felt like, I don't know, Demi Moore. And then, a few years later, living in New York, I developed a Friday manicure habit. I'd get off the subway after work on Friday and slip into the nail salon, slap down seven bucks, and leave feeling fancy and groomed for the weekend.

And only a few years ago, I discovered eyebrow threading. After my first appointment, I looked in the mirror and said, "Well, hello, face!"

Now the occasional overdue manicure or even more belated trip to threading date is a treat. These silly little things make me feel that I'm loving my body. They remain on my self-care to-do list.

What are you doing to take care of yourself?

April 29

Lose Yourself on the Cross

He will provide the way and the means, such as you could never have imagined. Leave it all to Him, let go of yourself, lose yourself on the Cross, and you will find yourself entirely.

—St. Catherine of Siena

Today is the feast day of Catherine of Siena. A writer, mystic, and saint, Catherine died on this day in 1380. Catherine was such a happy little girl that her nickname at home was "Euphrosyne," the Greek word for joy. When she was five or six years old, she began to have supernatural visions and mystical conversations with God.

As a teenager, Catherine dedicated her life to prayer, penance, and caring for the sick. Intensely compassionate, Catherine was said to have "the gift of tears"; the suffering of others affected her greatly. She also had the gift of healing.

Although she wasn't formally educated, Catherine was a prolific writer and dictated hundreds of letters. Most have survived to this day. Her book, *The Dialogue of Divine Providence,* was said to be dictated to a scribe while she was in a transcendent state, talking with God.

So what does the life of St. Catherine have to do with taking care of ourselves?

As Catherine shows us, our bodies are instruments through which we can love and serve others. Self-care and self-absorption are not the same.

May we, like Catherine, be awake to the presence of the Divine.

Healthy Self-Esteem

If you want to be happy, be.
—Leo Tolstoy

When I walked into her house, my niece's hands were clasped behind her back. She rocked forward and back on her heels, brimming with pride.

"Ooh," I said. "What do we have here?"

"Ta-da!" she said, thrusting a piece of paper into my hands.

Her kindergarten teacher had given the class unlined sheets of paper with one sentence typed at the bottom: "My favorite person is _____."

My niece's answer? "My favorite person is *me*." Above it, she'd drawn a big, smiling picture of herself.

That was about twenty-five years ago, and I'm glad to say, my niece is still someone who shines with healthy self-esteem. But if someone were to ask who her favorite person is today, I imagine she might name her mother, her husband, or one of her best friends. She would probably think it inappropriate or narcissistic to name herself.

But wouldn't it be great if, as adults, we were able to be so comfortable with our appearances, personalities, gifts—and even with our faults and shortcomings—that we could grin and say, "Me!" when pressed to name our favorite person?

Who are some of your favorite people? What about adding yourself to that list?

Risk

Do not be too timid and squeamish about your actions. All life is an experiment. The more experiments you make the better. What if they are a little coarse, and you may get your coat soiled or torn? What if you do fail, and get fairly rolled in the dirt once or twice. Up again, you shall nevermore be so afraid of a tumble.

—Ralph Waldo Emerson

May

Practice Forgiveness

Give Up Unforgiveness, Let Go

Letting Go of Resentment

*As I walked out the door toward the gate that would lead to my
freedom, I knew if I didn't leave my bitterness and hatred behind,
I'd still be in prison.*

—Nelson Mandela

The first third of this year was about reflection.

In January, we looked at the practice of patience and "living and
loving the questions." We then focused on connection and sharing
our "best strawberries" with those we love. March had us considering what it means to show up more fully in our lives, and last
month, we explored the gifts and challenges of taking good care of
ourselves.

Now that we have made it through the winter—perhaps both
metaphorically and literally—we will breathe in the spring air and
take some chances.

This month, as we look at forgiveness, we need to admit that it
is truly a risk to forgive someone, as it is when we offer an apology.
We might be rejected. Old wounds might be reopened. We might
have to look at parts of ourselves that we'd rather ignore. We might
have to let go of a painful part of our story.

Forgiveness takes the shame out of the mistakes we've made and
the disappointments we've accrued. It helps us make peace with the
real life we've been given.

Are you ready to risk?

Empty Unforgiveness

Forgiveness is the name of love practiced among people who love poorly. The hard truth is that all people love poorly. We need to forgive and be forgiven every day, every hour increasingly. That is the great work of love among the fellowship of the weak that is the human family.

—Henri Nouwen

Holding on to resentment damages us. Our "unforgiveness" confines us like an ill-fitting winter coat that we wear every day all year long, regardless of the weather. It's ugly. It makes us squirm and sweat. It doesn't go with anything.

Resentment does even more than that. It keeps us bound to the ones who hurt us. They're ever on our minds, and they still—often unbeknownst to them—have the power to rob us of joy.

But it can be agonizingly hard to forgive. When we are reeling from a betrayal or injury, we can't imagine what it would be like to forgive. We wonder, *Wouldn't forgiving mean that I had no right to be hurt in the first place? Aren't I letting them off too easily?*

I've held onto grievances as trivial as a dinner guest's bad manners and as weighty as my father exiting my family when I was a child (more on both to follow). But, big or small, my unforgiveness has never brought anything good into my life, and it has never evoked contrite responses from the people who have hurt or insulted me.

Make a list—either a mental one or in your journal—of the people who have hurt you. What did they do? How long have you been holding onto these wounds?

Soul-Clearing Forgiveness

Forgiveness is the key to action and freedom.
—Hannah Arendt

Even when we understand that forgiveness is essential to our health and happiness, it's still a challenge to forgive. My friend Rachael admits that, even after accepting an apology, she often continues to hold onto the injury and negative feelings.

"It is very difficult for me to forgive, and I'm not happy or proud about that," Rachael says. "I completely believe that forgiveness is the best way to go. But apparently my head knows things my heart cannot accomplish."

Rachael understands forgiveness as a spiritual practice: "We're supposed to forgive one another 'seventy times seven,' and that is just the beginning of how much God forgives us. We need to offer that soul-clearing forgiveness to others."

You know how difficult feats look simple when professionals perform them? Think of Olympic figure skaters leaping and gliding over the ice, or Yo-Yo Ma playing the cello. They're so graceful, so joyful. But what we never see is how many times the skaters have fallen or how many times a much less experienced Yo-Yo Ma messed up.

Like so many spiritual practices, we have to work at forgiveness to get better at it.

Have you ever experienced "soul-clearing" forgiveness?

Dinner-Party Misdemeanors

Watch out for each other. Love and forgive everybody. It's a good life, enjoy it.
—Jim Henson

More than twenty years ago, my husband and I had a group of friends to dinner. Not long after they arrived, I was startled to find one of the guests standing at the stove frying a chicken breast, cooking oil sizzling and splattering the wall. He said he was on a special diet and that was all he'd eat. (That my husband and I were vegetarians made it even worse.)

I hope that if the same thing happened today, I'd laugh it off, chalking it up to having a quirky friend. But back then? I said nothing but left him off the guest list from there on out. When we did finally run into each other years later, my unforgiveness and I blurted something about the chicken breast. He looked surprised and a little unimpressed by my sharp tone. I don't blame him.

When I look back on it now, I was angry that night because my ego was bruised, and I'd lost control over the dinner I'd planned. (Ego, ego, ego!) I forgave him this tiny offense long ago, but whenever I think of him, I wince, embarrassed that I lost a friendship over a piece of poultry.

What is the most trivial grudge you've ever held? Can you laugh about it now?

Peace with the Past

Forgiveness is an act of the will, and the will can function regardless of the temperature of the heart.
—Corrie ten Boom

A friend of mine came home one day to find a note from her husband sitting on the kitchen counter. It said that he had left, he didn't want anything further to do with her or their children, and he was moving in with his girlfriend. She would discover a day or two later that he'd cleared out their bank accounts. All of this came without warning.

My friend continues to travel through stages of forgiveness, but the process began with just feeling rotten. She indulged in some cursing, revenge fantasies, and snarky talk with her friends. But then she started to move on. She reevaluated her life, identifying where she needed more support. She started therapy. And as time passed, she was able to look honestly at what part she may have played in the broken marriage. She started to forgive.

Her process of forgiveness, however, doesn't progress in a straight line. Just when she thinks she is past feeling bitter, she'll find herself swimming in resentment. But with time, she is able—more and more—to let go.

Some people define forgiveness as no longer wishing to change the past but accepting the actual heartbreaks, as well as the joys, that have made up our lives.

What parts of your past do you wish you could change? Is there a way you can make peace with these things, accepting that they are part of who you are?

Grace for Strangers

It is surely better to pardon too much, than to condemn too much.
—George Eliot

After her father's funeral, my friend and her family came back to our house. I ordered pizza; when it arrived, my friend's nine-year-old son Matthew and I answered the door. An older gentleman stood outside.

"Well, don't you two look nice," he said.

"We were at a funeral," I explained.

"Were they saved?" the deliveryman asked, handing me the pizza. "Did the person who died know the Lord?"

"Yes, he did," I said.

"Well that's a relief!" He bent over, addressing Matthew. "Otherwise, you know, you'd have no hope of ever seeing him again."

I closed the door and stood in the hallway, stunned.

"That was weird," Matthew said.

"Inappropriate. Sorry about that," I said. "We ordered pizza, not a sermon." It had been an emotional day, and the man's remarks whipped my sadness into anger. It took me an hour or two, but I finally let it go.

When a stranger offends me, I try to remember that I'm imperfect, too, and say the wrong thing without meaning to, swerve in front of other drivers, and step on other people's toes. I need strangers to grant me grace, too. All the time.

⟿

When was the last time you were offended by someone you didn't know? How did you let it go?

The *H* Word

*Life appears to me too short to be spent in nursing animosity, or
registering wrongs.*
—Charlotte Brontë, *Jane Eyre*

I hate the word *hate*. No, really. I've taught my children that we
don't have the option to "hate" people because every person bears
the image of God. And if one of my kids uses the *h* word in refer-
ence to homework or the opera I'm listening to or eggplant Parme-
san, I ask them to rephrase.

Given this aversion to the *h* word, when a friend told me that
someone we both know had said that I "absolutely hated" him, I
protested.

"But you have to admit he's not your favorite person in the
world," my friend teased.

"Just because I find him arrogant does not mean I hate him."
Our conversation moved on, but my conscience was jabbed. We'd
served together in an organization years before, and I'd felt
offended by some of his attitudes and choices. (I'm sure he wasn't
in love with mine, either.) Although I didn't hate him, my trust
had been broken; my heart was icy toward him, at best.

Given that I didn't want to renew our friendship, I decided to
start praying for him: for the well-being of his wife and son, for
success in his work, and that he has a sense of God's loving presence. Doing so softened my heart toward him.

And maybe that's enough.

*Do you hold a grudge against someone for a long-ago offense? Can you
hope that good comes to that person?*

Temper, Temper

*Anybody can become angry—that is easy, but to be angry with the
right person, and to the right degree, and at the right time, for the
right purpose, and in the right way, that is not within everybody's
power and is not easy.*

—Aristotle

My middle two children—a son and a daughter—are eighteen
months apart, but they have functioned more like twins since the
younger one was a toddler. Well, twins, or an old, cranky married
couple, but more about that in a minute.

They are usually delighted to be together, laughing and confid-
ing in each other like best friends. But when things are off between
them, it can get nasty. They take offense at real or imagined slights.
The tension between them is a gathering storm that ends in a
thunder of accusations.

While making breakfast recently, I thought I heard my son
say something unkind to his sister. I spun around from the stove.
"Grow up!" I snarled. *Grow up?* I'd never barked that phrase at any
of my kids. It's actually the opposite of what I feel these days: *slow
down.*

They were baffled by my outburst; I'd completely misunderstood my son. I could've blamed posttraumatic stress (remnants of
their more contentious middle school years), the noisy room (dog
barking, music playing), or the early hour (I'd not yet had coffee),
but I didn't.

It was just ordinary, imperfect me jumping to the wrong conclusion. I apologized, and my son forgave me, but those
words—and the ugly way I said them—echoed in my head all day.

*When's the last time you've had to apologize to your kids for
misjudging them?*

Genuine Apologies

Forgiveness is the answer to the child's dream of a miracle by which what is broken is made whole again, what is soiled is again made clean.

—Dag Hammarskjöld

It's happened a hundred times. *At least.* I instruct one of my kids to apologize to another and then take issue with the guilty party's mumbled "sorry." I ask the child to apologize again, but to "say it like you mean it this time."

What a silly instruction, right? Real apologies come from aching hearts. When we truly seek forgiveness, we empathize with the other person and acknowledge how our behavior has affected him or her. More than forgiveness, we want our relationship to be restored.

We want to be trusted again.

That's why a child's compulsory "sorry" or the faux "I'm sorry if you were hurt by anything I did" doesn't work. We can tell when people are taking responsibility for what they've done. We can feel it when their goal is to repair the relationship and not simply to be let off the hook.

Next time you apologize, slow down and think about how your action hurt the other person. Ask the person you've wronged how you can make it right between you two again.

Imperfect Love

To err is human; to forgive, divine.
—Alexander Pope

I don't think we hear it enough: loving another person is hard work. Grueling, you might say. Maybe not every day, but on many days that matter.

Love humbles us. It requires that we do the most difficult thing for human beings to do: learn to value another person's well-being and growth and happiness and hurt feelings as much as we value our own. And our egos don't much like that sort of thing. Or is that just me?

Even when you are doing your best—and you won't always try your best—you will fail, disappoint, and hurt each and every person with whom you are intimate. You'll be cranky or selfish or moody sometimes. You'll misjudge your children. You'll fail to recognize your husband's, children's, or friends' most exquisite gifts and most screaming needs. You'll often default to putting your own desires above those of others.

I will. You will. Everyone we know—if we get and stay close enough to them—will do the same. And we'll have the chance to offer others what my friend Rachael calls that "soul-clearing forgiveness."

And when we do offer that, however imperfectly, we'll be reflecting the love of God to those we love.

What's the hardest apology you've ever made?

Understanding the Stories of Our Lives

In three words I can sum up everything I've learned about life:
it goes on.
—Robert Frost

The thing about forgiveness (or lack of it) is that it changes the way we understand the stories of our lives. Resentment ties us to the past; binds us to the people who have hurt us; and keeps all the failures and wounds that we've experienced fresh, alive, and in living color.

And yet, and yet, and yet . . . it's still so hard to forgive.

Carolina is mother to three boys. Although she says that it's "very hard for me to forgive," she works to do so. She's been divorced, traverses a rocky landscape with her former husband, and navigates a relationship with an unstable family member. She says that she's had to learn to create healthy boundaries with those who have hurt her.

"I think the thing that is most misunderstood about forgiveness is that it doesn't mean that you erase the injury and everything goes back to normal," Carolina told me. "It's possible to forgive someone and still decide that the dynamics of the relationship aren't healthy."

To forgive, however, is a priority for her. "Forgiveness is at the center of my spiritual beliefs," she said. "I fail. God forgives. Without forgiveness, there is no grace. Without grace, there is no hope."

Is there anyone in your life whom you've forgiven but with whom you have to maintain careful boundaries?

Unaccepted Apologies

*It's all very well to tell us to forgive our enemies; our enemies can
never hurt us very much. But oh, what about forgiving
our friends?*
—Willa Cather, *My Mortal Enemy*

When he was little, I remember asking my son to apologize to his sister after roughly grabbing a toy from her. I might have added, "And say it like you mean it." He apologized, but his sister announced, "Well, I don't forgive you."

I had to stifle a laugh; it was a perfectly honest and human response. She wanted him to linger a while with his guilt.

Have you ever had an apology rejected by a friend? I have, and I was shocked by how fiercely it hurt. It ripped open old, unrelated wounds, and it took me years to get over.

As my friend Carolina says, "Rejected apologies are the worst. The worst, worst, worst, worst, worst!"

Why do we refuse to forgive? Sometimes, when the injury has been serious, it takes time to process it—maybe as long as decades. We need time to heal before we can let our pain go or restore the relationship. Other times, we like sitting in the powerful position of victim. We get to bask in others' sympathy. We aren't held accountable for our actions.

But getting stuck in this kind of indulgent unforgiveness keeps us from contending with whatever shadows lurk in our own hearts.

Have you ever rejected an apology?

We're an Imperfect Bunch

Children begin by loving their parents; as they grow older they
judge them; sometimes they forgive them.
—Oscar Wilde

The kids were talking about Steph, one of my son's classmates, at dinner again. Brash and funny, this girl has starred in many of our dinner conversations over the years. Our family is split right down the middle regarding whether we think Steph is wonderfully outspoken and original—or just opinionated and mean.

The new story about Steph had to do with a cutting comment she made to my older son. His brother, ever loyal, erupted into a rant. "You know," he said, "if a girl is mean in middle school she might grow out of it. But Steph? It's high school and she is pretty much set now. She's just a mean person."

My other son disagreed. "Nah. She's really okay," he said. "Just kind of insecure sometimes."

"No." His brother scowled. "It's too late for her."

I stepped in, ever grateful for the Stephs and Anjas and Zachs and the rest of the cast of characters that make our dinner conversations so interesting. "The truth is, no one ever completely grows out of being insecure or mean sometimes," I said. "Not me, not you, not Steph. We humans are an imperfect bunch. Even long after middle school."

How do you talk to your kids about your own faults?

Parenting with Forgiveness

My mother had a great deal of trouble with me but I think she enjoyed it.
—Mark Twain

The rules of parenting seem to change in a split second when our children become adolescents. The same kids who used to spend weekends at home playing out back or building pillow forts in the basement now go to high school football games, hang around at the mall, and have new friends whose parents—*gasp!*—you've never met. Worse, these friends can drive cars.

For the most part, I've felt fortunate about the choices my kids have made and the friends they've chosen as teens. Of course, my parenting story is not over and never will be.

But some of my friends have already been through grim times. Some kids have experimented with drugs. Others have been caught lying or stealing or driving drunk. It's heart-stopping stuff.

A friend of mine whose kids rebelled in high school says, "Little kids, little problems. Big kids, big problems." I resist the idea that "big problems" are inevitable when you have adolescents. Many teenagers bloom into healthy, compelling young adults without making their parents lose their minds.

But regardless, I find that the amount of forgiveness I need to offer, and accept, multiplies as my kids grow older. I misunderstand them. Embarrass them. Speak for them. Disappoint them.

And they do these things to me, too. Over and over, we must offer each other grace.

In what way does forgiveness play a part in your parenting?

Choosing to Forgive

The weak can never forgive. Forgiveness is the attribute of the strong.

—Mahatma Gandhi

My friend Barb says she learned to forgive only when she was in her late thirties. Her upbringing, as well as her "well-honed sense of justice," had been a recipe for resentment.

"My mother was the type of person who felt wronged at every turn," Barb said. "As I grew older, I began to see how easily I slipped into her patterns. I knew I didn't want to end up like her: bitter, with few friends and a long list of grievances."

Barb learned to forgive by deeply exploring the stories in which she cast herself as the victim. She realized that she had a choice of whether to keep retelling these narratives or just to let them go. She started to see where she'd been culpable in a rift.

"I realized that bitter people are drawn to people and situations that promote their sense of victimhood," she said. "They keep repeating the same patterns."

Barb says she now forgives others more easily than she used to. When she feels insulted or hurt, she steps back, is present with her feelings, and takes responsibility for her own part in the matter—even when it's just the way she reframes the story and whether she lets it go.

How does the way you were taught to forgive as a child affect you now?

Letting Go of Greater Hurts

Reflect upon your present blessings, of which every man has plenty;
not on your past misfortunes, of which all men have some.
—Charles Dickens

She had blue eyes, silver-gray hair with spiky bangs, and deep smile lines. And about fifteen years ago at a church retreat, she sat down beside me and, her voice tender, said, "Honey, you have a forgiveness problem."

My eyes flooded with tears. "I do?" We'd gone around the circle earlier, describing our life challenges. I hadn't said much, just mentioned my parents' divorce and estrangement from my father.

I was skilled at being quick about it. As a child, I'd shrug and say that I didn't care that my father wasn't around. By grad school: "I'm post-therapy on that." Indeed, I had explored in therapy the issues around growing up without a father, but I'd never considered that I had a forgiveness problem.

But I did. There was a part of me that didn't want to let my father off the hook for the way his choices had sent painful ripples into my life and those of my siblings.

That gentle confrontation started me down a new path. It wasn't one that brought my father and me to reconciliation, but—thanks to my wise friend—I began to let go of my chronic wish that the past had been different than it was. I started the process of letting it go.

Often it's our childhood losses that hold us captive.

May 17

In Process

I imagine one of the reasons people cling to their hates so stubbornly is because they sense, once hate is gone, they will be forced to deal with pain.
—James Baldwin

The movie *Millions*, released in 2004, is one of my favorites. It's the story of two brothers growing up with their widowed father. The boys discover a large amount of cash. The younger, Damian, wants to give it to the poor; Anthony, the elder, is more self-serving.

Before the money comes into their lives, wily Anthony teaches Damian a trick for getting free candy from shopkeepers. "You tell them your mam's dead and they give you stuff, every time," Anthony says.

"Our mam's dead," is a recurring line in the film and always results in the boys receiving treats or clemency.

In my process of forgiving my father, I realized that I, too, relied on a little cheat, a secret refrain. It was, essentially, "My dad left."

Why was I bad at handling conflict? My dad left. Why was I so misunderstood? My dad left. Why was I withdrawn from others? My dad left. Why did God feel distant? My dad left. Why was I risk averse? My dad left. Why did I struggle to feel loved? My dad left. And on it went.

These issues were touched by his leaving, to be sure, but to forgive, I had to wave good-bye to that old familiar way of coping.

What do you tell yourself is the reason for your unhappiness or faults?

Surprising Sources

When people talk listen completely. Most people never listen.
—Ernest Hemingway

When I was deep in the process of trying to forgive, I received a nudge forward (or you might call it a kick in the pants) from an improbable source.

At the time, I knew a woman whose arrogance and lack of empathy truly made me wonder whether she might be a narcissist. I mean diagnosably a narcissist. Let's call her Leslie. One afternoon Leslie and I were chatting with a few other women. In our conversation, I'd mentioned my parents' divorce (my dad left) as well as the story of how, years ago, I was very close to having a novel accepted for publication by a major publishing company.

Leslie interrupted, pointing at me. "You know what's wrong with you?" she asked. "You're all 'Boo hoo, boo hoo' about your childhood. How old are you, anyway? Your parents divorced. Big whoop."

I started to giggle. For months, I'd been earnestly praying to let go of resentment, and it was as if God had sent this unlikely messenger to tell me to move on.

"And you know what else?" Leslie said. "You've talked about that novel before. *Waaah, waaah, waaah.* So write another one."

"You're right," I said, laughing hard. "You are so right."

Have you ever gained wisdom from a surprising source?

May 19

Imperfect Forgiveness

*Sometimes small mercies are tender enough. We don't have to be
virtuosos at the forgiving game to make it work.*
—Lewis Smedes

In my quest to forgive my father, I searched out books on forgiveness, skimming through some and studying every word of others. The one that affected me most deeply was Lewis B. Smedes's *Forgive and Forget: Healing the Hurts We Don't Deserve.*

Smedes asserts that forgiveness is difficult (yes, yes, we know) and that it's usually only achieved in bits and pieces. Our falling-outs and rifts, he says, are tangled, rife with misunderstandings and snarling emotions. He also notes that forgiveness takes only one person, whereas reconciliation takes two.

We don't usually have a "gigantic monster" to forgive, Smedes reminds us, but a needy human being, one as weak and "silly" as we are. But he also acknowledges that, even after we forgive, we might still feel anger. And that's okay: we'll know that we've forgiven someone because we'll no longer feel hatred or malice toward that person.

Instead of supposing that we'll be close to the person we've hurt or who has wronged us, forgiveness might mean simply being able to be polite to each other and wish each other a Merry Christmas. And mean it.

*Does it help you release your hatred when you see the one who hurt
you as a wounded and weak person instead of cruel and
intimidating?*

May 20

Forgive and Forget?

What I cannot love, I overlook.

—Anaïs Nin

Three weeks earlier, I'd never have believed any of it.

There we were: my husband, my twelve-year-old son, and I sitting on folding chairs in the elementary school gym, my younger kids backstage, waiting to climb the risers and sing. None of this was unusual, except that two seats down from me, next to my husband, sat my father.

Until that day, he'd never met my children, but he'd come to town because my sister was dying. He wanted to say good-bye. The last weeks had been a blur for me. Learning that my sister was sick and back in the area. Visiting her in the oncology ward. Moving her home for hospice care. Introducing my children to an aunt they'd never known.

And then my father came to town. What I knew, at dinner and then as we shuffled into the school for the concert, was that I no longer had malice for him. He was old now and disconnected from my life. I had a strong marriage and four children whom I adored. I had no reason to let the past cloud my gratitude.

I knew I'd forgiven him, or forgiven him enough.

How do you describe the relationship between forgiving and forgetting?

Spring-Cleaning for the Soul

To gain freedom is to gain simplicity.
—Joan Miró

Yesterday, I cleaned out the pantry. I stood on a step stool, started on the highest shelf, and emptied everything onto the kitchen counter. The contents of the top shelf were the most random: rye flour, a couple of marshmallows shrunken in a bag, paper snow-cone holders, sheets of dried seaweed, a stray can of bamboo shoots hiding behind everything else.

The next shelf down held wholesome, sanctimonious items: lentils, quinoa, brown rice, farro. Below that were kid pleasers such as cookies, crackers, hot chocolate, and cereal. The lowest shelf was a jumble of tinfoil, plastic wrap, lunch bags, and mismatched paper plates. On every shelf, I found empty boxes and other cast-aways: unidentifiable crumbs in a plastic bag, wrinkled napkins, uncooked spaghetti, a plastic straw.

I washed down the bare shelves and stood a moment to admire them. And then I turned around to the mess, and the real work began.

Forgiveness is a thorough spring-cleaning for the soul. You upend your assumptions, examine the expiration dates on the narratives you tell yourself, toss out what's empty, and bring order to what remains.

It's much harder than just leaving the pantry door closed.

We have to make a mess when we start to clean out the grudges in our lives, but the simplicity and order we gain makes the hard work well worth it.

Taking What Comes

*If anyone tells you that a certain person speaks ill of you, do not
make excuses about what is said of you but answer, "He was
ignorant of my other faults, else he would not have mentioned
these alone."*

—Epictetus

As I write this, my daughters' new pitch-back waits in the backyard
for someone to wind up and let the softball fly. It's nylon, stretched
on a metal frame, and there is a human shape printed on it. When
the pitcher's aim is good, the ball lands in a net where the catcher's
glove would be. When it's wild, the pitch bounces back or off into
the grass.

I've named the pitch-back "Mitch." (Rhymes with . . .) Mitch
is so lifelike that this morning our dog ran out and barked menac-
ingly at him. Mitch didn't seem to mind. I've felt a little like Mitch
lately. I've been on the receiving end of some wild pitches: misunderstandings and wrist slappings; tricky issues with the kids; and
the usual May scrambling to keep up with end-of-school-year parties, teacher appreciation events, and orchestra concerts.

Mitch serves as a good example to me. He doesn't lose his balance or change what he's doing when he has to wait or when someone barks at him. He knows what his job is and steadfastly keeps
at it, one pitch at a time.

Oh, to be more like Mitch.

How do you keep balanced during demanding times?

We Might Be Mistaken

In all affairs it's a healthy thing now and then to hang a question
mark on the things you have long taken for granted.
—Bertrand Russell

One night as I was putting my daughters to bed, the older one, then ten years old, said, "I forgot to tell you. A man stopped his car and talked to us when we were walking to school today. He had a naked doll in his lap. It was creepy."

There had been a few recent abduction attempts in our neighborhood, so this was disturbing news, to say the least. The next morning I sat with my daughters, one at a time, as they described the incident to a police detective.

What astonished me was how differently the girls described what happened. One said the car was black and the other said it was light green. It had four doors, or two. They remembered his appearance and accent differently. Did he sound Russian or like a standard Midwesterner? One had seen a doll; the other hadn't. And so on.

Looking at mug shots, one of my girls plunked her finger down and said, "Him." The other didn't recognize him. As it turned out, the man one of my daughters identified had an arrest record and was not permitted to be in contact with children. It had been him.

I was stunned that my girls remembered it all so differently. The detective, however, wasn't surprised. "It's always like this," he said. "We all see and remember the same things differently."

As we look back over the stories we tell ourselves, it's wise to remember that the person who wronged us may remember things very differently than we do.

Remember that each of us perceives the world in our own unique way.

Remembering Differently

*No story is the same to us after a lapse of time; or rather we who
read it are no longer the same interpreters.*
—George Eliot

The "walking to school" incident was more upsetting to me than
to my girls. They liked the detective, and my older daughter was
delighted to receive a cell phone that Christmas, a year earlier than
she'd expected.

There were many different ways we could remember that day,
and I was careful about how I talked about it with them. I focused
less on what could have happened and more on what did: they
ignored him, they identified him, and he was arrested.

I like pointing out to my kids how many times we're told in
the Scriptures not to be afraid. Throughout the Psalms, in Isaiah,
and all through the Gospels, we hear those words: "Fear not! I am
with you."

I didn't want my girls to become fearful people, worried that
danger was lurking around every corner. The stories we tell ourselves shape our lives, and remembering the past with a brave and
generous heart helps us move on. "You're not still letting them
walk to school are you?" a friend asked when she heard about the
incident.

"You bet I am," I said. "They'll be fine." And they are.

Is there an event in your past that you could remember differently?

May 25

Watch for Cues

One ought to hold on to one's heart; for if one lets it go, one soon loses control of the head too.
—Friedrich Nietzsche

My circle of friends in college was special, and most of us remain close friends. But years ago, after one in our group died tragically, a second friend seemed to want nothing more to do with the rest of us. He wrote us puzzling letters, giving us our leave. Later, we'd joke about it, our laughter masking broken hearts.

I grieved that friendship in stages, skipping over denial and lingering for more than a decade in anger and hurt whenever I thought of him. I worked to rid myself of resentment, until, finally, I knew I'd forgiven him.

Another decade later, I received an email from that old friend. He apologized for the way he'd behaved. His guilt had been gnawing on his conscience. We met for coffee, and I accepted his apology. It was a sweet time, and the last little thorns of resentment were plucked out of my heart.

Sometimes, though, when I think of those lost years, that old habit of bitterness is triggered. My face flushes. My chest clenches up. These are cues that I need to breathe, be present with my feelings, and again look on my friend with grace.

Forgiveness, even true forgiveness, sometimes has its lapses.

What are your physical cues that you are angry or resentful?

Changing Hate to Understanding

Try to understand men, if you understand each other you will be
kind to each other. Knowing a man well never leads to hate and
nearly always leads to love.
—John Steinbeck

At the beginning of May, we made a list of the people who have hurt us. If you haven't done it yet, take a few minutes now. Be as comprehensive as possible, and write down tiny insults and major grievances.

When I wrote mine, my sixth-grade teacher's face came to mind. My older siblings had idolized him, and I longed to impress him. But it wasn't meant to be. Early in the year I was chosen to be in a choir he directed, but when I was late to the first rehearsal, he cut me.

"You're late; you're out." (He was a tough love kind of guy.)

Cue the violin music, but I'd been the only kid who didn't have a ride. I'd jogged across town to the rehearsal but was dismissed before I could explain. This was not long after my parents split up, so there was a "my dad left" element as well. I hung back from that teacher for the rest of the school year.

But is that offense really worth its weight in grudge? He didn't know my family situation. He was trying to teach excellence. He was fallible, just like the rest of us.

⌒

Can you better understand slights you experienced as a child now that
you are an adult?

Releasing Those Who Hurt Us

The man who opts for revenge should dig two graves.
—Chinese proverb

Maybe it's a teacher who didn't believe in you or a former friend who gossips about you. It could be a parent, an ex-husband, or even an institution that quashed your spirits. We all know people who make our hearts drop, but when we are unforgiving, we're hostage not only to those who hurt us but also to bitterness.

Forgiveness is the only good option, even when the person who hurt you doesn't acknowledge having done so, won't ever apologize, and may have even forgotten your name.

Several years ago, I realized I had an unpleasant cluster of people loitering around in my memories. Each of them had hurt or offended me at some point in my life. I wanted them gone.

Daydreaming one morning not long after waking up, I imagined us all standing together on a dock beside a river. One by one, I took them by the hand and carefully helped them into a rowboat. As each stepped into it, I said, "I release you."

And when they were all aboard, I untied the boat from the dock and they began to paddle off, away from me. From then on, when any of those people came to mind, I knew I was free of them.

Is there anyone you need to release?

As the Lord Forgave You

Bear with each other and forgive whatever grievances you have against one another. Forgive as the Lord forgave you.
—Colossians 3:13 NIV

My friend Tim admits that he's been working "for decades" on being quick to forgive but that he "still can nurse past wrongs like a warm beer." I love how he puts that. Isn't there something lazy and somehow comforting about hanging onto pet resentments?

Sure, it's simple for me to forgive the teacher who kicked me out of choir thirty years ago. And yes, in the quotidian give-and-take of marriage, it's even easy (most of the time) to forgive my husband when he hurts my feelings.

It's trickier, though, to release people who are, to be honest, sort of fun to vilify. Mean girls who never grew up. The serially cantankerous. The no-kidding, really, truly jerks.

In the end, though, I have to concede that my lack of grace doesn't prevent any further wrongs from being committed. It has no power over anyone else but only feeds what is petty and small in me and blinds me to the fact that the one who hurt me *is like me*: imperfect, frail sometimes, and made in the image of God.

Who's the hardest person for you to forgive? The easiest?

No Blame

True humility is not thinking less of yourself; it is thinking of yourself less.
—C. S. Lewis

As I've gotten older, I've gotten better at forgiveness.

Maybe it's noticing harsh lines on the faces of unforgiving people and not wanting my own face to tell that kind of story. Maybe it's learning how heavy grudges are to hold, how bulky and awkward they are to carry. Maybe it's that, with a college-age child and three others racing up behind him, I see how quickly time passes. I'm selective about how I expend my energy.

But if I had to guess, I think I'm better at extending forgiveness because my pride has been chipped away and worn down by all the times I've had to ask for forgiveness myself.

When we were newlyweds, my husband and I picked up a good habit: when we had a disagreement, we didn't talk about who was to blame. After many late-night arguments, teary and tied up in knots, one of us would say, "There's no one to blame. There's nothing to blame."

At those moments, we acknowledged that the argument needed to be over, that we needed to sleep, and that one of the trickier parts of being human is having to wrangle through conflicts like that.

"No blame."

Forgiveness is the opposite of blame. It's about not making a fist around our wounds but opening our hands and letting them go.

May 30

Otherworldly Forgiveness

Jesus said, "Father, forgive them, for they do not know what they are doing."

—Luke 23:34 NIV

It was a breathtaking lesson in forgiveness.

On October 2, 2006, a gunman entered an Amish schoolhouse in Lancaster County, Pennsylvania, barricaded the door, and shot ten girls ages six to thirteen, killing five of them. He then killed himself.

The story of the massacre at the West Nickel Mines School is a true horror. What's astounding is the way the Amish community immediately responded.

Within hours of the incident, family members of the deceased and their neighbors offered forgiveness and love to the shooter's widow and children. They organized a charitable fund for the family. Many attended the shooter's funeral a day after attending the funerals of their own children.

The rest of the country sat back, astonished.

The shooter didn't ask for forgiveness. How could they absolve him so quickly? How could they comfort the killer's family on the same day their own hearts were broken? The Amish are quick to explain that the God they love offered forgiveness to those who unrepentantly abused and killed him. How could they not do the same?

Can you imagine such generosity and faith?

Sweet Forgiveness

I love you and I forgive you. I am like you and you are like me. I
love all people. I love the world. I love creating. Everything in our
life should be based on love.

—Ray Bradbury

The five Amish girls who survived the shootings in Lancaster County live with disabilities caused by their injuries. At least one of them now uses a wheelchair and feeding tube and is unable to speak. As has been the case for years, every week this young teen receives a visit from a friend who bathes her, sings to her, and reads her stories.

The friend is the mother of the man who tried to kill her, a woman who says that she had to forgive her son or she'd have "the same hole in her heart that he had."

That Amish community points to a God who is more loving and full of grace than I almost dare to imagine. If they could so automatically forgive the man who wreaked such violence and death in their community, and if the killer's mother can face the consequences of her son's actions and forgive him, what about you and me?

Can we decide to be open to forgiving our friends, our parents, our neighbors, and even our own personal histories for the insults, disappointments, and injuries that they have brought us?

Could we reflect some of God's grace in that way?

What has this month of practicing forgiveness been like for you?

June

Practice Your Principles

Surrender Your False Self, Commit to
Living True

.

My New Philosophy

Our true reality is in our identity and unity with all life.
—Joseph Campbell, *The Power of Myth*

The Amish were just as distraught as any community would be after the schoolhouse shooting that took the lives of five girls and horribly altered the lives of five more. But they knew who they truly were and, as so many said afterward, they are "simply not a people who hold grudges."

That's part of their "rule of life."

Wouldn't it be a gift to have such a clear sense of identity that, regardless of what happens, you'd spontaneously respond as your finest self?

This month we are going to take a look at our personalities, articulate our values, and maybe even strip away some of the falseness we hide behind so we can better commit to living authentically.

Talk about taking risks, right?

By writing down what we're about—crafting a personal statement, or rule of life, if you will—we'll be able to stay focused on what matters to us most and live into the unique life we were created for.

Did you ever see *You're a Good Man, Charlie Brown*, the musical based on Charles Schultz's comic strip? I love Sally Brown's song "My New Philosophy." In the span of a few minutes, Sally's dictums hopscotch all over the map, from "That's what you think" to "No!" to "Live every day as if it were the last."

Your own "new philosophy" can be just as unique, just as brief, and just as fluid as hers.

Are you ready to take a look at the person you were truly created to be?

June 2
Back-Timing

If you want to identify me, ask me not where I live, or what I like to eat, or how I comb my hair, but ask me what I am living for, in detail, and ask me what I think is keeping me from living fully for the thing I want to live for.

—Thomas Merton

A few years ago, a friend and I were commiserating about the myriad tasks that splinter our days. I mumbled something about how important it is to plan ahead and to be organized, but my friend had a much more specific strategy.

"It's all about back-timing," she said. For years, she worked as a television news director. Every day when she planned the evening news, she back-timed, or worked back from the exact time the broadcast would end.

She then plugged in chunks of time for commercial breaks, weather, and sports. With those pieces in place, she could choose which stories to cover.

"I looked at which stories were priorities and saved some of the less pressing, more 'gee-whiz' stories for pad," she said. "Pad" is the nonessential news that can be cut for a breaking story or if a reporter goes long in an interview.

"I use the back-timing technique with everything in my life," my friend said. "I figure out the goal and the deadlines and work backward from there. It keeps me on time and helps me assess what's nonessential, what can be dropped."

Consider your personal statement a back-timing exercise. What are your end goals?

Back-Timing Relationships

*We have to dare to be ourselves, however frightening or strange
that self may prove to be.*
—May Sarton

Back-timing not only helps me better manage discrete tasks such as meeting work deadlines, helping my children get college applications in on time, or preparing the week's meals; it also informs my relationships.

For instance, if I want to remain close to my children, I need to treat them as "top stories" and not as nonessential fluff. If I want to be close to them when they are my age, how can I back-time our relationships now?

When I speak to adult friends who aren't close to their parents, they often chalk it up to trust issues or say, "Oh, they never understood me." So, right now, while most of my children are still at home with me, I need to pluck out the padding, connect authentically with them, and make sure they know I can be trusted. I fail, of course, but hope it's more like smudging their trust than breaking it.

By being intentional—and back-timing—I can work to nurture lasting relationships with my children.

*Think of how you want an important relationship to end up. Is there
a way you can back-time it?*

Personality Tests

What I'm looking for is not out there, it is in me.
—Helen Keller

I love taking personality tests. At the moment, a spate of new and incredibly silly tests is making the rounds. Which Harry Potter character are you? Which US president are you most like? Are you a hipster? ("Luna Lovegood," "Thomas Jefferson," and "no," in case you are wondering.)

Obviously those quizzes don't shed light on who I really am. They don't help me clarify my values or point me toward that mysterious "finest self" I'm always hoping to discover. They're just for fun.

There are personality assessments, however, that can offer real insight into the distinct ways each of us perceives the world. The Myers-Briggs Type Indicator (MBTI) is one. Of the MBTI's sixteen types, I'm an INFP (introversion, intuition, feeling, perception). INFPs tend to be reserved and spiritual. We trust our instincts, have an aversion to conflict, and abhor boring details. (Ah, so that's why I never read product manuals.)

Honestly, I know that if there is a finest self for me to find, it's not hidden in my personality but is a matter of the habits I cultivate.

My finest self is revealed only in how I relate to and treat other people.

Have you ever taken a personality assessment? As you think about your core values and goals, it's helpful to keep your unique personality type in mind.

Transcending Ourselves

We know what we are, but know not what we may be.
—William Shakespeare (from *Hamlet*)

My Myers-Briggs results excuse my tendency to dodge conflict, and they pat me on the back for being a good listener, but another personality assessment—the Enneagram—digs deeper and helps me better understand my inherent limitations, motivations, and true self.

It unmasks what I might call my "original sin," if you will.

The Enneagram describes nine basic personality types, illustrating each one in relationship to the other eight. The Enneagram is ancient but has been elaborated on and is widely used in modern times. It's currently growing in popularity among Christians who view it as a tool for spiritual discernment. "Yes, the truth will set you free," Franciscan friar Richard Rohr says, referring to the Enneagram. "But first it will make you miserable."

Reading about my type (I'm a nine) indeed made me miserable. I felt exposed. Yes, I do want to put my fingers in my ears and say, "La, la, la" when I'm overwhelmed by all the suffering in the world or the hurt inside me. Yes, I default to numbing myself, staying quiet, and sleeping too much. Yes, strong emotions frighten me—especially my own. I struggle with feeling overlooked, insignificant.

But thanks to having taken that test, I am growing healthier spiritually: taking more risks, telling God what I really feel, and focusing on all the ways I truly am loved.

Bit by little bit.

⌒

Have you ever taken a test or had someone describe you in a way that helped you know yourself better?

June 6
What Moves You

The tree which moves some to tears of joy is in the Eyes of others only a Green thing that stands in the way.
—William Blake

As you begin crafting your "new philosophy," brainstorm a list of what moves you.

Think about the following:

What work of art feels comforting and familiar, as if it somehow belongs to you or was created with you in mind?

Are there lines from a hymn or poem or movie that you've carried around with you for the past decade or two?

When's the last time you felt truly seen, loved, and accepted?

After a weekend away with friends, a woman I know said she felt a renewed sense of identity. Something was awakened in her. "I want to be in a place where I feel surrounded by joy and a sense of belonging," she said, succinctly naming her intention, rule of life, or "new philosophy."

Now that she's expressed this desire, she's beginning to consider how she can get herself to such a place. It might mean moving nearer to close friends, or it could require taking the time to invest more deeply in the people who live nearby. She noticed and named what stirred her, articulated her desires, and now can begin to effect positive change in her life.

What moves you? How could you be truer to your deepest desires?

June 7
A River of Joy

When you do things from your soul, you feel a river moving in
you, a joy.
—Rumi

My husband and I were out west on a camping trip and had stopped for supplies in a small town in Oregon. A man sat outside the general store on a folding chair. A cardboard box of spotted brown puppies was on the sidewalk beside him.

"They're not purebred," the man said as we approached, waving his hand over the box. "The mother is. German shorthaired pointer." He eyed my husband. "They'd make fine hunting dogs." But then, given our Birkenstock sandals and bandanas, he seemed to realize that this wasn't a selling point.

"Look at the runt," he said, directing his gaze at me. "Oddball. Black-and-white and half the size of the rest of 'em. You could have him for nothing."

So, along with propane canisters, we drove off with Percy, named for our favorite writer, Walker Percy. Unlike the novelist, however, Percy the dog wasn't given to existential questioning. He was all about joy.

Several years later, I was walking Percy in Prospect Park, Brooklyn, with my friend Julian. The Long Meadow was nearly empty, so we let him off the leash. Percy took off, running great circles around us, a blur of black and white, smiling as big as he ever did.

"Wouldn't it be great," Julian asked, "if all it took for us to be happy was to run like that? As fast as we can?"

What makes you feel joyful and free?

A Healing Spirit

There is a light in this world, a healing spirit more powerful than
any darkness we may encounter. We sometimes lose sight of this
force when there is suffering, too much pain. Then suddenly, the
spirit will emerge through the lives of ordinary people who hear a
call and answer in extraordinary ways.
—Richard Attenborough, *Mother Teresa*

Pentecost is the Christian festival celebrating the descent of the Holy Spirit on Jesus' disciples.

In chapter 2 of Acts, St. Paul writes that Christ's first followers—just over a hundred people—were together when a sound "came from heaven, like a strong wind." What appeared to be tiny flames then flickered above their heads, "and they were all filled with the Holy Spirit" (Acts 2:4, ESV).

The Trinity is a central mystery of our faith. Christians understand God as one being, with three distinct parts or persons, like a braid. Some people use the analogy of water—liquid, frozen, and vapor—to understand the Trinity.

In the year 1213, the Fourth Lateran Council in Rome stated, "It is the Father who generates, the Son who is begotten, and the Holy Spirit who proceeds."

We can think of God as the Creator; of Jesus as God-made-human; and of the Spirit as the muse, or the source of inspiration, for our lives. The Spirit fills us, inspires us, convicts us, and, "intercedes for us with groanings too deep for words" (Romans 8:26, 27, ESV).

Which member of the Trinity—the Creator, the Near One, or the
Inspiring Muse—feels most real to you today?

June 9
Painted Just for Her

*It is good to love many things, for therein lies the true strength,
and whosoever loves much performs much, and can accomplish
much, and what is done in love, is well done.*

—Vincent van Gogh

When she was about three, my daughter Mia came running through the house to me, holding an open book. "This!" she said, pointing to a picture of Vincent van Gogh's *Starry Night*. She'd apparently just come upon it, and it was love at first sight. I sat down with her, told her the name of the work, and turned the page. She turned it back.

"I want this, Mama," She traced van Gogh's swirling stars with her finger. "Please, Mama."

"You want that painting?"

She nodded, smiling at the picture as though it were an old friend. I ordered a print of *Starry Night*, hoping she'd still be interested in it when it arrived. When it did, it was as though I'd somehow procured the original. At the sight of it, Mia gasped and clapped both hands over her mouth. I leaned it up against the couch, and she sat down before it, transfixed.

Almost a decade later, the painting still hangs in her room. And when she sees an image of that work—on a sweatshirt or coffee mug or in a book—she smiles, often breathing out a delicious sigh. It's as though van Gogh painted it just for her.

Does any painting work this kind of magic on you? Take a few minutes to remember when you first saw it, what emotions it stirs in you, and to try to articulate why you love it.

June 10
Defining Success

*"You shall love the Lord your God with all your heart and with all
your soul and with all your mind and with all your strength." The
second is this: "you shall love your neighbor as yourself."*
—Mark 12:30–31 NASB

The Bible verses above and the poem below are two of my favorite
rules of life. In the Gospel of Mark, Jesus says that the greatest
commandments are to love God and to love others. Following
Christ isn't about morality or "right thinking." It's about love.

Bessie Stanley's poem "To Have Succeeded," is often falsely
attributed to Ralph Waldo Emerson. Written in 1904 for a contest,
Stanley's poem won first prize. The definition of success that she
offers is, like the verses from Mark, clear and unpretentious:

> To laugh often and love much;
> To win the respect of intelligent people
> And the affection of children;
> To earn the approbation of honest critics
> And endure the betrayal of false friends,
>
> . . . .
>
> To leave the world a little better,
> Whether by a healthy child,
> A garden patch,
> Or redeemed social condition;
> To know even one life has breathed easier
> Because you have lived.
> This is to have succeeded.

As I craft my "new philosophy" this month, maybe I'll include
something about loving God and others and hoping to leave the
world a little better because I was here.

*Have you begun crafting your life's statement of purpose? Start by
thinking about a few quotes that mean the most to you.*

June 11
Personality and Purpose

Make your work to be in keeping with your purpose.
—Leonardo da Vinci

Whether or not you've taken tests such as the Myers-Briggs Type Indicator or the Enneagram, you probably identify as either introverted or extroverted. You know whether you tend to "fly off the handle" or if you move more calmly through life. You know if you're a risk taker or someone who plays it safe. Highly pragmatic or a daydreamer. And so on.

Once we know these things about ourselves, the trick is not only accepting them but also finding a way to transcend the obstacles our dispositions can put in our way.

Something I know about myself—and yes, this corresponds to my personality test results—is that I find it excruciatingly hard to confront or cast aspersions on other people's actions. My friend Keiko summed it up years ago: "Telling Jen that she's being 'judgy' is her Kryptonite."

When I'm being easy on myself, I frame this as my being tolerant and open minded. When I'm being harsh, I reproach myself for being weak, a people pleaser. My challenge, however, has been to accept that confronting others is part of life. Maybe part of my "new philosophy" should include being brave and speaking the truth, even when it's very hard.

⌒

How do your natural gifts or weaknesses affect your work or the way you organize your life?

Being Judgy

Accepting oneself does not preclude an attempt to become better.
—Flannery O'Connor

Years ago, I hired a house cleaner I'll call Marilyn. When Marilyn came to clean, she'd talk about her husband's poor health, financial insecurity, and a legal battle raging with their landlord.

As the months passed, Marilyn would leave more of the house untouched. I would write her a check and then finish cleaning the house myself. Increasingly, I wondered whether she was manipulating me: helping herself to lunch, taking frequent breaks, talking on the phone, cutting out early.

But who was I to judge? And besides, I was terrified to confront her.

Then one day, I knew it had to end. I'd spent the afternoon cleaning, even though I'd just paid Marilyn that day. I wore the baby in the sling while my sons—then ages one and three—clambered for my attention. Hands shaking, I left Marilyn a message saying we didn't need her services anymore. That was fifteen years ago.

Today, I'd keep better boundaries with Marilyn, be clear about my expectations, and know that my pity wouldn't solve her problems. I wouldn't be so panicked about letting her go. I know I still default to shrinking away from conflict, but I'm glad that I'm at least a bit bolder and more truthful than I was.

What is one of your core weaknesses or faults? Can you trace how you've grown and matured over the years?

June 13

Home Is Where Your Story Begins

When a man does not know what harbor he is making for, no wind is the right wind.

—Seneca

Walking through Target, my son Theo hoists a large, lettered sign into our cart. "You Make Me Happy When Skies Are Gray," he reads. "You can never have too many inspirational signs, right, Mom?"

I laugh and take it out of the cart. It's true that, lettered on wood or tin, positive messages abound in our house:

"Home is where your story begins."

"In everything, give thanks."

"Believe in the wonder of tomorrow!"

"Be kind, for everyone you meet is fighting a hard battle."

And stamped on a large, square piece of wood in our kitchen is the mother of all lettered signs. Its directives include: "Say Your Prayers. Use Your Napkin. Never Run with Scissors. Tell the Truth. Don't Believe Everything You Hear. Play Fair. Respect Your Elders."

When I first became a parent, I was ever on the lookout for a magic formula for creating a loving and happy home. Of course, there isn't such a formula, but these messages, sign by sign, seemed to provide some clues.

What message would you like to post on a sign in your home?

June 14

Scratch Where It Itches

I have a simple philosophy. Fill what's empty. Empty what's full.
And scratch where it itches.

—Alice Roosevelt Longworth

You don't need to get it stenciled on a piece of wood to hang in the kitchen, but writing down your personal philosophy is a key strategy for living with intention.

Remember Henry David Thoreau's *Walden*? "I went to the woods because I wished to live deliberately. . . . I wanted to live deep and suck out all the marrow of life, to live so sturdily and Spartan-like as to put to rout all that was not life," he wrote.

Writing out our thoughts helps us determine our core values and encourages us to choose people and activities that are consistent with them.

In April, I mentioned a friend who is vigilant about saying no to whatever "does not have my name on it." Among other things, McKenna declines hosting "loud boy sleepovers." Only by specifically naming what truly appeals (and what doesn't) can she "put to rout all that is not life," to borrow Thoreau's phrase.

How would any of these objectives affect your day-to-day life?

"I want to be the kind of person my dog thinks I am."

"I want to live creatively and love selflessly."

"I want to model intelligence, kindness, and authenticity for my children."

⌒

Create a one-line "I want" personal statement or rule of life. We will continue to work with it, but today just jot down the first thing that pops into your mind. (Use paper, make a note on your cell phone, or just scratch it into the back of this book.)

Know Thyself

He who knows others is wise; he who knows himself is enlightened.
—Lao-tzu

Years ago, my friend Samantha and I joked that, as mothers of young children, we were wandering around with brain fog. We'd forget why we'd entered a room. Put a box of Cheerios away in the freezer. Scour the house for the sunglasses that were perched on our heads. That kind of thing.

"Bryce was coloring in the kitchen when I was making dinner last night, and he asked me my favorite color," Samantha said. "I just stood there. I couldn't remember."

If it's hard even to remember your favorite color, being asked to craft a "life rule" might feel like trying to do trigonometry when you're in the second grade. Try this:

> Start by listing basic words you use to describe yourself. I'd use *wife, mother, writer, dog lover, foodie, friend.*
>
> Circle the three or four most essential roles you play. No offense to my dog Shiloh, but I'd choose mother, wife, writer, friend.
>
> Briefly describe how you'd like to be described in each of these roles. Loving, creative mother. Supportive, kind wife. Top-notch writer. Loyal friend who shows up.
>
> Give details and write actionable statements for each. "By listening and knowing my children well, cultivating their unique gifts, and accepting their flaws, I will be a loving mother."

Take a few minutes today to begin crafting your own personal statement.

Follow Your Instincts

The more people have studied different methods of bringing up children the more they have come to the conclusion that what good mother and fathers instinctively feel like doing for their babies is usually best after all.

—Benjamin Spock

When my friend Annika was a new mother, her sister-in-law gave her a subscription to a natural parenting magazine. There were advertisements for fragrance-free diaper cream, organic cloth diapers, and herbal remedies for everything from colic to PMS. She pored over articles on baby wearing, breast-feeding, and the family bed.

The editorial tone indicated that being a perfectly consistent, all-natural attachment mama was the only respectable way to be a mother. The problem was, Annika never got the hang of the baby carrier that the magazine recommended. She despised washing diapers and stared longingly at packages of Pampers at the grocery store. She ran herself ragged following all the magazine's instructions and never just relaxed in her son's company.

She felt like an imposter, a failure as a mother. "I was completely stressed out," Annika says. "If I could do it all over again, I'd just follow my own instincts. And enjoy him more."

Happily, when her daughter was born four years later, Annika had let the subscription lapse, and she was able to rely on her own unique gifts and instincts as a mother.

Do you ever feel pressure to pretend to be a different kind of mother than you are?

June 17

Picturing God

For God is good—or rather, of all goodness He is the
Fountainhead.

—Athanasius of Alexandria

I didn't know much about middle school kids when I agreed to teach the class at church. My oldest was only six years old, and "middle school" still evoked the musty smell of the janitor's mop at my junior high, older girls spraying their "feathered" hair in the locker room, and ill-fated sewing projects in home economics class.

But week after week, I had a roomful of them.

It was a year after the terrorist attacks of September 11, 2001, and the events of that day haunted my students. I read that kids this age begin to grasp the permanence and inevitability of death; I wanted to offer them some sense of God's love for them. I needed it as desperately as they did.

One Sunday, we talked about what face, if any, they pictured when they thought of God. We paged through magazines and sketched our ideas. A few chose images that represented an outdoorsy, hippy-looking Jesus. Others drew bearded wizards. One chose a photograph of outer space, galaxies twirling. Another drew Christ on the cross. One student left his page blank.

The exercise helped me know these students more intimately as we talked about our faith.

How do you picture God when you pray? Do you most connect with
the Creator, the Son, or the Spirit?

Welcome!

All true friendliness begins with fire and food and drink and the
recognition of rain or frost. . . . Each human soul has in a sense to
enact for itself the gigantic humility of the Incarnation. Every man
must descend into the flesh to meet mankind.

—G. K. Chesterton

My friend Tricia sent me a text: "Remind me: What is David's favorite garnish for his martini?"

"Blue-cheese olives," I wrote back.

My husband and I were going to her house for dinner that evening, and although it was barely noon, she was already thinking about his drink and making sure it would be exactly as he likes it. I shouldn't have been surprised. Tricia and her husband are excellent hosts. When we arrive for dinner at their place, we feel welcome. Hors d'oeuvres are laid out, the table is set, and our hosts are relaxed.

In his homily a few weeks ago, the priest told a story about a restaurant owner who has a passion for making customers feel welcomed and embraced, just as they are. Whether customers are dressed shabbily or in formal attire, the staff greets them enthusiastically.

"Welcome! We've been waiting for you!" they say.

This is what our parish should be like, our priest told us. When people come through the doors, they should know that we've been waiting, expectantly, for them. They should feel that their authentic selves are embraced and that we're delighted that they're here.

What makes you feel eagerly welcomed? Where do you feel you
most belong?

Like a Little Child

[Jesus] said, "Truly, I say to you, unless you turn and become like children, you will never enter the kingdom of heaven."
—Matthew 18:3 RSV

When I was a girl, Christ's instruction to "become like little children" seemed like one of the strangest of his teachings. I ached to fit in with my older siblings. I was restless to grow up and enter that tantalizing place called "the real world."

But increasingly, especially since I became a mother, Jesus' words make sense to me.

One morning, when my son was five, he and I were in his bedroom making the bed, chatting about kindergarten, planning the day. "Mom," he said, his voice suddenly grave. "Sometimes my heart feels white and lovely like Christmas. Sometimes it feels heavy and dark. What can I do about the dark feelings?"

I told him that Christ forgives our sins and makes our hearts beautiful again. I asked him if he wanted to pray, right then, for forgiveness and peace. He prayed a simple prayer and then flashed me a smile.

"I feel different," he said. That kind of faith—faith that we are fully loved and can be reconciled with God—is indeed the realm of those who are trusting, open, unencumbered. Childlike.

What could "becoming like a little child" mean to you?

Solstice

Farther in summer than the birds,
Pathetic from the grass,
A minor nation celebrates
Its unobtrusive Mass.
—Emily Dickinson

The summer solstice falls around this day every June; it's the day when those of us who live north of the equator are tilted closest to the sun. Even if it has felt like summer for weeks—the kids out of school; the sink littered with popsicle sticks; and our schedules off-kilter, tailored to work around vacations and summer camps and visiting friends—the solstice is the first day of summer.

The solstice is the longest day of the year. Here in the Midwest, it's usually not gotten hot enough for the air to echo with the chirping of crickets. That "minor nation" is indeed stealthy, out of sight, as Emily Dickinson indicates in the poem excerpted above. It will be a month or so before I begin to hear their creaking symphonies.

After the solstice, the days get shorter and colder; and in just over a week, we'll be halfway through the calendar year. The word *solstice* comes from the Latin words for "sun" and "to stand still," because on the days around the solstice, the sun appears to stand still in the sky.

If you could make time truly stand still, how would you spend the afternoon? Savor this longest day today.

Best and Worst

And so is the world put back by the death of everyone who has to sacrifice the development of his or her peculiar gifts to conventionality!
—Florence Nightingale

When I admitted to being allergic to conflict, I said that, depending on my mood, I either think it's an admirable trait (I'm good natured!) or a flaw (I'm a cowardly people pleaser!). But, could it be both?

My friend Nadine taught me to think that way after telling me about her struggles with one of her children. "I want to tell you the wisest words anyone ever spoke to me about my son," she said. "They were: 'What's good about him is what's bad about him.'"

Her son had been a "hurricane of a child." He was stubborn, had hour-long tantrums, and was "an adrenaline junkie. My husband and I used to wonder if we'd end up visiting him in jail," she said.

They decided to homeschool him, knowing he did better with less stimulation and more routine. Long story short, he graduated summa cum laude from college, is now nearly thirty, and is happily married.

"His intensity and stubbornness were not problems but gifts," Nadine said. "Though, honestly, he was a very difficult child to raise."

In what ways could you view your "issues" as gifts?

June 22

Not What You Expected

Happiness! Can any human being undertake to define it
for another?
—Dinah Craik, *A Woman's Thoughts about Women*

When our older kids were two, three, and five years old, my husband and I began the adoption process. It was a new undertaking. I'd lost a baby to miscarriage and felt that someone was missing from the family. We both wanted a fourth child, and were sure this time she'd come to us by adoption. I felt like it was meant to be.

From the start, we were asked many versions of the same question: "What if she isn't what you expect?" Sometimes people got more specific: "What if she's not smart? Not attractive? What if she has health problems?"

What I knew—and still know—to be true, is that regardless of how children come to us, they rarely meet our expectations. Type A mothers can give birth to type B kids. Children are born with disabilities no one expected.

Kids go through unpleasant phases, and every parent at some point must admit, "I don't like this child right now." But the point of our relationships isn't to make us happy but to transform us. When we become parents, we're forced to put others first, and we grow.

We learn, more than ever before, what it is to love.

⌒

Do you think of happiness as a goal or more like a consequence, or
by-product, in your life?

June 23
Trade Stories

Experience keeps a dear school, yet Fools will learn in no other.
—Benjamin Franklin

We all have high hopes as parents. I want to connect authentically with my children and to model kindness. I don't want my kids to be screen addicted; I want them to be lifelong readers. And less sugar and more time outdoors is good for everyone.

My application of these goals, however, is patchy:

Some days their lips are stained blue from the ice-cream truck's rocket pops.

Even on dazzling June days, some afternoons my kids lie around listening to music on their iPods or watching a movie instead of embracing the great outdoors.

Patience hurdles away from me, and I lose my temper.

Oh, well. I remind myself that there are many, many ways to be a good-enough parent. As we work to lead more authentic lives, let's not try to look like or measure up to anyone else's standards.

And when we talk shop as parents, let's just trade stories, commiserate, and laugh with one another about how infuriating, rewarding, confounding, and what a gift it is to be a mother.

Do you ever feel pressure from in-laws or other family or friends to be a kind of mother you aren't?

June 24
No "There" There

Above all the grace and the gifts that Christ gives to his beloved is that of overcoming self.
—St. Francis of Assisi

We often don't even notice how self-absorbed we are. At least I don't. I feel entitled to resentment if someone has truly hurt me. If my thoughts generally center on my own well-being, I chalk it up to having healthy self-esteem.

And when my conscience is snagged by the fact that so many people in the world live in poverty, I look away and remind myself that I've worked hard for what I've got. (And, as you know, my dad left when I was young. It's not a picnic being me.)

The problem is, sooner or later, I come crashing up against the limits of this kind of thinking. It's like an elaborately painted backdrop in a movie. You think there are real roads jetting off into the distance and a three-dimensional world out there, but actually it's just a painted wall. "There's no 'there' there," Gertrude Stein said of her hometown, a place she felt lacked life, groundedness, culture.

It's inevitable: living for self is a recipe for despair. Every day this is dramatized in the news: child stars who burn out at nineteen; politicians who seek comfort, immortality, or escape (or all three) in extramarital affairs; gifted people drowning in greed or debt or substance abuse.

It's because our selves can never sustain us.

Do you ever catch yourself living a more one-dimensional life than you'd like?

Spiritual Identity

We are not the healers, we are not the reconcilers, we are not the givers of life. We are sinful, broken, vulnerable people who need as much care as anyone we care for.

—Henri Nouwen, *In the Name of Jesus*

This month, we've been taking on the risky project of delving into identity and looking at who we might possibly be as our finest selves.

We've explored how we can gather clues about ourselves from personality tests. We've thought about what makes us want to run with joyful abandon, like my old dog Percy at the park.

We've acknowledged our weaknesses and allowed the possibility that our gifts and our faults might just be intricately connected.

We've been reminded by my friend Annika and her futile attempts to become a crunchy Earth Mama to be authentic in our parenting and to resist other people's attempts to make us into something we aren't.

And we've chipped away at sculpting a new philosophy or life rule.

All this work has left me with a renewed desire to better understand what rooting my identity in Christ really looks like. I'm drawn to the idea that I just might be in the process of being formed more and more into God's image. I haven't quite taken full hold of it, but the possibility of this kind of transformation excites me.

∼

What new insights about yourself, or about God's love for you, have you glimpsed this month?

Cramming

My pitching philosophy is simple: keep the ball away from the bat.
—Satchel Paige

Okay, no pressure, but time's running short; June's nearly over. If you're still resisting writing down a personal statement, I'm going to make one or two last pitches (pun intended, see Satchel Paige quote above) that you take the risk and do it.

You might be reticent to write down your new philosophy because you're a journal avoider, irritated by the idea of keeping one. Or you might be one of the wistful, would-be journal keepers we discussed, and it just feels like too much pressure. Maybe you'll get it wrong. Maybe you'll change your mind. Maybe someone won't think it's as meaningful as you think it is. Or whoever you are, you might feel that it's too vulnerable a statement to put on paper.

Try not to worry about these things. According to neuroscientists, the time it takes to write down a goal or objective is the minimum amount needed to create an easily retrievable memory. You can always change it later, but by writing down your thoughts, you will have access to them. You'll be able to look back and remember where you were at this moment.

Take a few minutes to jot down a personal statement, life rule, or new philosophy. Use your journal, a sticky note, or just scribble it down right here on this page. Have fun with it; think about what brings you joy and which aspects of yourself you'd like to cultivate.

Finding Your Tribe

The bond that links your true family is not one of blood, but of respect and joy in each other's life.
—Richard Bach, *Illusions*

Marketers, psychologists, and daytime talk-show hosts talk a lot these days about "finding your tribe." Bloggers, organic farmers, and at-home moms are told that finding their tribes is the key to success. By "tribe," they mean a group of people who share interests and accept one another as they really are, and with whom they work toward a common goal.

I have a friend who's found her tribe at a local college in the art department. Year after year, she and several other adults—none of whom is pursuing a degree—enroll in an independent study and spend a few days a week together in the studio. Their ages vary. They have different personalities and go home to very different situations. But together they work, side by side, as they grow as artists. They've become close; they are on each other's sides.

My friend wouldn't have found this tribe had she not first identified what makes her feel most free. An artist throughout high school and college, she set aside her work after having kids. But she had an itch, a longing, to return to it. And she has.

And now she even has a tribe.

Have you ever felt that you had identified your "tribe"? Where might it be found?

Be Salty

The cure for anything is salt water: sweat, tears or the sea.
—Karen Blixen (Isak Dinesen)

I've been asking friends about the statements they live by:

"You can't please everyone."

"It's not my business what other people think of me."

"Life's short; eat dessert first."

One friend recited the Golden Rule. My friend Mary hurried from the room and returned with a hymnal, flipped it open, and read, "Take my life and let it be, consecrated Lord to Thee."

Earlier this month, I thought my new philosophy would detail the mother and writer I want to be. But I've changed course. It is "Be salty."

Salt brings out flavor, melts the ice in winter. Christ said, "You are the salt of the world."

That never meant much to me until I heard my priest give a homily in which he said that, by itself, salt isn't good to eat. But the right amount—a sprinkle—brings out the natural flavor of food. In the ancient world, it was also used to clean wounds. "Salt doesn't change what it touches into more salt," he said. "It doesn't overpower but revives what it comes into contact with."

That sounds like an okay-enough goal for someone like me.

What's your new philosophy?

God's Masterpieces

Give up your self, and you will find your real self. Lose your life and you will save it. Submit to death, death of your ambitions and favourite wishes every day and death of your whole body in the end: submit with every fibre of your being, and you will find eternal life.

—C. S. Lewis

It couldn't have been all that superfantastic to be Paul, the apostle formerly known as Saul. He had a wince-worthy past, and it took God's literally blinding him to convince him that he wasn't as morally superior as he thought. He later walked thousands of miles to talk about this God whose love so dazzled him. For his troubles, he'd spend a lot of time in jail—oh, and be beheaded on this date somewhere between AD 62 and 67.

It's no wonder that he said that to die was a "win" for him. But what does it mean for us?

Maybe it means that dying to ourselves, to our egos, is a gift even though it comes wrapped in pain. But once we've accepted it, we can begin to understand how undependable our feelings are, how unimportant other people's opinions about us are, and how deeply God loves us.

As Christians, we are ever asked to turn strange incongruities like this over in our minds. We're supposed to remember Christ's crucifixion and to "rejoice always." We are told that we are ashes and to ashes we'll return, and that we're "God's masterpieces" (Ephesians 2:10, NLT).

No wonder it takes so long even to begin to grasp these mysteries.

What does "to live in Christ" mean to you?

Put Your Brave On

We must walk consciously only part way toward our goal, and
then leap in the dark to our success.
—Henry David Thoreau

After spending a month doing some risky soul-searching, acknowledging what's false in ourselves, and seeking ways to live less ego-driven and more intentional lives, it's time to have some fun. After all, it's summer.

In July, keeping in mind the life rules we've been tinkering with this month, we'll look at what taking creative chances can look like. You'll hear stories about women who took astonishing chances on love. (Spoiler alert: some stories have happier endings than others.)

I'll tell you about people whose stories prove that it's (almost) never too late do that thing you always dreamed of doing. And we'll see examples of how switching up our daily lives can be a life-giving thing.

In short, you'll be cheered on to "put your brave on," as a friend of mine calls it.

So, kick off your shoes, step into those flip-flops, and get ready to dive into what makes your heart sing. Ready?

What comes to mind when you hear the phrase "put your brave on"?

July

Practice Taking Chances

Switch It Up and Put Your Brave On

July 1
Don't Play It Safe

Life shrinks or expands according to one's courage.
—Anaïs Nin

The other chaperones and I sat along the back wall of the practice room, with laptops or knitting balanced on our knees. Our children would soon perform in an orchestra competition, but they were punchy and bleary eyed from travel and staying up too late in their hotel rooms the night before.

After stopping them—again—for playing sloppily, their conductor told them to put down their bows. "This is not the day for you to play it safe," he said, his words carefully selected, almost metrical. "You might be the best orchestra here, but that doesn't matter. What does matter is who you are and what you mean to each other."

He told them that their performance would be both short lived and somehow also permanent, the music forever echoing through the cosmos.

All of us hung on his every word.

"What I need you to do is get more energy. Sweep it up into the dustpan, scrape it together for another hour," he said. "Then we can make the trip home and remember what we did and not have an 'I wish' attached to this day."

"Create euphoria," he said. "Do what you need to do."

Let July be a month of scraping together your energy and getting unstuck.

Time for Nothing

*I pray thee, spare thyself at times: for it becomes a wise man
sometimes to relax the high pressure of his attention to work.*
—St. Thomas Aquinas

Back in March, I described asking a roomful of mothers to schedule ten minutes every day for doing nothing at all. When I told them they could use the time to stare into space like children, they looked at me as if I'd lost my mind.

We get out of the habit of daydreaming, imagining, and carefully examining the natural world as we grow older. Yes, our lives get busier as we manage, day by day, our children and homes and work and relationships. There's not much time anymore for daydreaming, is there?

How about the parts of the day that lend themselves to being put to no good use? Those in-between moments, like when we're waiting for a child's soccer practice or school day to end.

What if, the next time you had a spare moment, you left your phone in the car, stepped out, and sat up against a tree? What if you spent those five unproductive minutes watching the clouds or crumbling a piece of bark between your fingers? When was the last time you lay in the grass and just stared up at the sky?

*Take some time for nothing today and notice something that won't be
visible to you when winter comes again.*

July 3
Someday

Hold fast to dreams,
For if dreams die
Life is a broken-winged bird
That cannot fly.
—Langston Hughes

When our children show even the slightest hint of self-doubt, it seems we can't help ourselves from turning into peppy cheerleaders. Even introverted types like me do it. "Never give up on your dreams!" we say, beaming. "Be the best you can be!"

Do we ever motivate ourselves like that? No, but our kids have their whole lives ahead of them, right? Isn't it too late for us to take risks or try something new?

Well, Julia Child was forty-nine when she published her first cookbook, *Mastering the Art of French Cooking*, and fifty-one at the debut of her television program. Those kinds of stories abound.

If you're feeling like you're stuck, consider back-timing your life. What do you want your life to hold when you're sixty? What will you regret not having done? It could be something as simple as having a container garden or learning to bake bread, or as complex as going back to school or moving somewhere new.

What risk could you take that would be an effective palate cleanser for your life?

⌒

Write the words, "Someday I'd love to . . ." in your journal or the back of this book and then brainstorm a list. Could you choose one item and try it this summer?

Independence Day

*Together with a culture of work, there must be a culture of leisure
as gratification. To put it another way: people who work must take
the time to relax, to be with their families, to enjoy themselves,
read, listen to music, play a sport.*

—Pope Francis

Unless we are traveling, my family and I celebrate the Fourth of July the same way every year. In the morning, folding chairs in hand, we walk the two blocks to our friends' house on Main Street to watch the parade.

By the time we arrive, their front lawn is crowded with neighbors and friends, some of whom we see only once a year on that day. Little kids crouch on the curb, flags in hand, as floats and local politicians, business owners, and firefighters go by. Older kids wander; adults chat.

We stand when the flag or veterans pass. We cover our ears when fire trucks blare their horns and turn on their sirens. We cheer for the kids we know in marching bands or Scout troops. It's small-town America at its finest.

And then we go home, often bringing friends along, for a lazy day of eating, chatting, and playing badminton out back until nightfall, when fireworks fill the sky.

July 4 is a day off, set aside for compulsory leisure for many of us, and one on which I am grateful for my life's simplest pleasures.

Today, take a moment to see God's hand in the blessings you enjoy.

Risking for Love

*There is no intensity of love or feeling that does not involve the risk
of crippling hurt. It is a duty to take this risk, to love and feel
without defense or reserve.*
—William S. Burroughs

When her children were very young, my friend Bethany's husband died, just months after receiving his cancer diagnosis. For the next few years, Bethany cared for her children, increased her hours at work, and tried to help her kids remember the father whose voice and face they would soon forget.

She said she went on autopilot: unloading groceries, showering, cleaning the house, working to pay the bills. *This is how it's going to be from now on*, she thought.

Then she met Dan. Single after a painful divorce, Dan fell in love with Bethany and her family. He had always longed to have children and, as she had, had assumed he'd be single from then on. Initially Bethany was hesitant to see him. Was dating Dan somehow disloyal to her husband? And how could she risk suffering another loss?

"But there was a moment when I knew, and I didn't question it," she said. "I knew God had something great planned, and I just had to wait."

Later, they married. Opening her heart to Dan and taking that risk has brought healing and companionship to Bethany and a loving father to her children. Yes, she's exposed herself to the possibility of more loss, but loving someone else always does.

When has loving someone felt like a risk in your life?

July 6
What If?

You never climb the same mountain twice, not even in memory.
Memory rebuilds the mountain, changes the weather, retells the
jokes, remakes all the moves.
—Lito Tejada-Flores

A few nights ago my husband and I were at a dinner party. Over dessert, the guests took turns asking one another questions. Kind of like truth or dare for adults, minus the dares. "What's something you always wanted to do but haven't done?" our host asked. The responses included skydiving, becoming a beekeeper, and living overseas. I admitted to a secret dream of learning to throw pots on a pottery wheel. The last person to answer was our friend Gabe.

"I'm doing what I've always wanted to do this Wednesday," he announced cheerfully. "I'm going to Florida to visit cousins I haven't seen since I was a child."

"What?" we all shouted. How was that comparable to jumping from a plane or moving somewhere like Budapest?

"It is!" Gabe insisted. He said he'd lost touch with this part of the family and had wanted to reach out for years but was afraid of being rejected. "What if they don't want to have a relationship?" he asked. "What if our being cousins doesn't mean anything to them the way it does to me?"

We agreed that Gabe's answer was the riskiest of them all.

What did you write on your "Someday I'd love to . . ." list? What feels like the biggest risk to take? The smallest?

July 7

Excuses, Excuses

The real man is one who always finds excuses for others, but never excuses himself.

—Henry Ward Beecher

So what if Julia Child was almost fifty when her cookbook was published? Or that Peter Roget wrote his eponymous thesaurus in his seventies? And what of Mother Teresa establishing the Missionaries of Charity when she was forty or receiving the Nobel Peace Prize at seventy-nine?

That's them, right? Even with examples of people older than ourselves taking risks—and doing wonderful things—you and I have no shortage of reasons we shouldn't even try.

We can't picture what our new life might look like. We worry that we'll fail. We fear what others will think. And, anyway, maybe we don't have an idea as clear cut as writing a cookbook or moving to Calcutta. Instead, we just have this vague idea that something is missing. We have an ongoing hunch that maybe God has something special for us to do.

On the day of an orchestra competition, my son's conductor said: "This is not the day for you to play it safe. Do what you need to do."

And they did. They gathered up all their energy and focus, played well, and won. I don't think any of us expected that would happen.

Maybe today's not the day for playing safe for you—or for me, either.

⌒

What's the first thing that comes to mind when you read the phrase "Do what you need to do?"

211

But They Make Funny Stories

You grow up the day you have your first real laugh—at yourself.
—Ethel Barrymore

Not all of the risks we take result in best-selling books or the Nobel Prize; some just end badly.

A woman I recently met told me that, while traveling in Central America in her early twenties, she was obsessed with "romantic stories about people discovering the loves of their lives" and ended up marrying a virtual stranger. A few days later, she realized her mistake, and they parted. She returned home to the States, moved in with her parents, and began therapy to discover what it was she was really looking for.

My most foolish choice at that age involved caffeine and a brown polyester uniform. I was working and in college and anxious about money. It had occurred to me—light bulb moment!—that I really didn't need sleep and could instead work at an all-night diner. After a couple of disastrous nights (and days), I quit by having my roommate return my uniform to the restaurant.

My traveling friend's shortest marriage ever and my brief misadventure as a late-night waitress were not the result of careful, rational thought. But, as they say, the road to maturity is paved with mistakes.

What is the most foolish risk you have ever taken? What do you know now that you didn't know then?

Delicious

*Another glorious day, the air as delicious to the lungs as nectar
to the tongue.*
—John Muir

Getting out of a rut can be as simple as breaking routine and
unplugging from rote behavior. When I've felt stuck, I've done
some of the following:

Tried new recipes. Once, on a whim, I made an English trifle.
 You know the layered dessert made with berries, pudding,
 cake, and cream? I'd never done it before, and haven't since,
 but enjoyed the novelty.

Swapped out the pictures on the walls.

Dug into the Christmas bins and hung twinkly lights outside in
 the summer.

Ordered a meal I had never tried.

Gone to a remote corner of the library and chosen a book.
 That's how I happened upon the Scottish writer Muriel
 Spark. I went back to that spot week after week for more of
 her mysteries.

Driven home by another way, winding through unfamiliar
 neighborhoods, really noticing where I'm going.

These little choices remind me that I'm not stuck. I have options.
I can be creative and add color to my life.

 You can, too.

*This month, try something new. Wear an outfit that's been stuck in
your closet for too long. Bake something you've never baked before.
Take your dog for a walk, and surprise him or her by taking a
different route. Try something from one of life's endlessly
delicious choices.*

Going Purple

Security is a superstition. It does not exist in nature. . . . Avoiding
danger is no safer in the long run than outright exposure.
—Helen Keller

My friend's teenage daughter dyed her hair purple. Not a muted magenta or deep maroon, but purple, like a grape Popsicle. (It looks terrific.) This is a girl who is so funny and self-possessed that someone should give her a TV show. The first time I saw her after she'd gone purple, it seemed rude not to mention it. "Wow, Claire," I said. "Now that's purple!"

"Yep!" she said.

"It looks great."

"I know!" She grinned. "Bad news is I've got to dye it back before the choir concert. Rules. But then after that, I'll do something else."

"Like?"

"Oh, I don't know. A green stripe maybe." And with that, she left me standing on the sidewalk in front of the grocery store. I caught my reflection in the window. My hair is dark brown, like Claire's used to be. I thought about how if a woman my age went purple, it would be seen as a statement or, more likely—at least in my tidy suburb—a sign of instability.

But when you're fifteen, it's just a whim, a lark, a funny little experiment. You're free to reinvent yourself, as long as the choir director approves.

What could playfully reinventing yourself look like?

July 11
What Fits?

And so with the sunshine and the great bursts of leaves growing on the trees—just as things grow in fast movies—I had that familiar conviction that life was beginning over again with the summer.
—F. Scott Fitzgerald, *The Great Gatsby*

My six-year-old daughter squatted on the back porch, rifling around in the basket that holds flip-flops and plastic clogs. My children love the lightweight clogs in the summer. At the beach, sand magically shoots out of the ventilation holes; and, after tramping around in the mud, they can be hosed off and left to dry in the sun.

"Hey, Mom!" she shouted, holding up her pink pair. "You shrunk my Crocs. They used to be too big, but they're perfect now. Thanks!"

I asked my daughter if she thought anything might be different about her feet since last summer. Maybe the shoes were exactly the same. She slipped one foot out of her shoe and raised it into the air. Pivoting her ankle, she studied her foot for a second or two. "Nope, it's my same foot," she said, sliding the shoe back on.

I'm like that, often unaware of the ways I'm growing into, or out of, parts of my life: friendships, routines, and who I was created to be.

⌒

Have you ever realized that something in your life "fits" that didn't fit before?

Bohemian Romantic

You're never too old to become younger.
—Mae West

I'm not much into fashion. In college, I mostly shopped at resale shops. One was called Weeds, playing on how Shakespeare used that word to mean "attire" in *Twelfth Night.* I favored men's blazers worn over T-shirts, rolled-up jeans, and the occasional long prairie skirt. Think Molly Ringwald in *Pretty in Pink.*

These clothes were comfortable and made me feel like myself. My *Pretty in Pink* look was replaced with sensible-looking dress clothes (straight skirts, crisp white blouses, the occasional silky scarf) when I took an office job in Manhattan.

My wardrobe changed again with pregnancy and as a new mother; all that mattered was that clothes were large, stretchy, and had those convenient nursing slits.

Now, though, I'm not sure what I'd call my look—maybe suburban-mom wallflower chic?

My friend Aimee is in her forties, like me. She recently told me that she was changing her look. Bohemian romantic, she explained, tossing a floral scarf over her shoulder. "I've been wearing the same conservative suits for decades. It was time for a change."

What whimsical name could you give your style? Do your clothes make you feel like "you," or might it be time to change things up?

Hello, Chef

I am growing up. I am losing some illusions.
—Virginia Woolf, *Orlando*

Michelle told me that five years as an at-home mom with her two children had taken a toll. She felt bored, unsatisfied. Her spirit was restless for change. She remembers thinking: *If I have one more conversation with another mom at a playground about what stroller we purchased or how we selected our pediatrician, I'm going to lose it.*

Michelle rallied her courage and took a leap. "Although I had zero intention of becoming a chef, I went to culinary school. I did have a pie-in-the-sky idea of becoming a culinary nutritionist at some point, but that never happened." (Her unpremeditated use of the term *pie-in-the-sky* makes me smile.)

Now, a few years after finishing her program, Michelle says she isn't using—and will likely never use—the degree professionally and continues to pay off her student loans. "And that's no fun," she admits.

But was it worth it? Would she do it all over again? "Absolutely," she says. "It was one of the best things I've ever done for my psyche."

Reading about Michelle, did a dream pop into your mind? Could you take a leap as she did?

More Like Yourself

Mrs. Darling put her hand to her heart and cried, "Oh, why can't you remain like this for ever!" This was all that passed between them on the subject, but henceforth Wendy knew that she must grow up.

—J. M. Barrie, *Peter Pan*

Being a parent, to state the obvious, is difficult. A woman I know puts it more bluntly: "No one tells you how much of a drag motherhood can be."

Over the past few years, she's felt increasingly isolated and at odds with herself. She says she's lost her professional edge by working from home, and friendships that were once important to her have faded away. "I want to feel like me again."

I don't know any women who wouldn't sympathize.

"My advice to moms who feel stuck is to take up martial arts," my friend Dana said. "Or if they don't have the time for that big of a commitment, get some boxing gloves and get into a gym where you can hit a heavy bag a couple of times a week."

Dana said boxing plus listening to AC/DC "really loud" has kept her sane as a mother. "Get someone to show you how to throw a real punch—it's so empowering. You'll sweat a lot and will feel like a badass when you walk out," Dana said. "For me, it's just a different way to meditate."

What makes you feel empowered or "more like yourself"?

July 15
They Call Me Mother

Those who are happiest are those who do the most for others.
—Booker T. Washington

Today is the feast day of Anne-Marie Jahouvey, a nun who took enormous risks throughout her adult life. Her story is relevant to us as we look for ways, big and small, to put our brave on.

Anne-Marie Jahouvey was born in France into a wealthy family in 1779. As a girl, she had a vision in which Teresa of Ávila entrusted her with many children of different races. Later, Nanette, as she was called, would devote her life to the poor and to educating children all over the globe.

Mother Javouhey's most celebrated achievements are founding the Sisters of St. Joseph of Cluny and being acknowledged as their "mother" by hundreds of emancipated slaves in French Guiana after teaching them to live prosperous and independent lives.

Her life wasn't easy. She made arduous journeys to South America, islands in the Indian Ocean, and West Africa. Some resented her work to empower former slaves and plotted to kill her. She also faced opposition within the church at home.

Nanette could have lived in comfort in France but instead gave her life to God. In return, she lived a varied and meaningful life.

How would you like to be remembered by the people who call you "Mother"?

Road Construction

Deep summer is when laziness finds respectability.
—Sam Keen

There's a saying where I live that there are two seasons here in the Chicago area: winter and road construction.

It's true: as soon as the streets are cleared of snow and ice, detour signs start appearing. Notification boards pop up beside highways: "Road Construction Next Ten Miles. Expect Delays" (or the grimmer message: "Injure/Kill a Worker $7500 + 15 Years").

During construction, potholes and divots are covered over with asphalt and smoothed with mammoth steamrollers. The patches of new road, scars as black as licorice, reveal the parts of the road that bear the most weight and get driven over the most.

Fissures are created when parts of the road bear the weight of traffic, over and over again. That's what ruts are, after all. Indicators that we are repeating the same things, traveling the same routes, over and over and over again.

That's why taking martial arts or dying our hair purple or changing the pictures on the walls can feel so satisfying. We're reminding ourselves that we're alive, we have room to experiment, and we aren't destined to keep traveling the same paths again and again.

Where in your life is repetition creating potholes and ruts?

Moving House

Where Thou art—that—is Home.
—Emily Dickinson

I would bet that Blessed Anne-Marie Jahouvey (aka "Nanette"), whose story I shared on July 15, never had the opportunity to get into a rut; she didn't live anywhere long enough. Among the places she called home were Senegal, Gambia, France, French Guiana, and—in her final years—Tahiti and Madagascar.

Color me, as person with acute wanderlust, envious.

Changing location, for any of us, can be an effective way to spring ourselves from ruts. Even if it's just a weekend getaway.

"My favorite trick is picking up and moving to a new city when I am stuck," Bonnie said. "When I found myself floundering in a stale, bad relationship and bored with a job I used to like, I moved back to Vermont from Boston."

Bonnie's friend Mila does the same. "I'm another frequent mover. When I was younger, I subscribed to the belief that geographical change would improve whatever was wrong where I was. Now I suspect I just like the challenge of trying to make a new home in a new place."

For me, a week in Florida or even a few nights tucked away on a friend's basement futon can do the trick.

How long have you lived in your current home? Do you feel restless to live somewhere else?

July 18
The Hair We Wear

I'm undaunted in my quest to amuse myself by constantly changing my hair.
—Hillary Clinton

I knew that Eileen and I would be fast friends when, minutes after we met, I confessed to having just trimmed my own bangs—as though their lopsided witness way above my eyebrows wasn't confession enough. "Oh, I get it," she said. "You get mad, and you cut your hair. Me, too."

Her words were so spot-on. Indeed, I'd been in a foul mood the day I did it, and I'd made the quickest, most satisfying change I could make without leaving the house or spending a dime. I chopped off my bangs.

When women are feeling restless or depressed, many of us consider changing our hair. Hair has meaning. Some say that short hair on a woman is a feminist statement and long hair a signal to men that we'd make good lovers. (Mine's medium length. What could that mean?)

But any way you look at it, from Rapunzel's ropelike locks cascading from the tower in which she is held captive to Britney Spears's head-shaving incident to cultures in which women's hair is always covered, people attach layers of meaning to women's hair.

Have you ever cut your hair because you're mad or out of sorts? Would cutting your hair or growing it out be liberating for you?

Get Unstuck

We are taught you must blame your father, your sisters, your brothers, the school, the teachers—you can blame anyone, but never blame yourself. It's never your fault. But it's always your fault, because if you wanted to change, you're the one who has got to change.

—Katharine Hepburn

Let's say you're itching for change but absolutely cannot ditch your real life for culinary school or make a cross-country move. I've mentioned that taking a different route to and from regular destinations, playing musical chairs—literally—with furniture, and other low-impact but changed-up choices can help roust us out of ruts.

One friend says that reaching out to others yanked her out of a "depressed fog." "For almost a year after college, I lived at home with my parents, worked for my stepdad, and hated my life. I was miserable!" she said. "To pull myself out, I started volunteering—and eventually signed up to train—for a marathon to raise money for the San Francisco AIDS Foundation."

She said she "got in shape, met a ton of people, and lost weight," but more important, she gained a sense of purpose. "The experience gave me confidence, and that confidence enabled me to get super aggressive with finding a job. I eventually found a great one and moved out of my folks' place. Plus, I ran a freaking marathon!"

Could reaching out and volunteering for a good cause with others help you get unstuck?

July 20
Change Haters

Taking a new step, uttering a new word is what they fear most.
—Fyodor Dostoyevsky, *Crime and Punishment*

One of my sons says he's "not a huge fan" of change. This was plain
to all of us early on. If his preschool teacher was out sick and a sub-
stitute filled in, he'd speak of little else the rest of the day. "They
could have told us," he'd moan. "Why did it have to be someone
different? They should have canceled school."

A challenge for him has been to accept that life is always in flux.
Teachers call in sick. Businesses fail. Birthday parties get canceled.
Friendships fizzle out. Interests shift.

"I don't like change," confessed Jess, a mother of two. "Even
when things are bad, I'm reluctant to rock the boat or go outside
my comfort zone. I joined a gym two years ago. It was the single
most terrifying, change-it-up kind of thing this painfully shy, completely out-of-shape bookworm has ever done. I've never encoun-
tered a more daunting atmosphere."

Jess took a beginner's class but found herself in the company of
several athletes and even a soldier on leave. "The workouts literally
made me cry," she said. "But I've experienced an amazing surge of
self-esteem; my body can actually do the things I ask it to do."

*What's the most frightening change you can imagine doing? Can you
risk going there?*

Change Junkies

It takes a very long time to become young.
—Pablo Picasso

Patti loves change, but says that, as a wife and at-home mother, she doesn't have the luxury of controlling the way she spends her time. "The only thing within my complete control is my body," she says. "So, I've taken up Pilates, cut out added sugar, and gotten a tattoo."

She admits to feeling "itchy again" and is looking for new ways to switch things up.

We describe feeling stuck in so many evocative ways: "I'm itchy," "Things feel stale," "I've got the blahs." When you find yourself using language like that, jot down a list of your very favorite people and things. Are you making sure they're in your life? Are you doing anything that helps you live out your purpose?

Ruts are an inevitable part of life. No matter how sunny your attitude or focused your rule of life, that feeling of being stuck will sneak in, catlike, from time to time. It's up to you whether you let it curl up and make itself at home, or shoo it outside again.

How do you know when you're in a rut? Pay attention to those feelings.

July 22

St. Peter's Charms

I love the man that can smile in trouble, that can gather strength
from distress, and grow brave by reflection.
—Thomas Paine

When an experience is going well for me—a friendship, a collaboration, even a really good meal—my mind flits around like a dragonfly, trying to figure out how I can land on this exact situation again.

It's one of the reasons I identify so much with St. Peter; he was just the same.

In good times, Peter ached to make time stand still. Remember the transfiguration? Christ's face "changed" and his clothing "became as bright as a flash of lightning." Moses and Elijah even appeared—"in glorious splendor," apparently. We don't know what James and John had to say, but Peter?

"Let's stay here forever!" (Luke 9:28–33, NIV). He was just as fervent about avoiding pain. When Jesus told the disciples that he would be crucified, Peter said, "Never, Lord! This shall never happen to you. God forbid it!"

Then Jesus got a little testy. He said, "Get behind me, Satan! You . . . do not have in mind the concerns of God, but merely human concerns" (Matthew 16:21–23, ESV).

Ouch. As a "Peter" myself, that reprimand is also directed at me. Stop being so risk averse; focus on more important matters.

Do you identify with St. Peter in these stories?

Your Name, Your Beginning

What's in a name? That is what we ask ourselves in childhood
when we write the name that we are told is ours.
—James Joyce, *Ulysses*

I have a brand new niece, and all I can think about is what her parents are going to call her. They haven't yet decided.

I start at the top of the alphabet, nudging my memory for favorite names beginning with *A*. Adelaide? Amadea? Aurelia? Her mother is a painter. What about Georgia (O'Keeffe), Frida (Kahlo), or Berthe (Morisot)?

It took my husband and me days after they were born to name our children. Finally, the right name came for each of them, and we never looked back.

My niece exists, but somehow she will be even more herself once she has a name.

In some cultures, a child isn't named until she or he is seven days old. In others, naming takes place after the remaining bit of umbilical cord drops off, signifying that the baby is ready to be an independent person. Some people wait much longer.

And then, like a butterfly alighting on a leaf, an email arrives. I open it and am met with the exquisite *Winifred*; the name means "blessed peace; fair reconciliation."

Gazing at the photo of her tiny sleeping self, I know that the name, like the baby herself, is perfect.

To whom or what have you given names? What does your own name mean to you?

July 24

Past Successes

*Perhaps all the dragons of our lives are princesses who are only
waiting to see us act, just once, with beauty and courage.*
—Rainer Maria Rilke

My daughter Isabel, when she was eleven, was sorting through a box of certificates, ribbons, and other accolades—a reading award, a softball trophy, that sort of thing. "I think I'll just get rid of this stuff," she said, tossing it all back into the box.

"No!" I said. "Don't do that!"

"Why not?" She looked surprised. Usually I'm the anti-hoarder mom trying to get the kids to toss things out.

"Well, look at it this way," I said. "When you're forty and if you're feeling low, you could look through these things. You could remember that you once were singled out as being special."

"You think when I'm forty years old, these will still be the only awards I ever got?" she said. "And that will cheer me up?"

Since then, of course, whenever any of the kids gets so much as a sticker from the pediatrician, another will say, "Keep that! When you're forty you might need it to feel special!" Cue uproarious laughter.

Truth is, though, our past successes can bolster our confidence. Looking back can make us feel braver about moving forward.

⌣

*If you are feeling insecure, revisit your past accomplishments and
remember that you faced challenges before and overcame them (even,
I bet, in the fifth grade).*

Preferring the Given

*His will be done, as done it surely will be, whether we humble
ourselves to resignation or not. The impulse of creation forwards it;
the strength of powers, seen and unseen, has its fulfillment
in charge.*

—Charlotte Brontë, *Villette*

British novelist and theologian Charles Williams, who, with C. S.
Lewis and J. R. R. Tolkien, was a member of the literary club the
Inklings, had an exceptional life rule. Instead of being devoted to
his own idea of where his life would go, he chose to "prefer the
given" of his present reality, letting the divine plan unfold before
him. He knew that it might be very different from his own.

"Preferring the given" is about presence, acceptance, and trust.
It's one of my favorite spiritual concepts. There's a tension between
making bold changes and being content with things as they are.
But I think we can manage both.

When we're stuck, we can be present and acknowledge the rut
we're in. We can be open to what God might be teaching us in a
moment we didn't choose for ourselves. It doesn't mean we have to
wallow in stuck places or give up hope that things will change; we
can simply trust that the waiting, the slow traffic, and the bumpy
road have something to teach us.

Maybe we'll end up on a detour that will take us to a new des-
tination, one we were meant to discover all along.

*Have you ever come out of a stuck place into a brand new kind of life
or with new perspective?*

Admiration

The wicked envy and hate; it is their way of admiring.
—Victor Hugo

Pay attention to what makes you feel a pinprick of envy or fills you with heart-tugging admiration.

If a friend tells me she's going on a cruise, I say, "Bon voyage!" There is no pricking or tugging. I'm afraid I'd be seasick, the movie *Titanic* scarred me, and recent cruise debacles (viruses that sicken everyone on board, power outages, and even episodes of boats sinking—their captains jumping ship) leave me feeling that my life would be more than complete if I never set foot on a gangplank.

When a colleague is hired as the keynote speaker at a conference, I give her a fist bump and my heartiest congratulations. Again, no envy or jealousy. Public speaking isn't my favorite.

But—and I think this is true without exception—when someone tells me she is getting a puppy, going to Paris, publishing a novel, taking a girls' weekend with friends, or training to become a spiritual director, then the tugging and pricking commence in full force.

You see, I'd truly love another dog. I long to visit Paris. I want to make time to write fiction. I find weekends away with friends scrumptious. And secretly (a bit less secretly now), I think I'd love to be a spiritual director someday.

What pulls at your heart when you hear about someone else doing it?

Spiritual Ruts

It seemed to me that where others had prayed before to their God,
in their joy or in their agony, was of itself a sacred place.
—Elizabeth Gaskell, *Cranford*

I've heard, from the pulpit and from the pages of books, that we should feel flattered when the only answer to our prayers is silence. God's silence, we're told, is a gift.

I think that's a disingenuous message. It's not a privilege to feel spiritually alone; it's disheartening.

Although I've had spiritual encounters that were so crystal clear, so visceral, I can't imagine ever giving up on my faith, I've been in spiritual ruts more often than I'd like to admit. I'm no expert for getting out of them, but I do think they aren't so very different from ruts we get into with the people we love: God and I need quality time together.

One colossal difference: we get to see and touch and snuggle with the people we love; we must have faith in order to interact with God. So there's that.

It has helped me to take a walk and notice the beauty of creation, read the Psalms, receive the Eucharist, or talk to close friends about how God has answered my prayers in the past.

Like any kind of rut, spiritual ones can be tricky to navigate. But no, they absolutely do not feel like a gift.

What do you do when you feel spiritually stuck?

July 28
Bad Days

Every heart has its secret sorrows, which the world knows not, and often times we call a man cold, when he is only sad.
—Henry Wadsworth Longfellow

Everyone has rotten days on which we feel unable to "get our brave on," take risks, or even walk out in nature to listen to the crickets sing or look for shapes in the clouds. In fact, the thought of even attempting either of those things will make us laugh, and sardonically.

These days don't necessarily mean we're in a rut, only that our mood is low. Our moods are affected by variables including hormones, sleep, vitamin deficiencies, and stress levels. Sometimes we feel low because the past has come creeping up from behind us, taps us on the shoulder, and recaps our bad memories.

About three years ago, I went to my doctor for a checkup. I casually mentioned that I'd been feeling weak and more tired than usual. I was understating it; I'd felt truly frail. A few blood tests later, I learned that I was vitamin D deficient, a rather common ailment here in the Midwest.

After a few weeks of taking megadoses of D, I felt more like myself again—and was reminded, for the millionth time, how we humans are such science experiments. I wasn't depressed or in a rut, I just needed to get my chemistry right.

Do you ever worry on bad days that you are stuck or in a rut? Remember that everyone has rotten days, and be kind to yourself.

Dangers of Navel-Gazing

I tell people to monitor their self-pity. Self-pity is very unattractive.
—Patty Duke

The word *omphaloskepsis* comes from the Greek *omphalos* (navel) and *skepsis* (act of looking). It means—yep—the contemplation of one's navel. In the context of yoga, navel-gazing refers to being present in the moment, compassionate with the thoughts that arise during meditation, and aware of one's breathing.

But in common usage, navel-gazing is derogatory. "He's a navel-gazer," means that someone is self-absorbed, narcissistic, and/or given to self-pity. He's so focused on himself that he cannot even notice what other people experience—in his family, the wider community, or the world.

Navel-gazing is not the same as daydreaming. Daydreaming is letting the mind wander and wonder. It's thinking about possibilities. It's noticing. It's letting go. Navel-gazing is about being stuck in our heads.

Our egos are strong and athletic; they are happy to let us forget that there is a world outside, full of people as three-dimensional; complicated; and deserving of dignity, love, comfort, and compassion as we are. Navel-gazing can get us into a rut.

Sometimes the only way out is to straighten our backs, lift our heads, and look out and away from ourselves.

Have you ever found yourself navel-gazing?

Courage over Fear

Courage is found in unlikely places.
—J. R. R. Tolkien, *The Hobbit*

We all deal with fear differently. Some of us are more dramatic and express it by shouting out or cowering behind our feelings—or maybe we do a bit of both. Others hold our fear in and act cool, thinking that somehow if we pretend we aren't terrified, everyone else will believe it. Maybe we'll even believe it, too.

As far as I can tell, neither strategy works.

My tendency is to pretend that everything is all right when I'm suffering. I don't want to be any trouble. I scramble to tidy up my heartbreaks privately and try to say I'm fine, even when I'm not.

It's healthier when we can say we're afraid, that we feel like we're drowning in whatever sadness has accosted our lives: a scary diagnosis, financial worries, a relationship that is teetering on the edge of brokenness. It helps us heal more fully when we ask for, and accept, help.

How do you manage when you feel fearful?

Reach Out

I suppose I have found it easier to identify with the characters who
verge upon hysteria, who were frightened of life, who were
desperate to reach out to another person. But these seemingly
fragile people are the strong people really.
—Tennessee Williams

This month, we looked at what it means to be brave and take risks when we find ourselves feeling numb or stuck. We explored low-impact, as well as more drastic, ways to jolt ourselves out of the ruts in which we land from time to time.

Whether you get a tattoo or change around your furniture or cut your hair or go back to school or move across the country or just go on a walk outdoors so you can be in touch with creation, you have options.

You can open yourself up and work to rouse yourself from a sleepy, weary time in your life. You can also look at down times as seasons when you will wait upon God, trusting in God's goodness. We'll delve into that further next month, as we practice trusting and letting go.

We ended this month by defining navel-gazing and by looking at how opening our hearts to others can liberate us from a too-narrow focus on ourselves.

When we devote our time, financial resources, and hearts to helping others—working to empower others so that they might move out of poverty, loneliness, or whatever else marginalizes them—we free ourselves from the inevitable unhappiness that self-absorption brings.

Look back at your rule of life from June. How can you promote that
new philosophy by reaching out to others?

August

Practice Trust

Detach, Let Go, and Trust That You're
Good Enough

Freeing Ourselves

Act as if everything depended on you; trust as if everything depended on God.

—St. Ignatius of Loyola

Yesterday was the feast day of St. Ignatius of Loyola.

Iñigo López de Oñaz y Loyola, later known as St. Ignatius, was born into a distinguished family in northeastern Spain in 1491. As a boy, Iñigo was infatuated with stories of King Arthur's Camelot and was later known as a swordsman and womanizer. At nineteen, he joined the Spanish army.

After being wounded in battle at age thirty, Iñigo spent his extended recovery reading *De vita Christi*, a commentary on the life of Christ, and books about the saints. He resolved to become a "soldier" of the faith; some accounts describe him entering a chapel in full armor and laying his sword before the altar.

Ignatius established the Society of Jesus, or the Jesuits. One of his key teachings is that in order to follow God wholeheartedly, we should free ourselves from cherished preferences, opinions, and attachments.

After exploring forgiveness, then our truest selves, and, last month, making brave choices, this month's reflections center around detaching from the things that keep us wary, unable to trust.

We'll look at what makes us feel that we're unworthy so we can begin to move beyond these things, see ourselves more clearly, and more fully trust in God.

What makes you feel unworthy or not good enough?

Captive to Mistrust

The best way to find out if you can trust somebody is to trust them.
—Ernest Hemingway

Not long after we met, Heidi told me that it would take a long time for us to become friends, if we ever did. "I'm not a trusting person," she said. "My assumption is that you're guilty until proven innocent. It takes time to gain my trust, and I don't give it out easily."

In my twenties, I found her philosophy intriguing. I assumed the best of people to a fault, and indeed have learned to enter relationships with more caution. But I don't find it intriguing anymore. Just sad.

Heidi and I are still friendly, but our friendship has never grown deep. Although we meet for coffee once in a while and catch up about our kids and work, it's hard to be open and free with someone who is always on her guard.

Trusting others is a risk, but when we let fear hold us captive, we cheat ourselves. Sadly, that seems to be Heidi's experience all these years later. She still keeps life at arm's length, eyes new acquaintances with mistrust, and misses out on intimacy.

Do past hurts keep you from being vulnerable with others?

August 3

Hang in There

Moderate strength is shown in violence, supreme strength is shown in levity.
—G. K. Chesterton, *The Man Who Was Thursday*

The hallway outside my elementary school library was decorated with inspirational posters. (Remember Ziggy?) "Pobody's Nerfect," read one. One featured a kitten clinging to a tree branch; the caption read: "Hang in There." Another showed a galloping horse and the words: "If you love somebody, let them go, for if they return, they were always yours. If they don't, they never were."

Buddhism puts it another way: "You only lose what you cling to."

It's hard to let go and trust, despite how marvelous that wild mustang looked with the sun glinting off his back. If only loosening our hold on the things that matter most were as easy as turning horses loose in a meadow.

Just as I did on my children's first days of kindergarten or when I retreated down a dirt road after dropping them off at camp when they were nine, I must practice trust and let go when they go off to college, one by one, over the next several years.

Will our relationships survive? Will my sons and daughters be eager to come home for breaks and family vacations? Will being in a new place change them, change the tenderness and love they feel for their siblings and their father and me?

Like all the parents I know, I have to hang in there, take deep breaths, and let my children go, as best as I can. I'll mess it up sometimes, but you know what they say: "Pobody's . . ."

What's hardest for you to let go of?

August 4
Trust and Love

To be trusted is a greater compliment than being loved.
—George MacDonald

What are the differences between love and trust? Well, one is that love can be defined in many more ways than trust. Love is often described as "intense affection." For others, it implies commitment and attachment.

Some say—or, rather, Bette Midler sings—that love "is a river that drowns the tender reed." (She also describes it as a razor, a hunger, and a flower in her song "The Rose.")

Trust is more straightforward. When we trust people, we confidently rely on them. When we trust an idea, we believe it to be true. We *depend* on the people and things we trust.

I have friends and family members whom I love but on whom I don't rely. No matter how much affection I have for them, I would never have confidence that they'd follow through on taking care of something important. I don't ask them to dog-sit, manage my finances, or pick up my children from school.

We can love people we don't completely trust. And we can trust people we don't love, like, say, our gynecologists.

⌒

Think about the people you are closest to; do you both love and trust them?

August 5
Earning Trust

I cannot love where I cannot trust.
—Oscar Wilde, *The Sphinx Without a Secret*

When my daughter Mia's adoption was finalized and we were able to bring her home from Guatemala, she was snuggly and affectionate from the start.

But trust took time. She was a toddler at her homecoming and found herself suddenly transplanted into a home full of strangers eating foods she'd never seen, speaking a foreign language, and with a completely different set of habits and expectations.

Every bath time was an exercise in building trust. She was happy to splash around with her sister, but when it came time to rinse the shampoo out of her hair, she panicked. Whether I used the shower nozzle or poured water from a plastic cup, she screamed, as they say, "bloody murder."

She also balked and usually howled when I'd try to cut her nails, trim her bangs, or even wipe her nose. It took time—years, really—before she happily let me do these little tasks. It was only after she learned to trust me.

When have you had to earn another person's trust?

August 6
Healing after Betrayal

After all, damn it, what does being in love mean if you can't
trust a person.
—Evelyn Waugh, *Vile Bodies*

It's inevitable: the people with whom we share lasting relationships will almost certainly break—or at least rigorously bend—our trust.

Our children will take advantage of our blind confidence in them and slip cash from our wallets, lie about where they've been, or convince us that whatever-it-is was their sibling's doing.

Friends will sometimes hurt us, discounting our feelings or carelessly sharing our secrets. Some spouses cheat, their infidelity shattering trust like a cinder block hurled through a stained-glass window.

When we learn that we've been betrayed, we may feel so hurt that we resolve never to trust that person fully, or trust anyone, ever again.

But if you want to trust someone again, start with being honest about your feelings. If the disloyalty is minor, reflect on whether you have ever done something similar to someone you love. Did you deceive your parents? Tell another person's secret? Does that mean you should never be trusted again?

If the betrayal has left you traumatized, consider talking to a therapist who can guide you toward healing.

Accept that it takes time to rebuild trust.

Do you have healing work to do right now? Be gentle with yourself,
and know that you are capable of trusting again.

Who Are You?

Attachment is the great fabricator of illusions; reality can be
obtained only by someone who is detached.
—Simone Weil

From the looks of it, most college application essay prompts aren't written by Buddhists—or by Jesuits, for that matter. High school seniors are asked to share stories of past hardships or to wax eloquent about how their academic and extracurricular pursuits will help them succeed in their eventual careers.

If we imagine Buddha and St. Ignatius conferring at a mystical admissions meeting, the two of them might write a prompt asking students to forget the past and instead consider what it means to be in the moment and to empty themselves.

Buddhists call that kind of emptying nonattachment; Ignatians, holy indifference.

None of us is, after all, the items we list on college or job applications. We're not whether we can tie our shoes or remember to fill up the dog's water bowl. We're not our emotions or personalities, preferred sports teams and political views, or the sum of our successes and failures.

And high school students know that. Ever notice how excruciating it is for them to respond to those prompts? Sadly, as the years pass, many people begin to believe that they *are* the roles they play: athlete, journalist, artist, spouse, breadwinner, at-home parent, caregiver, investor.

They forget that they—like all of us—are truly spiritual selves, created, known, and loved by God.

Do you ever mistake the roles you play with who you really are?

Souls with Bodies

Never tell a child, "You have a soul." Teach him, you are a soul;
you have a body.
—George MacDonald

Glancing at the cover model on a magazine in the grocery check-out line, we yank our backs straight, suck in our stomachs, and remember our physical imperfections.

All of us lose touch with the reality that we *are* souls and we *have* bodies. We flip it around. Too often we not only think of ourselves as bodies with souls but also that one of the things that matters most about us is how our bodies look. And this occurs in a culture where the definition of what is physically attractive is unattainable for most of us, as well as the result of leading-edge photo-editing software.

Of course, women care about much, much more than our looks. Loving relationships, our children's well-being, and fulfilling work are infinitely more important to us than how attractive we are. But still, it's hard to escape the constant barrage of messages that our bodies should be thinner, our hair thicker, our skin glowier (whatever that means), and so on.

It can trip us up and keep us from remembering that we are souls first and bodies second.

How do you feel about your body? Do the images you see and messages you receive make you focus more than you'd like on your appearance?

August 9

Body Image

The really frightening thing about middle age is that you know you'll grow out of it.
—Doris Day

I asked a few close friends to describe their current body image. Rachael, who's approaching fifty, said that she "honestly can't think of one thing" she currently likes about her body. She is unhappy with her energy level, body shape, and weight.

"I'm stiff and easily hurt. I do not recover from things quickly," she said. "I feel saggy and like I'm falling apart. It's like my body is plotting my demise."

Like Rachael, Nora is a mother of three, but is about fifteen years younger than her friend. "My thirties hit me like a beast, with three babies—bam, bam, bam. I'm sometimes surprised when I see my jean size, but honestly, I love that my kids love my body—my veins and bumps and lumps. Sometimes they come into the bathroom when I'm showering and ask why I have big breasts when I don't have a baby anymore."

"I love my body for all the comfort and intrigue it has afforded these little people," Nora said. "Not to mention, the life it has given them."

What do you like best and least about your body?

New Constellations of Womanhood

*We do not grow absolutely, chronologically. We grow sometimes in
one dimension, and not in another, unevenly. . . . The past,
present, and future mingle and pull us backward, forward, or fix
us in the present.*

—Anaïs Nin

My friend Barb said that, after menopause, she has a different relationship with her body from when she was younger. "There's a
point in a girl's life when people start to see her as a sexual being,"
Barb said. "There's also a point when people stop seeing her that
way. These two events more or less coincide with menstruation and
menopause."

Barb said that when women are about fifty, they no longer are
viewed primarily as sexual beings. She found this upsetting at first;
she'd liked that kind of attention when she was younger. But she's
come to see advantages to it.

"There is a strange comfort that comes from no longer seeing
your body in such a sexual way," she said. "Men in their thirties
and early forties—older than your children but almost young
enough to be your kids—seek out your company. They aren't competing with you or afraid of you. You see that your sexuality was an
unintended barrier to some friendships along the way."

Barb views women older than herself in new ways, too: as role
models. Her favorites are fierce, unafraid, truth tellers: "I want to
be like that."

*How do you experience your body and others' responses to it differently
now than you did ten or fifteen years ago?*

What Your Body Can Do

The body is a sacred garment.
—Martha Graham

Most of the women I've spoken to about their relationships with their bodies mention the sense of wonder that has at times overwhelmed them when they look at what their bodies have done, particularly in ushering children into the world.

Julia is fifty-two and the mother of three teenagers. She says she feels as physically strong as she did in her thirties and, of her body, says, "It isn't giving me any trouble—and never has."

Her one surprise is catching her reflection in a mirror. She says it surprises her, that she looks older than she feels. However, Julia is more attached to what her body does than how it appears. She said that having children made her aware of it as "an amazing, complicated machine."

"I breast-fed each of my kids for a little over a year, and I was surprised at how natural it felt," Julia said. "I felt like a mammal, an animal, a purely physical being for the first time in my life. Maybe athletes feel that way, like their body is the most important part of them, whereas I've always been so much in my head."

Have you ever felt amazed by what your body can do, whether it's giving birth, running a marathon, or bringing order and beauty to a garden?

Coming into Power

The afternoon knows what the morning never suspected.
—Swedish proverb

Although my friend Julia's most serious objection to aging is that she looks older than she feels, many women bemoan items from the usual shopping list of grievances about aging bodies: weight gain, stretch marks, fatigue, creaky knees, graying hair, various forms of the verb *sag*.

"I guiltily find myself wishing I could have my old body back," Katelyn said. "I hate admitting that; it feels yucky and indulgent and sad."

But for many women, a new sense of authority accompanies the less charming effects of aging. "All this sounds so troubled and doomsday," Katelyn said. "But the paradox that I hold is that turning forty was the best. I feel my power growing in so many ways. I have never felt fuller of ideas and creative energy and so on the cusp of great things."

As we approach and then move beyond forty, many of us become engaged in new, artistic endeavors, deepen spiritually, and also feel more sexually responsive than ever.

So, despite the sag, it's good for our souls.

What do you most fear or most look forward to about getting older?

Alive within You

*I like trees because they seem more resigned to the way they have to
live than other things do. I feel as if this tree knows everything I
ever think of when I sit here. When I come back to it, I never have
to remind it of anything; I begin just where I left off.*
—Willa Cather

The lawn at our new house was scattered with oaks, black elms,
and honey locusts. Not long after moving in, I noticed dead
branches on one of the trees. "Let's call a service," I said to my
husband.

"And let's get rid of that one," he said, pointing at a short,
scrawny tree. "It's ugly."

When the arborist came to survey the trees, he pointed at one
of the tallest. "We need to take this one down," he said. "Look up
at its limbs—no leaves. It's completely dead."

"What about that?" I asked, pointing at the twisted little tree.

"No reason to lose it," he said.

So it remained there, a runty thing, year after year.

But then one August, that tree surprised us. On a hot afternoon, I looked out to see my children sitting beneath it, eating
pears. I hurried outdoors and found that its branches held dozens
of pears, ripe for picking.

Throughout the summer and into the fall, we filled baskets with
the fruit.

It can take time for us to bloom and yield fruit.

Can you trust that something is alive within you?

Soul Shine

*Everybody is unique. Compare not yourself with anybody else lest
you spoil God's curriculum.*
—Rabbi Israel ben Eliezer

The eighty-something nun who can be found, most of the time, in a trailer on the grounds of an English monastery is a respected art critic as well as my all-time favorite TV star. Reportedly, Sister Wendy Beckett converses with only two people when she's home: the nun who brings her daily provisions and the prioress of the monastery. She speaks mostly to God and spends her days in prayer.

Over the past twenty years, through her numerous books and documentaries on art and faith, Sister Wendy has made profound—though admittedly occasional—forays into my life via her work.

Observing her humility—she describes herself as "shabby and cowardly"—I have found my shallow faith and self-absorption challenged. Listening to her whimsical and astute reflections on art, my swirling, elusive ideas about particular works have been captured and beautifully articulated.

And although both do, it's neither her winning personality nor her overbite that most charm me. It's that she makes the God to whom she's given her life more appealing to me every time I come into contact with her work—the God with whom she chats in that trailer who, likely bursting with pride over this stunning creation, has kindly given the rest of us the opportunity to feel her soul shine its light on us.

Whose faith makes God feel more appealing to you?

August 15

Trust Yourself

Trust yourself. You know more than you think you do.
—Benjamin Spock

As mothers, it's hard to pluck off all the tendrils of disapproving messages that coil up and wrap themselves around us. From the start, we hear that we're doing something wrong. Putting newborns down in the crib on their sides instead of their backs, for instance. And as soon as we get it right, the recommendation changes. Again.

Our kids somehow survive the sleep-position fiasco and enter school. We are dutiful about their homework but then learn that doing homework is ineffective, and there is a national epidemic of stressed-out children. We ease up, only to be told that our kids are coddled and won't be ready to "compete in the global economy."

And on it goes.

It's an enormous responsibility to be a mother. We long to do it well. We want our children to be healthy, smart, creative, and kind. Mostly, we want them to become excellent adults.

Maybe the reason Dr. Benjamin Spock's iconic book on caring for babies and children, *Babies and Child Care*, published in 1946, has sold more than fifty million copies has to do with its first line: "Trust yourself. You know more than you think you do."

How can you more fully trust your instincts as a mother?

August 16

Resilient Children

There is in every true woman's heart a spark of heavenly fire,
which lies dormant in the broad daylight of prosperity; but which
kindles up, and beams and blazes in the dark hour of adversity.

—Washington Irving

My four children all use mobile phones, and consequently my own cell is abuzz with requests for rides, money, or permission to stay out later or see this movie or that. Occasionally, they buzz with little affectionate hellos and whatnots. Thank God for younger children. Seriously.

One Saturday, in the flurry of a text storm, one of my sons let me know he'd lost in the final round of a high school competition. I responded with something like, "I'm sorry. You okay about it? You did great."

My phone continued chiming with messages from the other kids. Yes, no, maybe, no.

Later I saw that the son who had lost the contest had sent me a message with a word count that rivaled the Gettysburg Address, but with none of its diplomacy. His message seethed with anger. He didn't need my pity, he told me. Failure is part of life. My response to his loss had been the worst thing about it.

I responded, telling him that I didn't pity him, and that some conversations are better in person than via text. He sheepishly agreed.

Our misunderstanding reminded me how important it is to my children to know that I see them as resilient, that I trust them to cope with the inevitable disappointments they'll face.

Do you ever feel that you have to protect your kids from feeling upset?

August 17

Pressure to Perform

A prig is a fellow who is always making you a present of his opinions.

—George Eliot

My friend Jane and her husband were wrangled into throwing a "couples" baby shower for some friends of friends. Jane and Ari's apartment is larger and more easily accessible than others in their circle, and they are relaxed and welcoming hosts.

The expectant parents are ardent football fans, and their favorite team, Alabama's Crimson Tide, would be playing on the afternoon of the proposed event. "We'll get some pizza and beer," said Jane's husband, Ari, with a shrug. "And we'll put on the game."

But hours after they agreed to host, Jane found her email glutted with messages. One friend offered to contribute to the "decorating budget." Another suggested that Jane call a bakery that specializes in custom-made cupcakes and ask that they do the team's mascot, "Big Al." And on it went.

"Why does everything have to be so fancy and customized?" Jane said, telling me about it. "I thought this was just going to be about pizza and beer, and maybe a few onesies for the baby. Why can't we just relax and be together?"

"It's the dark underbelly of social media," I said, laughing. "You have to make it a show so everybody can show off those Big Al cupcakes."

⌒

Can you think of times when you feel you perform for others? How does that make you feel?

Texting, Texting, Texting

Do not despise your inner world.
—Martha Nussbaum, *Take My Advice*

I assumed that the hefty packet from our mobile phone company contained manuals in incomprehensible legalese about our new plan. But later my husband approached me, stunned, the torn envelope in his hand. The bulk of it was a record of phone numbers to which one of our children had sent texts the previous month. Several thousand messages.

When we confronted our child, it wasn't to complain about the cost; the plan offers unlimited texting. The messages hadn't been sent at odd hours or to suspicious numbers. It was the sheer *volume* of these messages that concerned us.

How could we enlighten a teenager in a text-addicted world about why this was out of balance?

We ended up talking about what it means to have an *inner* life, not one simply defined by articulating every passing thought or remaining in constant contact with one's friends. We talked about trusting that it is okay—even truly beneficial—to be alone. We talked about keeping some things unsaid, our thoughts still.

Today, how can you embrace silence and nurture your inner life?

August 19
A Good-Enough Life

Health is the greatest possession. Contentment is the greatest treasure. Confidence is the greatest friend. Non-being is the greatest joy.
—Lao-tzu

When we believe the myth that there is an ideal way to be a parent, our expectations—and stress levels—skyrocket. We compare ourselves to other moms. We obsess over what's imperfect in our lives: scuff marks on the wall, saggy post-nursing breasts, sullen teens, or whatever else dismays us. We believe the cruel lie that we're the only ones whose lives are so cracked, dirty, and beat up.

But honestly, we aren't.

Everyone has crumbs in the silverware drawer, dusty baseboards, and globs of toothpaste stuck to the bathroom sink. All of us second-guess ourselves sometimes, show up late, get cranky with our husbands, and screw up in countless other ways.

There's a pretty straightforward strategy for letting go of guilt about these things: tell another mom about them. Tell her you shouted at your toddler, nagged your husband, forgot to show up to chaperone the field trip—explain in great detail the indignity of getting wrinkles when you still use acne cream.

Trusting someone with our secret burdens, large or small, helps us gain perspective and let them go.

Do you have a trusted friend with whom you share your real experience of motherhood?

August 20
Everyone's Broken

The wound is the place where the Light enters you.
—Rumi

Rain was beating down, and lightning shattered the night sky into pieces. That summer night, every woman who hurried into the church was stooped over, protecting what she held—a purse, a bottle of wine, a plate of hors d'oeuvres—valiantly trying to keep it dry. As each woman entered, another relieved her of whatever she was carrying.

I was the evening's speaker that night for a mothers' group; my topic was bearing one another's burdens. The rough weather—and that we scurried to help each other in out of the rain—seemed a fitting backdrop.

And, it might have been the pleasure of lingering over a glass of wine, the cozy atmosphere, or simply that no one was eager to go back into the storm, but we stayed late that night, and women who usually just smiled and nodded across the church parking lot began to open up with one another.

One revealed that she and her husband were considering divorce. Another said her child was out of control. Others talked about the weight of caring for aging parents or worrying over finances.

Safely inside, sheltered from the storm, they shared the weight of burdens and offered real help to one another.

Is it hard for you to admit when you are broken? Is there a trusted friend or group who can help bear your burdens?

Let It Be (Good Enough)

The best is the enemy of the good.
—Voltaire

I was tempted to smack Owen for what he said, but the fact that he's eighty and has one of the kindest hearts I know stopped me.

The week had been packed. The kids and I had gone back-to-school shopping. They'd had softball, lacrosse, and soccer games. I'd washed armloads of sweaty jerseys and beach towels damp and sandy from the town pool.

A family friend, Owen has been widowed for many years and sometimes drops by. That Saturday, we chatted as I made macaroni and cheese for the kids. When my husband entered the room holding a piece of paper and a pencil, Owen asked him what he had.

"My task list," David said. "Hook up sprinkler, drop off dry cleaning, help kids change their sheets." He crossed one of the items off the list.

"I have a secret for you," Owen said. "Next time she gives you one of those, do everything badly, and as slowly as you can. She'll stop asking."

"Owen!" I shouted. But I was able to laugh because I have a secret, too. I've learned not to mind if the chores other people do aren't done as quickly or the same way I'd do them.

I'm just happy for the help.

‿

Is it hard for you to delegate and let go of certain jobs around the house? Remember that perfect is the enemy of good enough.

August 22

It Will Be All Right

All I have seen teaches me to trust the Creator for all
I have not seen.
—Ralph Waldo Emerson

It was one of those hot days that fling themselves against you from the second you go outdoors. So hot, your eyes sting.

There were about thirty of us, including a dozen kids, crammed in the photographer's attic studio. The children were arranged on a raised platform while a lone box fan feebly attempted to keep air moving. Some of the children stepped off the platform and blew into the fan, producing high insectlike sounds.

We parents grinned ourselves silly and used gummy bears to bribe our kids to smile.

All the children posing for this photograph, including my daughter, had been adopted internationally; the photo would accompany a magazine story on the topic.

I thought about the anxiety I'd had, just a few years before when I was waiting for Mia to come home, wondering whether I'd ever feel like her mother. Later I'd fret about whether she would ever trust me to trim her nails or rinse her off in the tub.

But there we were, together, four years after her homecoming, exchanging private, conspiratorial smiles on a sizzling day. It had all worked out.

Can you imagine a positive outcome for something you are worrying about today?

August 23
Time Flies

How did it get so late so soon?
—Dr. Seuss

Sometime near the beginning of my eldest child's junior year of high school, I had the unnerving realization that his time at home with us was truly almost over. It was like an alarm going off in the middle of the night, the sound jarring and unpleasant.

Of course, I knew all along that he'd grow up. And over the years, I'd felt tidal waves of gratitude for the ways he was developing. I've watched families battle mightily for their children's health, and I've attended funerals for children I've known. Having a healthy, growing child is a precious gift.

But all of a sudden, his departure felt imminent. So much would change. I'd have a new de facto eldest child. Instead of counting to four every time we were out together or when I laid out their breakfast plates, I'd be counting to three. I knew I'd miss him so much.

To prepare us both, I decided to give him more space to take risks and be independent. I said yes more often, even when it made me squirm: "Yes you can go to that concert in the city," "Yes you can stay at home overnight on your own." Yes, yes, yes.

It was a good start, for both of us.

How long is it until your children are grown? Might it be time to start giving them more room to roam?

August 24
What's Left?

Just trust yourself, then you will know how to live.
—Goethe

Following that first shock—realizing that my son would soon be grown—came a pestering question: had his father and I taught him everything he needed to know to go off into the big, bad world?

I remembered those helpful milestone charts I consulted when my children were little. They stated things like:

Most fourteen-month-olds can feed themselves with their fingers.

Some can point to their mouths when asked to do so.

A few can even use spoons and forks.

What would the corresponding chart for seventeen-year-olds look like? Maybe:

Most can order a pizza.

Some can scramble eggs.

A few can even perfectly render the Milanese minestrone from *The Silver Spoon* cookbook.

My eldest had never changed a tire, done a load of laundry from beginning to end, or cooked a meal other than frozen pizza or boxed macaroni and cheese. What else had we forgotten to teach him?

But we're not frozen in time at age eighteen. He will learn so much on his own—while becoming a beautiful work-in-progress.

Do you ever feel pressured to prepare your kids for each and every eventuality that they could encounter in their adult lives? What are you most grateful that you knew at eighteen?

Managing a Guesthouse

*All children must look after their own upbringing. Parents can
only give good advice or put them on the right paths, but the final
forming of a person's character lies in their own hands.*
—Anne Frank, *Diary of a Young Girl*

While she was raising her daughters, Liza said she had a "metaphor
running through her head" that she was just someone managing a
guesthouse and her girls were "travelers from a distant land."

"They arrived not speaking the language or knowing the local
customs," she said. "It was my job to house and feed and care for
them and to teach them how to get on in the world, but I knew
they would eventually move on."

She said that seeing herself in that role helped her remember
that she didn't own her daughters. She said she could see them for
who they really were instead of the people she wanted or thought
them to be.

Now they're adults, and I love seeing her with them and the
deep friendship they share. One daughter is married, the other finishing college. And they choose, at seemingly every opportunity, to
return to that "guesthouse" and be home again with Liza.

That metaphor was helpful to me as I saw my first guest pack-
ing up and getting ready to move on.

*What do you think of the "just running a guesthouse" metaphor for
parenting? Would it make you feel distant from your kids, or do you
think it would give them more room to be their distinctive selves?*

Trust in Silence

The ego gets what it wants with words. The soul finds what it needs in silence.

—Richard Rohr

She was laughing about getting the ticket, but it was obvious Kim didn't find it funny that she'd been pulled over for talking on her cell phone while driving. "So, now what I need is to spend even more money and get a wireless headset," she said. "I can't be without my phone when I'm in the car."

A few friends and I were chatting at a coffee shop when she made this announcement.

"But what about just leaving it off when you're driving," Tracey suggested. "You know, let everything be quiet?"

"Oh, I can't!" Kim said. "I need my phone."

As if on cue, a phone started ringing nearby, and the woman at the next table took the call. I looked around the room. At every table, customers tapped at their phones, laptops, or other devices. Kim got progressively irritated as the stranger next to us described what happened on a television show the night before.

"It's getting too loud in here," Kim said. "Why do people need to be on the phone all the time?"

"Yeah, that was our point," Tracey said. "About you. And your car."

Kim waved the air as if she was shooing away Tracey's words. "That's different. Then I'm all by myself. There's nothing else to do."

Do you have opportunities for silence every day? Do you take them?

August 27

God with Us

Soon as the ev'ning shades prevail,
The Moon takes up the wondrous tale,
And nightly to the list'ning Earth
Repeats the story of her birth.

—Joseph Addison

I used those lines, an excerpt from Joseph Addison's poem "Ode," on my daughter's combination birth-and-adoption announcement. During the adoption process, it struck me that no one had yet officially celebrated Mia's birth. It broke my heart. Crafting her announcement became my obsession in the months before she came home.

Thoughts raced in my mind as I worked on it. Had I heard right that God had told us to adopt? Would the Guatemala program close before her adoption was finalized? Would four children be too many for me to handle?

I scoured books of poetry for just the right lines. Finally, I came across "Ode." I was sure they were just the ones to honor her early history—her birth was of great significance—and to celebrate her adoption.

And then, something amazing happened. At the end of the church service on the first Sunday Mia was home with us, the organist began playing the closing hymn. Opening to the page, I saw that the hymn's words were Addison's "Ode."

No one had seen the announcement yet. Besides us, only God knew the details.

Singing that morning, my little daughter in my arms, I trusted that yes, God had been, and would continue to be, with us.

Have you ever had a clear sense of God's love and presence?

God in Silence

We need to find God, and he cannot be found in noise and restlessness. God is the friend of silence. See how nature—trees, flowers, grass—grows in silence; see the stars, the moon and the sun, how they move in silence. . . . We need silence to be able to touch souls.

—Mother Teresa

We're conditioned to find silences uncomfortable and to fill them up. We distract ourselves to avoid them. We put on the radio, talk on the phone, watch TV. God doesn't shout over a phone chiming or blaring music, nor does God interrupt us when we are filling up the empty spaces with chatter. We can hear God's voice only in the silences.

A monk once told me that his community maintains silence most of the time, a fact that wasn't surprising. But what he said next stirred me and burned itself into my memory. "It's not that there's nothing to say," he said. "It's that there is so much to hear."

He said that they *listen* to God.

I have a colleague who is a very good listener. We live in different parts of the country, and we usually communicate by phone. One of the things I like best about him is his comfort with silence.

When we are brainstorming or trying to solve a problem, he'll often say, "Hmm . . . let's think about this," and then fall quiet. A full minute or two might pass. Maybe even three. And sure enough, when he speaks again, he has a new idea or solution.

It was waiting there in the silence.

Think over what a typical day sounds like for you. How often are you in a quiet place?

God Nods

Riches take wings, comforts vanish, hope withers away, but love stays with us. Love is God.
—Lew Wallace

My friend Cathi and I call them "God nods," those serendipitous moments that feel like answered prayer, leaving us trusting that God is with us after all.

And sometimes—probably much more than we know—we get to play a part in other people's God nods, too.

A few years ago, my daughter Isabel and I were out buying school supplies. As we walked the aisles of a dollar store, an image popped into my mind of a bin full of treats and activities that my friend Mary's kids could dip into on busy days. She had welcomed her fourth and fifth daughters by adoption only months before.

Once home, I put all the pieces together—stickers, lollipops, chunky crayons—and wrote Mary a note. I named a few of the things I'd seen her do—loving acts for each of the girls—and reminded her that this stressful time was temporary. Now isn't forever.

When she got home that day (from the pediatrician or ballet lessons or the grocery store), Mary called me, crying. She'd prayed earlier, asking God for encouragement and the assurance that life wouldn't always be this full.

And waiting on her porch, a God nod.

Do you remember ever getting a "God nod?"

Feller of Trees

Prayer is not asking. It is a longing of the soul. It is daily admission of one's weakness. . . . It is better in prayer to have a heart without words than words without a heart.

—Mahatma Gandhi

Once a month, the six of us gathered at church. One of us was seeking discernment about entering ordained ministry; the other five interviewed and prayed for him. One evening, one of our committee members said something very surprising. "I don't want to hear about your competence," he said to the candidate. "What I want to know is whether you know your own incompetence."

It's true that God has this peculiar habit of employing almost absurdly incompetent people. I'd recently taught my Sunday-school class about Gideon, a man whose name means "destroyer" and "feller of trees." But when we meet him in the book of Judges, Gideon is telling an angel that he feels abandoned, his clan is weak, and he's the puniest runt of them all. "Don't choose me to do mighty things," he begs. "I'm not your guy" (see Judges 6:13–15).

He keeps asking for a sign that the vision is real and not some "undigested bit of beef, blot of mustard, or underdone potato." (Okay, that's from *A Christmas Carol*, but same idea.)

God keeps proving that it's really God. Finally, with a little pack of men and only lamps and trumpets in his arsenal, pint-sized Gideon obeys God and defeats a huge army.

Do you feel as if God has asked you to do something that is too big for you? How well do you know your incompetence?

New Freedom

Life is real! Life is earnest!
And the grave is not its goal;
Dust thou art, to dust returnest,
Was not spoken of the soul.
—Henry Wadsworth Longfellow

We started the month with St. Ignatius's counsel to stop being so preoccupied with our preferences, opinions, and attachments.

We were then reminded that we are souls with bodies, and not the other way around, in hopes that we can begin to unplug from our lopsided and unhappy fixations on our appearances, parenting styles, or even the way we throw baby showers.

Having said all of this, remember that detaching and trusting are practices. Detachment isn't a onetime transaction: Voilà! Now we're nonattached! We'll never really get these things down perfectly.

Even when I have a peaceful moment and realize that I am enough, when I feel the warmth of God's love, and on those rare occasions I experience an almost blissful kind of amnesia about all the trivial things that worry me or ruin my day, I can suddenly find myself in a rain shower of insecurity, resentment, or fear.

But I believe that the more we practice these things, the more occasional and less violent our forays into anxiety will be.

Is there some worry in your life that you have been able to let go of this month?

Rest

*Consider the lilies, how they grow: they
neither toil nor spin; yet I tell you, even
Solomon in all his glory was not clothed like
one of these.*

—Luke 12:27 NRSV

September

Practice Simplicity

Step Away from What Entangles You

September 1

Why Simplify?

Life is really simple, but we insist on making it complicated.
—Confucius

Some of us welcome the invitation to live simply. Our minds flash on an imagined interior of a modest home. Tulips lounge in a clear vase. Countertops are bare. Open any drawer or closet and bask in the glory of its sparseness and order. Perhaps there are two young children kneeling on the floor, peacefully building block towers. It's a blissful vision. If only we could replicate it, our lives would be uncomplicated, more fulfilled.

But that's not everyone's idea of nirvana. Some of us are repelled by the kind of order that's glorified in home-design magazines. We find it not serene, but sanitized; not beautiful, but boring. We're messy deskers! We've read the research: tidy rooms encourage conformist thinking, whereas disorderly ones inspire originality. We want to show some personality in our surroundings, for crying out loud.

As we enter the last part of the year and focus on rest, we are going to look at what kinds of clutter—people, things, and behaviors—prevent us from what is most life-giving and matters most to us.

When you think of clutter, what image first comes into your mind?

What is Simplicity?

sim·plic·i·ty
freedom from complexity, absence of pretentiousness, freedom from
deceit or guile.
—Merriam-Webster Dictionary

Simplicity looks different on all of us, but it feels very much the same. When our lives are uncluttered, we feel free; when they are disordered, we feel that some part of our lives—our responsibilities, our possessions, our relationships—is holding us captive.

So, simplicity has got little to do with how messy your desk is; it's about freedom from the people and things that constrain us. Simplifying our lives, then, is the process of evaluating what we've got and how we spend our time, and then ridding ourselves of what isn't working.

Thoreau put it another way; he said simplicity is about keeping only "the necessary and the real."

This month, we'll look at practices that might help us distinguish what's of value to us and what can be let go. This can mean decluttering our homes and reducing our commitments, but it affects our friendships as well.

By being more intentional about our relationships, we will more likely dole out the best parts of ourselves to people we love.

Do you want to simplify an area of your life?

Just Say No

A "No" uttered from the deepest conviction is better than a "Yes"
merely uttered to please, or worse, to avoid trouble.
—Mahatma Gandhi

I think they could smell it on me, the way dogs smell fear: I wanted to be nice. When my oldest started kindergarten and I was asked to manage a project or plan a class party or work with kids who were struggling, if I possibly could do it, I did. It was win-win. I liked getting to know the other parents and being familiar with the school's culture.

I also liked being liked.

The problem was, by the time my youngest was in fourth grade, my kids attended three different schools, and life had become much busier. But I hadn't yet learned to say no. Of course I'd always declined tasks that I truly was incapable of doing—anything involving numbers, for instance. My friend Becky noticed this as I narrated baking math one day: "Let's see. I'm doubling the recipe and it's three-quarters of a cup of flour times two," I said, mumbling aloud. "So that's like if I had seventy-five cents and doubled it. A dollar fifty, so . . . a cup and a half!"

But, if a job was a good fit for me—class newspaper, anyone?—I was in. Maybe it was a math issue, but despite my "exponentially" busier life, I kept on with the "yesses."

Until, that is, I learned to say no.

Are you comfortable saying no when asked for favors or to volunteer?

Birthday Bags

We have all a better guide in ourselves, if we would attend to it,
than any other person can be.
—Jane Austen, *Mansfield Park*

My son's third-grade teacher had a brilliant idea for a class service project. She'd learned from the local food pantry that clients often asked for cake mixes and frosting for their children's birthday celebrations, but these things aren't typically donated.

"What if," she asked me one day, "we collect cake mixes, icing, candles, and small gifts and make birthday bags?" I'd come in some afternoon—it would be an hour or two, tops—and help the kids assemble them. Then I'd drive the bags over to the food pantry. I loved it!

What I'd learn, however, was that the job wasn't quite so simple. Although parents eagerly contributed and we'd end up making more than a hundred bags, uneven numbers of cake mixes and tubs of frosting were donated. A project that promised to require an hour or two filled up the spare moments of an entire week. And given my initial enthusiasm, the teacher asked me to manage it even after my kids were out of third grade.

That is, until I said no. I loved the project and hated to relinquish my "good mom" reputation, but it was time.

Do you have any recurring volunteer jobs that you could surrender?

Strategies for Saying No

Besides the noble art of getting things done, there is the noble art of leaving things undone. The wisdom of life consists in the elimination of non-essentials.
—Lin Yutang

Maybe, like me, you think of yourself as helpful, and you don't like conflict. The prospect of hurting another person's feelings makes you cringe. You want to make a positive impact on the places your children spend their time. You enjoy being liked, and you don't want to be seen as a slacker.

For those reasons, and maybe twenty more, you find it exceedingly hard to say no. I've gotten better, by the way. You might even say I've become a champion at it. I try to remember six simple rules when declining a request:

1. Be respectful of other people's time.
2. Don't let multiple voicemail or email messages go unanswered—say no as soon as you can.
3. Say no politely but resolutely.
4. Say you're honored to be considered, but it's not a good fit for you or that you have decided not to take on anything more at the moment.
5. Don't say you'll "think about it."
6. Thank the other person for all he or she is doing.

Chances are, the person who asked is a volunteer, too. You both care about the effort, so tell him or her that you are grateful.

What are your strategies for saying no?

Not My Dog

A child of five would understand this. Send someone to fetch a child of five.
—Groucho Marx

I first learned the expression "not my dog" from my friend Keiko and her husband, Rob. They have three sons and run a flourishing small business for which they often must travel. And yet one of their distinctive traits is their ability to unplug from work and enjoy the simple pleasures of life: going on a hike, preparing a meal, playing a game with the kids.

One of the ways I see them practicing simplicity is their refusal to get engaged with issues that don't affect them. If neighbors or extended family members or people in their circle of friends get their wires crossed and begin clashing, they shrug and say, "Not my dog."

I've also heard that idea expressed as, "Not my circus, not my monkey."

Rob and Keiko refuse to misplace their energies on problems that don't concern them. Consequently, they don't gossip or obsess over the details of other people's lives.

This leaves them free to be openhanded with their children, each other, and those whom they serve in their communities.

When do you feel emotionally dragged into someone else's trivial business?

Opt Out

Truth is ever to be found in simplicity, and not in the multiplicity
and confusion of things.
—Isaac Newton

The magazine sales reps are geniuses at persuading sixth graders that they'll be able to sell a hundred subscriptions and win an iPod or big-screen TV. The day my son came home from school holding the sales flyer, his eyes were ablaze with desire.

"How many will you order?" he asked. "It's a fund-raiser, for new computers at my school."

"Honey, I don't need any magazines," I said. "Sorry."

He wasn't deterred, working feverishly to sell subscriptions to his grandparents and our family friends. In the end, he sold about fifteen subscriptions. A few months later, he received his prize: a plastic wristband. He promptly threw it out.

When my kids come home with fund-raiser order forms, I opt out. If I believe in the effort, I'll write a check directly to it, evading hours of hassle as well as throwaway plastic incentives and other clutter we don't need.

Next time a fund-raising drive is thrust upon you, consider
contributing in another way. What are other busy-making,
clutter-generating activities from which you could opt out?

Noisy Clutter

Manifest plainness,
Embrace simplicity,
Reduce selfishness,
Have few desires.

—Lao-tzu

I derive great pleasure from organizing closets. I like creating new systems to make my home run more smoothly. And I wouldn't say that my label maker is my very best friend, but we are very close.

But honestly, keeping my house well organized is hardly my first priority, and real life doesn't afford me the time to indulge in unnecessary neatness. Not only that, but I live with five other people for whom neatness is even less urgent. Umbrellas are flung, half closed and still dripping, into the coat closet. Clean laundry is crammed into dresser drawers. Each child has secret black holes of clutter in his or her room; every few years I ask that the black holes be tackled.

However, in general, I'm fairly successful at keeping organized. I actually need to be because I work from home, and for me, clutter and mess make noise. Unsigned permission slips, dirty gym clothes, and piles of mail or newspapers buzz and beg for my attention.

Only after I've quieted them, or at least turned down the volume, I can get to my writing work.

How do clutter and messes affect you? Other people in your family?

September 9

Steadfast Saints

*Stop collecting treasures for your own benefit on earth, where moth
and rust eat them and where thieves break in and steal them.
Instead, collect treasures for yourselves in heaven, where moth and
rust don't eat them and where thieves don't break in and steal
them. Where your treasure is, there your heart will be also.*
—Matthew 6:19–21 CEB

The stories of Wulfthryth and Wulfhilda, two English nuns who lived in the late tenth and early eleventh centuries, seem to have merged somewhat since their deaths. It's understandable, given their similar but wildly unique names and the fact that both were unwilling objects of a king's affections.

Many accounts say that St. Wulfhilda was raised in an abbey and joined its religious order. But when she was an adolescent, King Edgar the Peaceful fell in love with her and asked her to marry him.

After she declined his offer, a relative tricked her into seeing the king. It was then that the king raped her. She later gave birth to a daughter, whom she raised with her sisters in the abbey. (Other stories indicate that King Edgar's son Edward raped Wulfthryth, and that it was she who conceived a child.)

In some legends, Wulfhilda eluded Edgar, pulling away from his grasp, leaving the sleeve of her dress in his hand, and escaping through the castle drains.

Regardless of the exact details, these two women of God knew what mattered to them most and refused to be entangled in lives—even lives of privilege in a time of scarcity—that would keep them from following their true callings.

⌒

*From what people or things could you separate yourself to live with
more spiritual clarity?*

September 10
Plastic-Covered Couches

When you consider things like the stars, our affairs don't seem to matter very much, do they?
—Virginia Woolf

There are reasons, of course, why one person prefers to live in an immaculate house while another is comfortable living in relative chaos. We're a complicated mix of predispositions and life histories.

A friend in college grew up in a home where the furniture was encased in thick, durable plastic sheets. Plastic runners served as mandatory footpaths throughout the house. His mother, he used to say with a laugh, had control issues. Perhaps that was an understatement.

While I've yet to cover anything in plastic, I've gotten more neat and organized with the addition of each child, and I've seen the same trend in some other mothers I know. When my label maker and I go to work on a file cabinet or closet shelf, I feel that we are conspiring to do me a huge favor, the fruits of which I'll reap later.

Perhaps it will come in handy when, out of the blue, I have four kids circling me like wild dogs needing lost cleats or a pack of index cards. The more prepared I am, the easier it is to address their requests.

In what ways do you organize your home similarly to the one in which you grew up? What's different?

Touch It Once

The art of art, the glory of expression and the sunshine of the light of letters is simplicity.
—Walt Whitman

An organization expert spoke to my mothers' group years ago about everything from typing up grocery lists that included the aisle numbers in which each item could be found (um, no thank you) to scheduling haircut appointments for the entire year in one fell swoop (but what if I want to grow it out?).

Much of what she said didn't appeal to me; I wanted more room to improvise. But one thing she said has stayed with me more than fifteen years later: "Touch it once," she said.

Ooh. It was as if a Zen master had spoken. The words echoed in my mind. *Touch it once.* And to this day, as much as possible, that is what I do. I hang up my jacket as soon as I take it off. I bring in the mail and immediately sort it: children's mail on beds, catalogs into recycling, husband's mail into a cabinet, and mine on the desk.

I'm mindful that the alternatives to "touching it once" are touching something many more times, losing it, or forgetting about it altogether.

What's your best—and simplest—organizational strategy?

September 12
Dreaming as Planning

*Without leaps of imagination, or dreaming, we lose the excitement
of possibilities. Dreaming, after all, is a form of planning.*
—Gloria Steinem

When people learn I'm a writer, they often respond in one of two ways: "I want to write! I've got a book I've been meaning to write for years," or "I love to read, but I can't ever find the time."

These remarks have something in common: there's a disconnect between what people say is important to them and how they actually spend their time. I've heard life coaches say that to reach our goals, we have to do only two simple things: pinpoint what's most important to us and eliminate everything else. Cogent advice, but of course easier said than done.

I recently received a very different response, though, after telling someone my occupation. I was getting my nails done (self-care!) and the technician—a young woman who recently emigrated from the Ukraine—asked me what I do.

"I'm a writer," I said.

She asked me if I'd ever published a book, and I said I had. She put down the polish, sat back in her chair, and smiled at me. "I've never worked with a writer before," she said. "This is, in fact, an honor."

Isn't that lovely?

*Do you want to read—or write, or paint, or ski, or dance—more
often than you do? What can you cull from your life to free
up the time?*

Collage of Experiences

One of the most beautiful qualities of true friendship is to understand and to be understood.

—Seneca

When an experience is brand new—first kiss, first ride on an airplane, first bite of sushi—our brains store it with great detail. Looking back, we can linger on those memories, see, smell, and taste them again. However, the next time we dip a piece of sashimi into the soy sauce, we're building on an earlier memory and the brain takes less careful notes.

Some people theorize that this is why time seems to go faster the older we get. When we look back on memories of our adult lives, they're a blur, a collage of experiences, in contrast to the slow-motion, distinct memories of firsts.

There's at least one benefit to this phenomenon: when time seems to be going faster, it's easier to pick up where we left off with friends. If you find yourself saying, "I miss my friend, but I never see her," consider scheduling regular times to do so, even if they're a year apart.

Close the gap between what you say you want and what you really do.

Is there a friend whose company you miss? Can you get her on your calendar?

Spirit-Led Restraint

'Tis the gift to be simple, 'tis the gift to be free
'tis the gift to come down where we ought to be,

. . . .

When true simplicity is gained,
To bow and to bend we shan't be ashamed,
To turn, turn, will be our delight,
till by turning, turning we come round right.

—Joseph Brackett

The Shaker hymn, above, introduces the Quaker notion of the testimony of simplicity.

Quakers don't seem to savor being mistaken as Shakers. Sure, their names rhyme, and yes, they share a common devotion to simple living. But since the Shakers broke off in the 1700s, theological differences between the two groups have been glaring. Among other things, Shakers believed that Ann Lee, their founder, was the female manifestation of Christ.

At last count, there were only three Shakers living (all in the United States), while there are about 90,000 Quakers in the States, and 350,000 globally. The Shakers, you see, require celibacy and are sustained only by converts, and they've not had any for decades.

Now, back to the Quakers' testimony of simplicity. Also called "spirit-led restraint," the testimony of simplicity describes their choice to minimize a focus on self by limiting consumption and living in service to others. They are frugal with financial and natural resources, encourage the use of public libraries and museums, celebrate acts of generosity in their communities, and designate as a top priority assisting those in need.

In what ways could living more simply be informed by
your spirituality?

Useful and Beautiful

Have nothing in your houses that you do not know to be useful, or believe to be beautiful.
—William Morris

Hmm . . . William Morris's advice is lovely and so well put, but it feels slightly out of our reach today—especially when our homes are populated by young children who seem to attract cheap, plastic junk the way porch lights attract flying bugs at night.

But still, he makes a good point. So if reducing clutter is on your to-do list this month, use his advice as a sort of litmus test. If every time you pull out that marred plastic spatula, you toss it back in the drawer and look for the "good" one, consider tossing it. If seeing the vase that your college roommate gave you brings to mind that broken friendship, give it away, regardless of how beautiful it is.

Inanimate objects can affect our feelings, funny as it sounds. Case in point: I once traded a love seat for a mixing bowl. My friend Patrice and I were talking about negative associations we had with certain things in our homes. I mentioned the love seat; it reminded me of a sad time. She described a yellow mixing bowl that had been a gift from someone who later betrayed her.

"Trade?" I said. We delightedly made the exchange. I still use the bowl, and she still flops down on the love seat; we find these things useful and beautiful.

They just needed new homes.

Are there any items around your house that make your heart sink? Consider donating them or doing a swap with a friend.

Rice-Paper Walls

Simplicity is the ultimate sophistication.
—William Gaddis

BK (before kids), I once stayed for the day in a Japanese hotel outside of Kyoto. I had been traveling in Asia for work, had a long layover, and my company suggested I escape the airport and rest before the long journey home.

At the hotel, I was guided to the door of my room and, once inside, found just enough space for a tiny bathroom, a twin bed, and a side table and lamp. There were no framed pictures on the walls, no TV, no room service menu, no notes from housekeeping. Just a varnished wood floor, white walls, white paper in the partition between the bed and bath. Clean, spare, silent.

I lay down in the bed, feeling as if I were in a dollhouse or a dream. And when I turned out the lamp, I was in complete darkness. Maybe it was the unfamiliarity of the place or just exhaustion, but I remember it as one of the most restorative periods of sleep I've ever had.

I've wondered whether it was the absence of noise, both aural and visual, that made my body settle into the bed the way it did. I don't know.

What is your favorite environment for sleeping? Do you remember ever having a spectacular sleep?

Mind Clutter

Don't compromise yourself. You are all you've got.
—Janis Joplin

Although my children watched *Chitty Chitty Bang Bang, Mary Poppins, The Sound of Music,* and other kids movies so often that they could recite them and perform every twist and turn in the choreography, they spent their early childhoods without TV.

We had DVDs, but unless we were at a hotel or at their grandparents' houses, they never saw "regular" television. I wanted to keep their minds free of the mental and spiritual clutter that advertisements introduce. Too often ads promote not only a desire for a particular item but also a false message that more stuff in general makes us happier. It is a lie I wanted to keep them from hearing for as long as possible.

Now that they're adolescents, they have iPods and YouTube, and they can stream clutter right into their own minds.

My wise friend Lisa gets a little peeved when I obsess over things. Years ago, I wondered aloud to her about whether I'd done enough to teach my kids values. (Cue her eye roll.) "You don't have to say anything," she said. "They're watching. And they'll probably follow suit. I mean unless you, like, beat them or they hate you or something."

So, there's that.

When do you feel mentally cluttered? How do you tidy up?

September 18

Heap of Thoughts

We write to taste life twice, in the moment and in retrospect.
—Anaïs Nin

When the kids and I purge their bedrooms, I set out four boxes in the upstairs hall. Above each is a sticky note: "Donate," "Fix/Clean," "Toss," "Ask Mom." We empty the contents of their desks, dressers, or closets onto the floor. They then sort the mound into the boxes, returning whatever's still "useful and beautiful" to its place, and I usually work through the "Fix/Clean" and "Ask Mom" boxes in a day or two.

Straightforward, right?

But what about the mental clutter that we stuff into drawers and that trips us up in the middle of the night? Consider pulling out your worries, wishes, and regrets, and dumping them down on paper, making a big heap on the page. Then label four separate sheets "Donate," "Fix/Clean," "Toss," and "Ask Mom."

Organize the heap of thoughts, one by one, onto the appropriate page:

Donate: duties at home or work you're ready to delegate

Fix/Clean: relationships and projects that need attention or
repair

Toss: regrets, resentments, and things to let go

Ask Mom (or God, a therapist, or friend): things with which
you need help

Could you pull out all the things that clutter your mind and put them on paper? Carve out time for those that need repair or for which you need advice.

Relational Clutter

The soul is placed in the body like a rough diamond; and must be
polished, or the lustre of it will never appear.
—Daniel Defoe, *The Education of Women*

Some people slip like vampires into your life; you didn't see them coming. They call and, inexplicably, you feel awash in dread. After time together, you need to recover. You feel as if the life's been sucked out of you.

Others are in a moment of life when what they need is very different from what you are able to give. Perhaps you are emotionally strained—caring for young children or aging parents, or both—and those friends want even more, blind to how hollowed out you already feel.

Still others are running from something inside of themselves. When you're together, you never get past surface talk. They seek distraction, and you are aware that it doesn't make a difference to them who's before them.

These are not people with whom we need to cultivate close relationships. Nurture friendships with people who see you and who make your soul soar.

~

Today, scroll through your contact list and identify relational clutter.
While you're at it, send one or two texts expressing love and gratitude
to friends with whom you have happy, healthy, reciprocal
relationships: ups and downs, give-and-take.

Former Friends

Well, half the people in this room are mad at me, and the other half only like me because they think I pushed somebody in front of a bus . . .
—Tina Fey, *Mean Girls*

Several years ago, I went through a rough patch with some women in my wider circle of friends. It felt as though, overnight, they ducked away when they saw me coming.

In some cases, the friendship had died a natural and unremarkable death. Schedules changed or our own children's attachments faded, leaving us mothers with little in common and out of touch. Others felt more sinister. Out shopping one afternoon, I saw two women whom I considered friends standing nearby. I called hello, but they just exchanged dark, knowing looks and walked out of the store.

"You know the mean girls from junior high?" the woman from behind the register asked as I smeared away tears. "I hate to tell you, but they're still with us."

I've come to see my role in these misadventures. I had spread myself too thin relationally. I didn't make the effort to communicate how adjusting to working full-time after my youngest started first grade had turned me upside down.

Unconsciously, although I clung to my most intimate friendships, I just sort of let the others drift off to sea. Maybe it had to be that way.

When have you had mishaps with your friendships? Did you feel that your life was more, or less, complicated afterward?

What Is Sabbath?

Sab·bath
a day of religious observance and abstinence from work, kept by
Jews from Friday evening to Saturday evening, and by most
Christians on Sunday
—Merriam-Webster Dictionary

I've got to say, the dictionary definition of *Sabbath* is a full-out lie.

I can't speak for my Jewish friends, but to say that "most Christians" observe Sabbath—on Sundays or otherwise—just isn't true. My family does the "religious observance" part on Sunday mornings, but abstain from work? Not so much, unless driving one's son to lacrosse practice, getting groceries, and doing the laundry are not Sabbath breakers.

> "Remember the Sabbath day, to keep it holy. Six days you shall labor, and do all your work, but the seventh day is a Sabbath to the Lord your God. On it you shall not do any work, you, or your son, or your daughter, your male servant, or your female servant, or your livestock, or the sojourner who is within your gates."
>
> —Exodus 20:8–11 ESV

Oops. At least we don't keep livestock, so we've got that part covered.

As we do in so many cases, all of us interpret this bit of Scripture in our own ways. Is it an optional, but recommended, simple living exercise? A holy stress reducer? (Holy stress reducer, Batman!) A sacrifice to God in thanks for blessings received?

What does "keeping the Sabbath" mean to you?

What's your understanding and experience of keeping the Sabbath?

Defining Sabbath

You've got to quit, one day a week, and just watch what God is doing when you're not doing anything.
—Eugene H. Peterson

Regarding the Sabbath, the catechism gives a more nuanced reading of the commandment. It says that we should "refrain from engaging in work or activities that hinder the worship owed to God." So if chores come after worship, it sounds like we're good. Doing "works of mercy" and relaxing the mind and body are also acceptable. (What a relief.)

For a long while, when friends much more pious than me bemoaned the fact that they weren't "keeping the Sabbath holy," I felt a combination of indifference and guilt. Indifference because Sundays are often catch-up days for me, and I like them that way. The guilt stemmed from, well, that commandment thing.

Don't worry—this story doesn't end with me working feverishly until midnight on Saturdays and then smiling beatifically from my rocking chair on Sunday afternoons. I continue to wrangle with how to keep the Sabbath.

And I do think carving out time for relaxation on Sundays is an excellent way not only to unclutter our minds but also to connect with our families.

And I imagine that both please God.

What does your Sunday look like?

September 23
Family Time

You don't choose your family. They are God's gift to you, as you are to them.

—Desmond Tutu

When my kids were younger, for better and worse, every night was family night. If one child had a baseball or soccer game, we'd all be there cheering him on. If there was a play or movie one of us wanted to attend, we'd all go. Our four kids are close in age; only five years separate the oldest and youngest. So activities were often one-size-fits-all.

But, of course, things change. It started with Friday night football. Starting in middle school, my kids all seem to be irresistibly drawn to the high-school games. I understand the appeal; they see friends; feast on popcorn and hot chocolate; and, from a safe enough distance, observe the intricacies of a culture into which they'll soon find themselves.

It's not, obviously, so much about the football. Saturday nights began filling up, too. There were school plays and birthday parties, and my boys began to date.

A couple of years ago, I decided that we'd need to set Sunday night apart as a regular family night so that, at least weekly, we all could connect and relax together. I now consider it part of what "keeping the Sabbath" means in our home.

⌒

Is it possible to reserve a block of time every week for you and your children to spend focused time together?

Welcome the Sabbath

*Arranging a bowl of flowers in the morning can give a sense of
quiet in a crowded day—like writing a poem, or saying a prayer.*
—Anne Morrow Lindbergh

Sabbath literally means "to cease," or stop.

My husband and I won't ever really be "done" as parents to our
children. Our careers don't offer much closure either. As a writer,
my work could always be edited more closely, polished more, carefully finessed. It's hard to know when something I'm writing is,
actually, "done." David often has reports to write and calls he must
take at home. There are fixes and patches and new releases in his
industry; software is never, really, "done."

When I sullenly considered the Sabbath as yet another admoni-
tion I didn't quite understand, it seemed dreary. But now? It feels
welcoming. And I am accepting the invitation to rest by keeping
my computer powered down on Sundays. I can consider things
"done" for the day.

Staying unplugged brings me perspective. The sky will not fall,
and the Internet will not come to a screeching halt if I don't check
my email or go online. Whatever it is, it will wait for tomorrow.

Today I am invited to be done, and to rest.

Does it feel inviting to you to take a digital Sabbath?

Simple Pleasures

When one door of happiness closes, another opens; but often we look so long at the closed door that we do not see the one which has been opened for us.
—Helen Keller

Sometimes simplicity is a choice, and sometimes it's thrust upon us.

The Great Recession of 2008 caused more financial insecurity than any other economic downturn since the Great Depression. Almost nine million people lost their jobs. Many drained their savings. Nearly everyone felt bruised.

But after the dust settled, we began to discern a few, small silver linings. Perhaps the brightest was that, as a culture, we were forced to question our consumeristic values and ask ourselves what really makes life "good."

Economist Juliet Schor decries the pitfalls of living in a society marked by excess consumption. She says that such a culture is unsustainable ecologically (deforestation, water depletion), socially (social exclusion, lack of community), and financially (household debt).

Might it also be spiritually unsustainable?

When we live more simply and get off what Schor calls the "work-spend cycle," we find ourselves less attached to what we look like, less interested in how our possessions (cars, houses, clothing) compare to those of others, and more attuned to the needs of others.

In short, we'll draw closer to God.

Are there ways you can distance yourself from cultural messages that insist that what you buy defines you?

Small Tasks

The simplification of life is one of the steps to inner peace. A persistent simplification will create an inner and outer well-being that places harmony in one's life.
—Peace Pilgrim

For the next few days, we'll focus on completing small tasks, none of which will take you more than about ten minutes to accomplish. Completing them, however, will open up room in your mind so you can focus on what most matters to you.

Your first ten-minute task is to take inventory of your living space. Grab a pad of paper and a pen, and start at the front door. If you look at the space and it works for you, leave it. If it bothers you, if it's taking up mental space, write it down and deal with it later.

Have your kids left shoes or dumped backpacks there? Are there cobwebs in the corners or library books on the table that you keep meaning to return?

Move through your home, jotting down notes. Note any items that make your heart sink, and consider trading them to a friend for something else. Your inventory is your own to-do list for a rainy Saturday or for little ten-minute snippets of time.

It's okay to do just one task a week; but try to let yourself, and even let this project, rest on the Sabbath.

Today, spend time noticing which places around your home cause you stress. Address the list as you are able, in ten-minute periods or in great swaths of time.

Assembly Line

*Whether you think that you can, or that you can't, you are
usually right.*
—Henry Ford

How many peanut butter and jelly sandwiches do you make every week during the school year? No, seriously, count them. (Or bologna, or whatever it is your kids prefer.) I make between ten and fifteen a week.

And when I'm smart, I take a whole loaf of bread from the freezer, make as many peanut butter and jelly sandwiches as it affords, slice the tall tower of them in half, and either stash each sandwich into its own plastic container or slip the entire stack into the bread bag, and freeze them. Total time: less than ten minutes.

Today your task is to write down all the mindless, menial tasks you do multiple times every week. Are there any that you can do ahead of time, once a week, and in bulk? If so, maybe you can do them today.

(And when you're preparing lunches try to avoid plastic baggies; they are costly to the environment. Instead, find alternate ways to package lunches such as using reusable dollar store containers.)

Your second simple, ten-minute task is to write down any of the tasks you do multiple times every week. Get creative about completing those tasks in a more efficient way.

Donation Box

*It is preoccupation with possessions, more than anything else, that
prevents us from living freely and nobly.*
—Bertrand Russell

Felicia and I were having coffee at her house not long after her
youngest was born. At one point in the morning, she laid the baby
in his bassinet and motioned for me to follow her. "I've got a stair-
well problem," she said. "Let me show you."

Sure enough, inside the back door where the stairs split to go up
to the kitchen or down to the basement, the landing was overflow-
ing with packed grocery bags. "We get so many hand-me-downs
from the neighbors," she said. "What I don't want, I throw in
a bag. To donate." It was the last bit that wasn't getting accom-
plished; she had more important things to do, such as caring for
little Christopher.

"It's the same upstairs," she said, walking to the front of the
house and pointing up the steps. "What do you think I
should do?"

Later, as she fed the baby, I looked around her basement, found
a large box, and shoved it into the back corner of the garage. I then
tossed all the bags into it. "Mark's going to love you," Felicia said.
"And he's got a Goodwill right by the office. Easy-peasy."

*Today, your third mission, if you choose to accept it, is to identify both
an out-of-the-way place and a container for donations. Take ten
minutes and create a new solution for dealing with it.*

Tangled

Oh, what a tangled web we weave
when first we practice to deceive.
—Sir Walter Scott

It's not a very mellifluous name, but we call it the "technology drawer." It holds batteries, cameras, and cords—but mostly cords. They are black and all look alike until you pull them out, let the plug fall to the floor, and examine the tiny prongs on one end. Untangling a great knot of them when I'm looking for one can take me from euphoria to a dark, homicidal state.

You can bet I've tried to keep them organized. I bought a drawer divider that had adorable little trap doors built right in, into which a neatly wrapped cord could be dropped. When that didn't work, I created, from toilet-paper rolls, a neatly marked container for each one. I've used rubber bands among other approaches. But each time, some malicious cord user simply pulls open the drawer and drops them in.

I've just found another system to try: I am going to get a large glass jar, label each cord with my label maker, wrap it tight, secure it with a twist tie, and drop it in.

This one ought to work, don't you think?

Maybe cords and cables don't bug you, but what does? Think about a new way to manage it. Know that not every new system you put into place will catch on right away, if at all. Be patient, know that decluttering is a process, and try to find the humor in it.

Muddling Through

*Never explain what you do. It speaks for itself. You only muddle it
by talking about it.*
—Shel Silverstein

It's a warm Saturday in autumn, and the four of us sit on Anna's
back porch watching her children play.

"What was it like to go back to work when you all had babies
at home?" Anna asks.

"Sticky," one friend says.

"Exhausting," says another.

"It was kind of a relief," I say. "To think, to be someone in the
outside world again."

Anna's just returned to work as a college professor. She's struggling—three kids ages six and younger, a house, a husband. "It's
confusing," she says. "I'm with you on sticky and exhausting and
that it's a kind of break to be back at work. But I sometimes
feel like an imposter. I feel that my students can tell I'm only
half there."

We assure her that it takes time to learn to act nonchalant about
the sour spit-up smell that radiates from your shoulder or when
papers stick to the back of your hand.

Anna sighs.

"It'll get better," I say. "For now, you'll just have to muddle
through."

"That's right," she said. "And this helps." She waves her hand,
drawing a circle in the air above our heads, almost like she is lasso-
ing us, all together.

To whom do you go when life feels complicated?

October

Practice Playfulness

Lighten Your Heart, Take Time to Play

Laugh and Grow Strong

Laugh and grow strong.
—(attributed to) St. Ignatius of Loyola

I can't tell you how relieved I am to find us in October. This month is going to be fun. We are going to look at how we played as children, what makes us laugh, and how we can recapture more light-heartedness in our lives.

Honestly, some of the exercises we've done together this year knocked me flat. It wouldn't be fair, after all, to ask hard questions of you if I hadn't explored them first. If you could see how many times I've been hunched over my laptop, raking over my resentments or regrets, wishing for easier questions:

Are you withholding forgiveness from someone?

Where, in your life, is repetition creating potholes and ruts?

What makes you feel unworthy?

Who comes up with this stuff? I've thought. (And then I remembered: *me.*)

I'm glad to have plumbed these because, yes, being an adult and living intentionally is serious business. But adding just a bit more play to our adult lives will surely connect us more fully to that true, wholehearted self we've been talking about all year.

Are you ready to play?

October 2

Who Me? Play?

Adults are just obsolete children.
—Dr. Seuss

If I were you, I might feel a little wary of the declaration, "This month we'll be playful!" Who doesn't do everything in her power to avoid the person who is trying to seem naive or childlike? It comes off as false.

You know, like the woman who's decided it's endearing to speak in faux baby talk and pretend to be much less intelligent than she is? (Paris Hilton allegedly once asked a reporter whether Walmart was "where they make walls.")

It's no better when a man bursts into a social situation, obviously intent on being "the fun guy." His nervous energy and lack of boundaries are as noxious as savagely bad breath, and without exception his stories and jokes are entirely unfunny.

Nothing like that is going on here. You won't have to play hopscotch on the sidewalk, chew globs of pink bubblegum, or pull your hair up in high pigtails. Well, not unless you want to.

It's just that we lose touch with the fact that play is just as necessary for adults as it is for kids. It makes us healthier and more creative, and it can transform our relationships. Most important, it's fun.

What's your definition of play?

October 3

Purposeless Pleasure

In every real man a child is hidden that wants to play.
—Friedrich Nietzsche

When I met Tina, one of the first things I noticed about her was her playfulness. Quick-witted and kind, she was the type of mom who played tag with her son at the park, laughing and chasing him around the equipment and running up the slide after him when he tried to make his escape.

I wasn't. I was the one on the bench, reading a novel. And that's okay enough, right?

Tina's still close to her son Ben, now fifteen, but recently—after the two of them played a game of pool—she realized how rarely she plays. "Ben and I were laughing that night, really uproariously, at how completely unskilled we are," she said. "But in that laughter, I was struck with the conviction that I don't play enough. When these happy asides happen, I feel so incredibly delighted, so surprised at how much fun I'm having."

Tina said she only infrequently feels that kind of gladness, and she worries she's "pushing Ben to the same playless·existence. It's not good," she said.

Play experts talk about play as "purposeless pleasure." Maybe that's why so many of us productivity-obsessed American adults are so bad at it. Does playing oppose our national values?

October 4

Varieties of Play

It is a happy talent to know how to play.
—Ralph Waldo Emerson

While most dictionary definitions simply define play as games and recreational activity, Dr. Scott Eberle, an expert at the Strong National Museum of Play in New York, has said that defining play is more difficult.

(Did you even know we had a National Museum of Play? I didn't.)

Play, Eberle said, is "a moving target, a process, not a thing." At the museum, the progression of play is charted; it begins in "anticipation" and ends in "poise."

If you're worried that, after being convinced of the value of play, you'll be relegated to voicing the action figures as your child drops them off the back of the couch, don't worry. At the Strong, examples of play include learning, imagining, competing, discovering, socializing, collecting, creating, reading, and writing.

Playing is reading a book, collecting leaves on an autumn day, telling knock-knock jokes, singing an impromptu song, or creating a silly video with your children.

We have many options when we give ourselves over to play.

What's your favorite way to play?

October 5

Just Joking

My fake plants died because I did not pretend to water them.
—Mitch Hedberg

I love verbal playfulness and kidding around. In college, Celia and I often pretended to be tourists from France when we went to the grocery store, puzzled by all the unfamiliar products, all "How you call it?" and "*Oui*, this looks *bon*." We don't even know French. Clearly.

When I first met Chloe, she casually mentioned that her husband was a roadie with the band Hall and Oates. My mind raced: *Were they even still performing?* I nodded and smiled, like most people do when she says that. (Her husband actually works in insurance and has never even heard them play.)

My friends, a married couple, used to tell people that on long car trips, they wore adult diapers so they wouldn't need to make stops. (Um, they never did that.) Joking around like that is the best.

Famously among my friends, I love question-and-answer games. Not the ones that ask if you'd rather lick a public toilet or eat a live worm, but those that open up serious, upstanding adults to talking about private thoughts as silly as who they think is their celebrity doppelgänger or as surprising as a desire to learn how to play the oboe or to speak Portuguese.

Who's the most verbally playful person you know?

Squirrel Obsession

A person reveals his character by nothing so clearly as the joke he resents.

—Georg Christoph Lichtenberg, *The Waste Books*

My neighbor was waging a multiple-front, coordinated military operation—on the squirrels. His arsenal included a BB gun, tree-trimming tools, and poison. Had I not had visual access to his yard, I'd never have believed he was anything but the serious, unassuming person I'd seen in public.

But when facing off with a squirrel, he was a maniac. He'd clench his fists and jump up and down like a toddler throwing a tantrum, red faced, cursing, sweat coursing down his neck. Or maybe my brain has embellished the memory all these years later.

As much as I am a lover of wildlife—I left bread out for squirrels the next place I lived, newly aware of the oppression their kind suffered—watching my neighbor was more entertaining to me than anything I could find on television.

And truly, it seemed that the squirrels chose to engage him. The neighborhood was rife with bird feeders. Many, including mine, were hardly squirrel-proof. But still, every day, I'd see the squirrels dangling from his, flipping their tails, feasting.

He'd burst out of the back door and the battle would rage again.

Are there any everyday, slapstick situations around you? Funny characters? Silly situations?

October 7

Say Yes

I am a child who is getting on.
—Marc Chagall

Kids' brains are flexible; adults', not so much. Sometimes, I stand back from myself and pay attention to the way I'm interacting with my children. I'm at once inside and outside of myself for a minute. In those admittedly rare moments when I get this kind of perspective, my rigidity can take me by surprise:

No, that outfit doesn't match. (*What's it to you?* I wonder.)

Yes, you have to shower tonight and not in the morning. (What difference does it make?)

No, we get this brand of peanut butter. (Really? You're a paid spokesperson?)

Not long ago, after experiencing myself that way, my daughters and I ran out for groceries. Such trips are, of course, full of requests: "Can I get these pens for school?" "Ooh, I've had these crackers at Lindsey's—can we get them?" "We need new headbands." And so on.

On that particular trip, I decided only to answer yes. At first my girls were surprised. Surprise gave way to delight. Delight turned into all-out hilarity. In the end, I probably spent less than ten dollars more than usual. They still laugh and love to tell the story about "that day Mom could only say yes."

Is there a way you can switch it up and be more playful with your kids today?

October 8

Meanie and Nicey

The playing adult steps sideward into another reality; the playing child advances forward to new stages of mastery.
—Paul Roazen, *Erik H. Erikson: The Power and Limits of a Vision*

We'd been sitting on the floor, building with magnetic blocks, when I let a handful of mine drop to the floor. My five-year-old niece glanced up at me. I scooted to her, squinted my eyes in mock anger, and gave her shoulder a little push.

She grinned; she knew I was starting some kind of game. (At the Strong National Museum of Play, anticipation is the word used to describe the moment when play begins.)

"Hey," I said, pushing her shoulder again. "I'm meanie. You're nicey. Those are mine." I grabbed the blocks from her hand. "You gonna cry about it? Huh? Are you?"

She pretended to pout. "Waaaaahh."

"Okay," I said. "Now you're meanie and I'm nicey."

"Hey, you!" she said, making her voice gruff and low. "Hey!"

I jumped back, obviously terrified, and commenced weeping. We went back and forth like that for an hour. I could tell it was liberating for her. Maybe, as a conscientious kid, she liked acting out and being "mean" without real consequences. Maybe she needed to let off a little steam after starting kindergarten and being newly burdened with a hundred rules.

Or maybe, for both of us, it was just fun.

How could being playful help you let loose?

October 9

Play as a Necessity

Play is a basic biological necessity.
—Stuart Brown

Psychiatrist and play expert Stuart Brown writes that play is all around us but "goes mostly unnoticed or unappreciated until it is missing." Brown is founder of the National Institute of Play and the author of *Play: How It Shapes the Brain, Opens the Imagination, and Invigorates the Soul.*

After studying the lives of incarcerated men who had been convicted of murder, Brown discovered that severe play deprivation was a common denominator in their lives. Play prevents violence, Brown asserts. Children and adults who enjoy spontaneous play develop skills and strengths that help them cope with stress in positive ways. They are far less likely to resort to violence when they experience extreme stress.

"Play is who we are," he writes. He notes that when victims of the terrorist attacks on September 11, 2001 were memorialized by the *New York Times*, the headlines—how their lives were lovingly summarized—had nothing to do with the work they did but with how they played. "A spitball-shooting executive," "a Frank Zappa fan," "a practical joker with a heart."

Brown writes that his favorite "player" is God, "who somehow put this marvelous divinely superfluous process into the cosmos for us to embrace."

How would you, or the people who know you, describe you in terms of the way you play or playfully interact with others?

October 10

Just for the Fun of It

Man is most nearly himself when he achieves the seriousness of a child at play.
—Heraclitus

"I have a hard time remembering to play, or playing period," Emily, a mother of two, admits. "It feels like there's just so much work to do and that we don't really value play time in our society."

She's right. Our culture values work and being productive almost more than anything else. After being introduced to someone for the first time, what is the very first thing we want to know? "What do you do?" we ask.

It's not that way everywhere. "Look at how much more vacation time Europeans get," Emily notes. "There is a lot of pressure on adults—maybe moms, in particular—to always be productive, and play is the opposite of being productive."

She defines play as "immersing oneself in the moment and reveling in the activity just for the sheer fun of it. Frankly, I can't remember the last time I allowed myself to truly relax into and be immersed by an activity that was sheer fun," Emily says. "Oh, my, I have some work to do!"

Or, actually, Emily has some "play" to do.

Do you resist playing because it's not "productive"?

October 11
Moments of Playfulness

Why, sometimes I've believed as many as six impossible things
before breakfast.
—Lewis Carroll

The truth is, the season of motherhood is one of the fullest in any woman's life. So, is it really fair—despite all the benefits of playing—to ask that moms add "play more" to their interminable to-do lists?

Well, I have good news for you. Dr. Stuart Brown, who has given his life to studying play, writes that just "a little bit of play" heightens creativity and increases feelings of happiness. And by "play" he means everything from taking part in organized games to role-playing to telling jokes to exercising to singing along to the radio when you're driving in the car.

I welcome this "a little bit will do" message.

Although I don't play with my kids—or engage in play myself—as much as I'd like, I am often play-full. Although my kids are no longer toddlers, for instance, sometimes I organize the food on their plates into smiley faces. I include unexpected items in their lunch boxes; recently, I slipped in tiny pumpkins. (How festive!) I tell them to take their vitamins but hand them a spoonful of Nutella instead.

These are only moments of playfulness, but they lighten our spirits.

What are some of the playful things you do?

October 12
Whimsical Bucket List

Everything you can imagine is real.
—Pablo Picasso

Okay, this might be going a little far afield for you, but how about we get a little silly?

Make a list (and I'm the only one who has to show hers) of the things you'd do if you had unlimited money, time, and talent, and if there would be no negative consequences. Maybe, before you were shrewd enough to limit your requests to things that your parents could buy you, your Christmas lists included impossible items such as a real leprechaun or a swimming pool full of dolphins.

Think that way again. Don't make a list of items you'd buy, but think about experiences or fun you'd like to have. Here are some of mine:

Pull the kids out of school and go to the Galapagos Islands

Work as a lounge singer in a hotel lobby

Be invisible and spend a week in the Oval Office witnessing what really goes on

Sleep over at the Smithsonian with one friend

Swim with a manatee

Your turn!

Write down the (perhaps improbable) things you'd like to do or be. The only stipulation is that what you list should be wonderfully appealing to you.

Play Histories

I doubt that the imagination can be suppressed. If you truly
eradicated it in a child, he would grow up to be an eggplant.
—Ursula K. Le Guin, *The Language of the Night*

In *Play: How It Shapes the Brain, Opens the Imagination, and Invigorates the Soul*, Dr. Stuart Brown advises adults to look back over their memories of play—to refresh their memories of their "play histories"—so that we can be reminded of what most delighted us as children and might delight us now.

"Generally, a person's purest emotional profile—temperament, talents, passions—is reflected in positive play experiences from childhood," he said. "If you can understand your own emotional profile when it was in its purest form, you can begin to apply it to your adult life."

When I was growing up, I enjoyed:

reading

imaginary play: dolls, dollhouse

arts and crafts: creating paper dolls, coloring, drawing

riding my bike

being alone in nature, exploring

daydreaming

taping my voice introducing songs, reading news, pretending to
    be a radio DJ

swinging

interacting with animals (our cats, the neighbors' dogs)

watching movies

What did you like to do when you were younger? Try to remember,
and write down a list in this book or elsewhere.

October 14

Blurry Snippets

If you carry your childhood with you, you never become older.
—Tom Stoppard

Yesterday we listed the ways we played when we were children not only to consider what kind of play might be appealing to us now but also to glimpse our purest emotional profile (temperament, talents, and passions).

Was it hard for you to remember what or how you played as a child? It was for me. My memories were blurry snippets, impossible to pull into focus. It helped me to think about specific rooms in the house I grew up in. Where did I sit? What was there to play with?

I recalled the toy closet in the family room. What did I take out of that closet? I looked into the drawer of the desk I had as a child and saw pencils, a box of crayons, and notebook paper. In another was a denim-covered three-ring binder where I kept my drawings and stories.

I pictured myself reading, riding a bike, playing alone with my dollhouse, and exploring undeveloped land near our house.

What I see in that "emotional profile" doesn't much surprise me: I see a girl who liked solitary play and who spent a lot of time with her imagination.

What does your childhood play tell you about yourself?

A Broader Understanding of Play

*We don't stop playing because we grow old; we grow old because
we stop playing.*
—George Bernard Shaw

There are many ways to understand what it means to play. When,
a few times a year, I go to an art museum, that's play. It's play when
I attend concerts or the theater, or when I fly out of town for a
few days to visit a far-away friend. It's play when I go to the library
just for the fun of it and not to do research or find a quiet place
to work.

It's play every year when I go on a writing retreat in New York
City, walking the sidewalks of my friend's familiar neighborhood,
taking the subway, buying bread and coffee from the corner store
as though I really do live down the block.

My family and I all play together when we have Sunday movie
nights, when a spontaneous dance party bubbles up out of an ordinary moment, when we carve pumpkins together, or when we go
on vacation and explore a new place.

These kinds of play follow the "rules" that play experts have
classified for play. That is, each event begins with anticipation and
ends in contentment, balance, and poise. Or jack-'o-lanterns.

*Look at the ways you play, alone or with your family. When you
define play more broadly, do you see that your life does, actually,
contain play?*

Anticipation

One can never consent to creep when one feels an impulse to soar.
—Helen Keller

"Play, for me, is something that I like to do that raises my endorphins," Sally said. "But I never actually call it play." Dinners out with her husband and long walks with a friend are examples of her endorphin lifters. She also makes a point of participating in play with her children.

"I swim with them, rather than watch them swim; build the snow fort with them, rather than watch them build it," she said. "Kids really enjoy it when we participate in play with them. And they can tell when we're having a good time."

For Sally, having something to look forward to also keeps her spirits high. "As an adult who gives all of her time and energy to three kids and a husband, I need to always be looking forward to something that I really want to do."

She tries to plan at least one or two special events a month. "This month it's a retreat; next month a family vacation and a moms' painting night. Looking forward to something keeps my endorphins up so I can handle the day-to-day in a positive manner."

What raises your endorphins? Look ahead to the next few months; what are you truly looking forward to?

October 17

Tucking In

We are such stuff as dreams are made on; and our little life is
rounded with a sleep.
—William Shakespeare, *The Tempest*

Each of my kids and I have developed our own customs and traditions: playful phrases and sayings of our own making, special places we go with only each other, and favorite movies we watch when no one else is around.

One of my sons is involved in about a half dozen clubs in high school. He's often out late at rehearsals or meetings. Often the only one-on-one time I have with him is just before he goes to sleep. I sit on the edge of his bed as he tells me something about his day before he slips off.

He's no longer a little boy. But sometimes I like to play like he is. After I straighten his covers, instead of leaving the room, I tuck one of the stuffed animals he most loved as a child in beside him. I interview them once in a while, asking the little tiger whether he remembers our trip to Williamsburg, Virginia, or a teddy bear whether he was afraid when my son spent a few days in intensive care as a baby.

My sleepy son pretends that he only tolerates these moments, but I know from his sleepy smile that he enjoys them.

Are rituals and customs developing between you and each of your
children? What's your favorite one?

Continue to Play

Work consists of whatever a body is obliged to do, and . . . Play consists of whatever a body is not obliged to do.
—Mark Twain, Tom Sawyer

Writing my "play history" a few days ago heightened my awareness about what my kids are playing now, and it caused me to reflect on what they loved to play when they were little. What "play" will lift their spirits and release their endorphins when they are adults and managing their homes and, presumably, families of their own some day?

From an early age, my oldest loved to run. By seven or eight, he ran 5Ks. Now he runs track, and I can tell by his bright eyes and smile when he comes home after practice that he's just been at play. Running, of course, is something he can easily bring along with him into adulthood.

His brother was always obsessed by swords. He'd go outside to play and, in seconds, was in possession of a long stick. Soon he'd be cutting through the air; he was a pirate, St. George slaying the dragon, or a knight of the Round Table. When he gave up all other sports for lacrosse, it made perfect sense.

I don't know how this will translate into adulthood. Maybe he'll take up fencing. I don't know, but I hope he'll continue to play.

What are your kids' favorite ways to play? Is there an adult equivalent?

October 19

Daydreaming as Play

To lose one's self in reverie, one must be either very happy, or very unhappy. Reverie is the child of extremes.

—Antoine Rivarol

More than my older three kids—and much like me as a child—my youngest is a daydreamer. While she can be as focused as a laser when she's pitching a softball or doing a math problem, sometimes she just stares. When she was younger, she called it "getting blurry eyes."

As a child, I'd go to a little woods near my house and sit on a fallen tree trunk. I'd close my eyes and listen. A dog's bark echoed off in the distance. I'd hear the low rumble of a garbage truck, the call-and-response of bird's songs.

I'd open my eyes, pull a blade of grass from the ground, and stare at it up close. I studied the gradations of green, and then its wet white stem. I'd run my finger over the coarse, perfect striations at its top. I don't know what I was hoping to find, and I couldn't have told you why it was such a rich time for me, but I loved to go there.

If, on coming home, my mother asked me what I'd been doing, I'm sure I'd have said, "Nothing." And that would be true.

Do you ever sit and just stare?

Food Play

Life is the combination of magic and pasta.
—Federico Fellini

On the cooking show *Chopped*, contestants, all fairly experienced cooks, are given baskets containing ingredients from which they must create an appetizing dish. Problem is, when they flip open the baskets at the start of the show, they discover items as obscure, inharmonious, and unappetizing as beef tongue, cheese puffs, broccoli rabe, and diet cola. (I made those up, but honestly, the combinations can be that nasty.) Then it's ready, set, go!

So, if you you're stumped about how to bring a little more levity into your home and if you and your friends to like to cook, what about hosting a competition something like that? Tailor it to work in your space; maybe each guest or team makes only one part of the meal.

For a more low-maintenance way to experiment with food, check out several cookbooks from the library, or go online, and find recipes or cuisines you've never tried.

Have a little fun with it.

When's the last time you played in the kitchen?

October 21

Pet Play

Money will buy a pretty good dog, but it won't buy the
wag of its tail.
—Josh Billings, *Josh Billings' Trump Kards*

I have a friend who spoils my dog. A religion writer, her nickname is "God Girl." Maybe it should be "Dog Girl." Every time Cathleen comes to town, she has gifts for Shiloh. If you twirl the red parrot she gave him in the air, it shrieks and moans like it's being tortured. Once, just before Halloween, he was bequeathed a King Arthur costume held together on his underside with Velcro.

I love my dog, but until Cathleen was smitten, his toy basket was uninspiring: a tennis ball, a few half-chewed rawhide bones, a hollow rubber toy that is meant to be filled with something that resembles sprayable cheese but is never supplied with the stuff because I find it so utterly revolting.

Shiloh's play life has improved greatly. I whip that parrot around for him just about every day. He vastly prefers this game to chasing the tennis ball.

Play experts, as you might imagine, are often advocates for pet ownership. Playing with pets, no matter how enthusiastically, is socially acceptable. And playing with dogs relaxes us quantifiably, lowering our blood pressure and boosting oxytocin levels.

So maybe those toys Cathleen spoils Shiloh with aren't, really, just for him.

Does interacting with pets relax you? How can watching animals play
teach you something about play?

Freedom from Self-Consciousness

A little nonsense now and then, is cherished by the wisest men.
—Roald Dahl, *Charlie and the Great Glass Elevator*

When we play, really play, we are released into a happy, unself-conscious state. Our self-reproach, reserve, and general "judginess" vanish. And playing with animals is particularly therapeutic because we never fear their judgment. We tangibly ("Look at that tail wag!") feel their unconditional love. It's a model for uninhibited play.

I don't know that I've ever thought of what I looked like or sounded like when I'm goofing around with my dog, Shiloh. I'm just twirling that ridiculous parrot around in the air or pretending to eat his rawhide ("Nom, nom, nom! Wow, this is tasty!") or acting shocked that the squeaky squirrel has somehow just snuck into the house again. "Oh, no, get it, get it!" I shout, kicking the squirrel to the other side of the room. "Go get that squirrel." (This game, not surprisingly brings my squirrel-hating neighbor to mind.)

When Shiloh gives me the international dog signal for play—extending his forelegs, bowing down, and then raising his rump in the air—I know what follows will be good for my soul.

When do you feel least self-conscious and most playful?

The Play's the Thing

While we look to the dramatist to give romance to realism, we ask
of the actor to give realism to romance.
—Oscar Wilde

My husband, David, before switching it up and going into software, received his graduate degree in acting and worked as a stage actor. He still performs when he can.

Truth is, whenever David is cast in a play, our family life goes lopsided for a few months. He does his regular job by day, talking telephony and software and whatnots, and then rushes home for a quick dinner before going off to rehearsal.

There is always some moment before the show opens when David pulls me aside and thanks me for supporting him. "I know this has been tough . . ."

But I don't let him go on saying such things. We do this for each other. When I go out of town to write or when I sequester myself upstairs to meet a deadline or when he's traveling for business or cast in a play, we cover for each other.

And for him, doing plays is his "play." He has other outlets: running with Shiloh around the park, listening to favorite podcasts, and cooking among them. But really, his greatest joy is theater.

And that joy spills over on the rest of us when he gets the chance to perform.

How do you balance work and family responsibilities with
other avocations?

October 24
Theater of the Dinner Table

Strange to see how a good dinner and feasting reconciles everybody.
—Samuel Pepys, *The Diary of Samuel Pepys*

In August, we talked about being stuck. We defined ruts—spiritual, geographic, and otherwise. But we didn't examine mealtime ruts: macaroni and cheese, burgers, spaghetti, tacos, lasagna. For many of us, this is what we default to when we can't think of what to make for dinner; they are some of the things we have over and over and over again when we're in a culinary rut.

If you have—as I have and pretty much every mother I know has—felt like all the fun has been sapped out of dinnertime, think about how to fold in even just a little bit of playfulness, regardless of the foods you serve.

Could you institute a new game? We play best and worst, sharing the highs and lows of our days. Could you assign one kid a week to make dinner? Could you eat one dinner a week without speaking in English, as though the family comprised visitors from all over the world?

What else might fold in a little fun?

⌒

What has been the most memorable family dinner you've had in the past couple of months? What made it special?

October 25

Letting Loose

With any child entering adolescence, one hunts for signs of health,
is desperate for the smallest indication that the child's problems
will never be important enough for a television movie.
—Delia Ephron, *Funny Sauce*

A few years ago, my daughter Isabel and I were shopping in what I recently learned is called a hypermarket, or one-stop grocery plus department store. The place seemed, to both of us, to be strangely quiet and too bright. Had there been a zombie apocalypse?

We fell into goofy, giggly moods. As we perused the spatulas, "Danny's Song," written by Kenny Loggins, suddenly broke the quiet, piping in from way up above our heads. When the chorus began, I sang it full voice, supplying *mah-mah-mahs* for lyrics I didn't know.

Even though we ain't got money . . .
(Mah, mah, mah, mah . . .)

At the time, my daughter was ten or eleven. Laughing, she grabbed the cart and pushed it around the corner from me. I stopped singing, but when I saw the edge of our cart returning around the corner, I fell to one knee, threw my hands in the air, and sang, "I'm so in love with you honey!"

Except it wasn't Isabel. It was a stranger who then sped away in a blur. Isabel had come around the other way. We could barely get off the floor, we laughed so hard.

Do you ever just let loose in song, at hypermarkets or elsewhere?

October 26

Playfulness Squelchers

The best way to keep children at home is to make the home atmosphere pleasant, and let the air out of the tires.
—Dorothy Parker

Although the incident of me belting out Kenny Loggins at a hypermart has made Isabel and me laugh for years, had it occurred at another time, in a certain window of her development, it may have turned out quite differently. That is, had Isabel been thirteen instead of eleven, I'd probably never have gotten to the throwing-myself-down-on-one-knee point of silliness. Instead of finding my singing funny, her thirteen-year old self likely would have issued a sharp "Stop it. You're embarrassing me!" from between clenched teeth.

(Happily, at fourteen, she is back to enjoying such moments. Phew.)

But, honestly, when my kids—each at slightly different moments of time—have been in that "my mother is the most awkward, embarrassing, ridiculous person in the whole wide world" phase, it has put a damper on my ability, or willingness, to let loose and play.

At first I thought their tween-age disdain wouldn't affect me. I just ignored it, thinking, "Oh. That's developmentally appropriate." But then it gets to you. Or, I should say, it got to me. It hurt, dampened my spirits. And it took time for me to be willing take the risk to be freer around them again, but I'm glad I did.

When have you felt like your playfulness was squelched?

October 27

Soup Season

*Anyone who tells a lie has not a pure heart, and cannot make
a good soup.*
—Ludwig van Beethoven

Late October feels like soup season to me. As the weather grows chillier and winter draws near, I become soup obsessed. The slow cooker is sprung from its home in the basement. I stock up on bouillons and broths and look for new recipes online.

My favorite soup to make in October is pumpkin porcini soup. I'd love to tell you that, along with pumpkins for carving, I buy them to cook and purée for this soup. I'd sound so virtuous! But that would be a lie. (The recipe I use, by the way, is in *The Moosewood Restaurant Cooks at Home*, one of my all-time favorite cookbooks.)

Chopping vegetables, opening jars of spices and breathing them in, and running my hand through dried rice or lentils engages my senses. Soups are flexible and forgiving—I truly get to play with them. They're healthy and wholesome, so even though they're simple, I feel noble filling the bowls and serving them to my family at dinner.

Isn't there something almost primal and deeply satisfying about their simplicity and serving them alongside hunks of good, crusty bread?

*What foods do you associate with autumn? When are you most
engaged as a cook?*

Play's Opposite

*Here is the sea, great and wide, which teems with creatures
innumerable, living things both small and great. There go the
ships, and Leviathan, which you formed to play in it.*
—Psalm 104:25–26 ESV

What's the opposite of play? "Work," right?

Dr. Stuart Brown, in his book *Play: How It Shapes the Brain,
Opens the Imagination, and Invigorates the Soul*, gives a different
answer. He says that the opposite of play is not work but
depression.

For more than forty years, Brown has studied the effects of
"play deprivation." Think back on times in your own life when
some combination of work or family responsibilities kept you from
play. Maybe you're in such a time now. In those times, we smile
less, laugh less, feel distant from God and from others. We're
heavyhearted.

Brown says that we can find our way back to play again. Thinking, as we did earlier this month, about how we played as a child
is a start. Identify one or two things you enjoyed then that can be
brought into adulthood. Brown writes that we can find opportunities to play every single day.

What can you do simply for the joy of it?

Psalm 104:25–26 states that God made the sea "to play in it."
When we play, then, we are reflecting the image of God in us.

Do you need to find your way back to joy?

October 29

Intimate Play

Love is composed of a single soul inhabiting two bodies.
—Aristotle

"I think flirting with each other is great play," said Bonnie, a mother of two young sons. "When Tom and I have not had sex in a while, he gets flirty with me—cute and funny. It's not even overtly sexual."

She said that she thinks husbands and wives "need to flirt, to giggle, to play" as they did when they were dating. "And then later," she said. "There is the joy that we share in intimacy."

Stuart Brown would agree; he's said that sex "counts big time in the world of play." Not that we need even more reasons to be intimate with our spouses, but sex also delivers many health benefits, including strengthening the pelvic floor, lowering blood pressure and the risk of heart attacks, and reducing stress.

But it's also play.

My friend Cassie includes sex in her top three ways to play. "Play for me includes sports that involve choices, such as mountain biking and skiing," she said. "Or aimless beach time, collecting sea glass and shells. And also, frankly, sexual stuff. It's great when neither my husband nor me is rushed and we both just enjoy all the fun little parts of the experience."

In what ways do you experience sexual intimacy as play?

October 30

Essential Self

Happy is he who still loves something that he loved in the nursery:
he has not been broken in two by time; he is not two men, but
one, and he has saved not only his soul but his life.

—G. K. Chesterton

I say of my kids, "They were always just who they are now." That is, from the moment they were born, our children show us something about their essential personalities and temperaments, something that's just intrinsically "them."

I saw it in the three kids to whom I gave birth, and I'm fortunate that the foster mother who cared for my youngest knew my daughter since she was only a few days old. "She was the sweetest of the sweet," she told me.

We watch our kids develop and mature, but we always keep that first sense of who they are in mind. But sometimes we forget that we have essential selves, too.

That's one of the benefits of doing the play history: we can get back in touch with our childhood self, embrace the activities we embraced, remember something fundamental about who we really are.

After our exploration this month, I feel a renewed interest—an urgent one, really—in bringing more play into my family's life, and into my own.

What did you learn, or remember, about your essential self
this month?

October 31

Shining a Light

No ghost was ever seen by two pair of eyes.
—Thomas Carlyle

When we take our kids trick-or-treating in the neighborhood tonight, our friends and I know which houses to skip and which ones we shouldn't miss. We've celebrated the holiday with them every year of our kids' lives, and we have the (adorable) pictures to prove it.

The children will want to stop by Veronica and Dan's house; they always give out king-size candy bars, but we'll pass by the white house around the corner. One year when we rang that bell, the couple who lives there shouted at us, telling us that they do not participate in Halloween and neither should we, saying it promotes witches and the occult. Our little astronauts, pirates, and mermaids stood and stared.

It's a personal choice, of course, whether and how to celebrate what can be a very play-filled holiday, but I find compelling the perspective of my friend, the writer Caryn Rivadeneira. Caryn has written numerous times about Halloween from a Christian perspective; she says it attracts her as a person of faith.

"If we can't face and admit what lurks about the dark, it's hard to appreciate and talk about the One who shines the light," she says.

Do you have strong feelings about celebrating Halloween?

November

Practice Gratitude

Be Grateful, on Purpose

November 1

Pondering Gratitude

grat·i·tude
the quality of being thankful; readiness to show appreciation for
and to return kindness, gratefulness, thanks, appreciation
—Merriam-Webster Dictionary

I hesitate to dedicate a month of reflections to practicing gratitude. Gratitude's rather overhyped these days, don't you think? Keep a gratitude journal, and the universe will grant all your wishes! Gratitude's an attitude! Change your thoughts, change your world!

My friend Nadine, a biblical scholar, says that people talk about gratitude as if it were a psychotropic drug. "We're told that giving thanks automatically flips an emotional switch inside of us," she says. "Like it will instantly turn us into calm, cheerful people who find ourselves making up new verses to 'these are a few of my favorite things.'"

Nadine and I agree: gratitude isn't a magic spell, but an act of the will.

Sure, sometimes when we express appreciation to a friend or to God in prayer, we feel a wave of blissful contentment wash over us. But that's not always the case. As Nadine so concisely puts it, sometimes "our emotions lag." We feel . . . nothing.

"Seeking an emotional payoff by offering thanks to God or others is an attempt at a quid pro quo arrangement," she says. "It shouldn't be. What's important is to acknowledge God as the giver of the gifts in our lives. Gratitude makes us a little less the center of our own universe."

Have you ever been promised that if you were just more "grateful,"
you'd surely be happy and that God would grant your desires?

Not Feeling It

Do any human beings ever realize life while they live it?—every,
every minute?
—Thornton Wilder, *Our Town*

Gratitude, of course, cannot be forced.

"You should be grateful," we growl at our kids, as they limply move the food around on their plates. "Do you know how many children in the world go to bed hungry? They would be overjoyed to have a dinner like that." Somehow this doesn't make the braised eggplant any more appetizing, at least to the children who sit around my dinner table.

We know that gratitude can't be forced, of course, but we still find ourselves trying to coerce our kids to be more grateful. And we do the same to ourselves, too.

We're aware that we have so much to be grateful for: my children's lives, a ready supply of food and water, cozy and secure homes. We enjoy these "basics"—and countless luxuries besides—while so many people in the world struggle just to survive the day. We secretly chide ourselves: *I should be more grateful.* But try as we may, we're just not feeling it. We wonder if there's something wrong with us.

Is my heart hardened somehow? Is it really not such a great gift to have these needs met? Will I ever feel content and satisfied?

Have you ever struggled with feelings of guilt about your own
ingratitude?

Starting from Scratch

Gratitude is not only the greatest of virtues but the parent of all others.

—Cicero

There are seasons in life when we feel utterly ungrateful. At those times, hearing shiny, happy stories about gratitude journals or testimonies about how someone has learned to embrace every moment as a fantastic gift make us feel ashamed and isolated.

When we're feeling that way, what are our options?

We can pretend to be grateful, all smiles and happy sentiments about living in the "now."

We can give up and embrace our ingratitude, maybe considering it inevitable in a skeptical, disaffected postrecession, postmodern era.

We can start small and explore what it might take to build up our gratitude muscles.

I vote for the third option. I don't want to pretend or give up. And cynicism depresses me.

Some of the most appealing people I have ever met nearly slosh over with gratitude, and to be more like them, I'm willing to take a few reticent baby steps.

Are you with me?

Do other people's expressions of gratitude and positivity ever grate on your last nerve? Or is it hard for you to understand why other people aren't more content?

November 4
What Could Have Been

Instead of complaining that the rose bush is full of thorns, be happy the thorn bush has roses.
—German Proverb

But what if you can't even recall what gratitude feels like? Where should you start?

Some would advise you to start being more mindful of all the blessings you enjoy. A well-meaning friend gives you a gratitude journal and a lovely new pen. You crack it open, and you give it a try:

I'm grateful for my cat. (Even though she ignores me.)

I'm grateful for that couch. (That I've never really liked.)

I'm grateful for my friends. (Even though I don't think they really care about me.)

And then you think, "*Nice list, bonehead. But who doesn't have couches or cats or friends? And guess what—everyone you know has something you don't.*" A husband, financial security, talent, beauty, kids who truly like them.

Your moment of gratitude has throttled you into a weepy mess.

Maybe instead of listing things we own, reflecting on past experiences of gratitude is a better way to practice gratefulness. Remember when, after that second mammogram, the doctor called to say there wasn't actually anything there? Or that the neighbor had found your dog after he got loose? Or that, after months of unemployment, you were being offered a job?

"Thank you, thank you, thank you," you say, your heart open, your body flushed in relief.

⌒

Can you think of a moment that came as a complete relief? Remember the lightness in your chest, the warmth that filled you? That is what gratitude feels like.

Redemption

Love of God is pure when joy and suffering inspire an equal degree of gratitude.
—Simone Weil

"I wonder . . ." Bonnie says slowly, tracing her index finger around the top of her water glass. "I wonder how we'd experience our lives differently if we paused long enough to notice the beautiful redemption that exists in our everyday lives."

The phrase captures my imagination. *Beautiful redemption.* "What do you mean by 'redemption'?" I ask.

"Just little things," she says. "Like how Charlie didn't fuss this morning about having to clean up his room. Or that bird out there on the feeder. Or that we're sitting here listening to the kids cheer and laugh their way through *Captain America.*"

Redemption. Renewal. Rebirth. Awakening. Her words make me notice the water in the pitcher that sits between us. The last few roasted pumpkin seeds lying in a bowl. The kids' laughter.

"I wonder," Bonnie says again, "if we reflected on it more often, how could redemption completely change our outlook, our disposition, our lives?"

I felt a flush of real gratitude for her gentle questions, her wisdom.

What, in your life today, feels like redemption?

Act First, Feel Later

Do all the good you can,
By all the means you can,
In all the ways you can,
In all the places you can,
At all the times you can,
To all the people you can,
As long as ever you can.

—John Wesley

Since bullying people into gratitude doesn't work, what are other ways we can we strengthen gratitude muscles?

One is to behave as though we're grateful even when we're not feeling it. We can choose to pay better attention to what is being done for us by others every single day and just say the words: "thank you."

Look into the eyes of the person bagging your groceries and say, "Thank you." You don't have to fall all over yourself; a simple "thank you" is sufficient. Actions precede emotions, even though we often think it's the other way around. We wait to do something until we "feel" like it. But our feelings come and go, the erratic little rotters.

We can't help what we feel, but we can choose how to behave. When one of my children seems less than, shall we say, appealing to me, I sometimes perform a loving act even when I don't feel like it. (Sometimes, of course, I just avoid the kid for a little while.)

But when I choose to show love by giving him a hug or making her hot chocolate, my feelings usually follow suit, and I feel a rush of affection for my child again.

How can you behave like a grateful person even when you don't feel like it?

Fake It?

If the only prayer you said was thank you, that would be enough.
—Meister Eckhart

You might wonder whether "actions precede emotions" is synonymous with the adage "fake it 'til you make it." I'd say . . . not really. That is, there's nothing bogus about saying "thank you" more frequently, and, to me, the word *fake* implies duplicity.

"Fake it 'til you make it" makes me think of old-time snake-oil peddlers or devious used-car salesmen: "Have I got a deal for you!" It sounds like what we're offering each other, and ourselves, is a sham.

But choosing to express thanks—even when we're not feeling it—doesn't have to be phony. It's not about acting like the most appreciative, self-effacing person in the whole wide world. It's simply choosing to speak the words "thank you" at the end of perfectly ordinary transactions.

You hold the door open, and I say, "Thank you." Someone schedules my kids' dentist appointments, delivers a package, or hands me my dry cleaning, and I say it again. It's about identifying ourselves as grateful people and deliberately acknowledging what others do for us.

Can you commit to paying attention and taking the opportunity to speak the words "thank you" more often?

November 8

Ingratitude

Be cheerful no matter what; pray all the time; thank God no matter what happens. This is the way God wants you who belong to Christ Jesus to live.

—1 Thessalonians 5:16–18 MSG

As counterproductive as it might seem, today we're going to explore all the things for which we are least thankful. Think about the parts of your life that never bring you pleasure. If you could make them vanish from your life right now, you would. Such as:

Cold, rainy weather

Mountains of laundry

When my daughter is sassy to me

A slow metabolism

Aging parents' poor health

Stained grout around the bathtub

Write down each complaint as well as reasons you so profoundly loathe it. "I am not grateful for this cold, rainy weather because it's not what autumn is supposed to look like. My kids won't play outside, and they are stir-crazy. The rain is making the leaves fall off the trees too soon, and I wanted to appreciate their colors longer."

We might be able to open a little space for gratitude by getting all that grumbling out. And maybe we'll find a little redemption. Is there anything, even on your "biggest annoyances" list, that nudges you toward gratitude? "Although I worry about them, I'm thankful that my parents are still living."

Can you look at each of your complaints and find anything redemptive in them?

Lack of Gratitude

*In daily life we must see that it is not happiness that makes us
grateful, but gratefulness that makes us happy.*
—Brother David Steindl-Rast

David was nearly weeping. Spectacular meals do that to him. (Full
disclosure: he's never cried over a meal I've prepared, even though
that pumpkin porcini soup I told you about last month is quite
delicious.)

For our twenty-fifth anniversary last summer, we'd splurged and
booked a weekend at an inn in Michigan whose nickname, promis-
ingly, was "Mini Versailles." I've not stayed at "original Versailles,"
so I can't compare the two, but it was as peaceful and beautiful a
place as I could have imagined.

One of the owners is a fabulous chef. One who makes
weep-worthy meals. Was it the shaved beets with Anjou pear?
Mussels in Pernod cream? Sweet-potato polenta? Each course was
exquisitely presented, flawlessly prepared; and David said it was the
best meal of his life.

Near the end of the evening, I noticed a woman a few tables
over from us signal the server. He leaned in, jogged off, and
returned with the chef. "That took too long," she said, scowling. I
decided I didn't like the pairing of a fedora with her velour track-
suit. Or, the flat affect of her voice, or most of all, her absolute lack
of gratitude.

Happily, David remained lost in his reverie.

Have you ever been dismayed by someone else's ingratitude?

Swimming in Thankfulness

Let us serve the world soulfully. The pay we will receive for our
service will be in the currency of gratitude. God's gratitude.
—Sri Chinmoy

As exasperated as I can get with my kids—for their sassiness or sullenness or failure to answer my texts or for forever asking for cash or leaving heaps of dirty clothes on the floor—all it takes for me to come crashing back to earth and fall head over heels in love with any one of them again is (1) worrying that they are ill, injured, or in any kind of danger or (2) learning about accidents, disease, or harm that have come to other children.

When, after I've heard about a school shooting or other tragedy, my children amble in the back door, what I feel—deeply feel—is gratitude. Suddenly that ten-dollar bill or extra load of laundry or sarcastic comment, or whatever else felt so infuriating before, no longer matters. At all.

I'm swimming in a sea of thankfulness. It's not that I don't usually realize how fortunate I am to be their mother. It's that I see our lives continuing along for decades, until—to quote Hamlet—it's time for me to "shuffle off this mortal coil."

And yet, for too many parents, events go another way.

When do you feel true, unmistakable gratitude?

Gratitude Journals

Take full account of what excellencies you possess, and in gratitude
remember how you would hanker after them, if you had them not.
—Marcus Aurelius

I have mixed feelings about gratitude journals. Consciously keeping track of the blessings in our lives is, of course, valuable. Too often, we overlook the everyday gifts—or "beautiful redemptions," as my friend Bonnie called them—that surround us.

Or we forget them, minutes after they light into our lives. Near misses on highways. Healthy children. Answered prayers. Wonderful friends and delightful surprises. A loaf of bread, a pitcher of water. The pink sunrise.

It's good for us to write these things down, revisit them, and remind ourselves that we are fortunate. Also, gratitude can be contagious. Maybe hearing about what you've recorded will inspire others to look at their lives from a different, more positive angle.

My issue with keeping gratitude journals (and dream boards, and the like) is that sometimes it almost seems that they are recommended as a means by which we can manipulate the universe (or God, or both) into giving us what we want.

And, after all, aren't we all inexpert at knowing what we truly want?

⌣

Looking back five, ten, or more years, can you identify something you
desperately wanted that you're now relieved not to have? A
relationship? A certain career?

November 12

Perspective

If the doors of perception were cleansed everything would appear to man as it is, infinite.
—William Blake

Gratitude is about getting perspective.

When I witness another mother's grief, I deeply appreciate my own kids' well-being. I'm grateful for my home after I see homeless families wait in line outside a local church to come in out of the cold.

Last year, I was visiting friends who live north of New York City, and I took the train down to Manhattan for the day. Before I left for the station, my friend said, "Oh, and don't worry—the trains seem to be moving again now." I hadn't heard, but there had been a derailment earlier in the morning, killing four people and injuring more than sixty.

I've taken the train a number of times from my friend's home to the city. Often—as it was that day—it's been jam packed and too hot. That morning, though, I didn't mind the crowded car. I felt grateful for the normalcy of it all: the frequent stops, doors opening and closing, even passengers who knocked into me on the way in and out of the train.

I thought of those whose lives had forever changed that day and who had only just begun to grieve.

Can you think of a time when you've seen your life from a different perspective and felt renewed gratitude?

Teaching Gratitude

All sanity depends on this: that it should be a delight to feel the
roughness of a carpet under smooth soles, a delight to feel heat
strike the skin, a delight to stand upright, knowing the bones are
moving easily under flesh.
—Doris Lessing, *The Golden Notebook*

How do we teach our children to be grateful? I think one key is not to spoil them. They need to be very accustomed to hearing no. Do you remember the story of—as my daughters refer to it—"that day Mom could only say yes"?

Walking with my girls through the grocery store that day, instead of saying, "No, no, no," to their requests for various treats, I said yes every time. It was fun for all three of us, but only because it was so unusual.

There are plenty of special occasions when my husband and I indulge our kids, including on their birthdays. Or, to be more specific, during their "birthday weeks." On the few days leading up to their birthdays, my kids get a pass from doing their regular chores.

"Hey, honey," I'll say. "Don't forget to load the dishwasher." I'll get a stunning smile in return, and a cheerful reminder: "Nope! Remember—birthday week!"

It's the novelty of it that makes it memorable.

How do you teach your children to be thankful?

Modeling Gratitude

Piglet noticed that even though he had a Very Small Heart, it
could hold a rather large amount of Gratitude.
—A. A. Milne, *Winnie-the-Pooh*

Another way to teach our children gratitude—one more potent than that ambiguous recommendation "not to spoil" them—is to model gratitude ourselves. When children hear their parents frequently saying "thank you," they will likely get into the habit of doing the same.

On a snowy afternoon last winter, my son had his first brush with the law, and I believe it was his good manners that saved him from getting a ticket. Red Riding Hood–like, he was on a mission to bring soup to my mother, who was recovering from pneumonia. Although no Big Bad Wolf would swallow him that day, the roads were icy, and after taking a turn too widely, he slid into the opposite lane. A police officer witnessed it, thought he was driving carelessly, and pulled him over.

My son apologized, and when the officer asked him where he was off to, my son mentioned his sick grandmother. (Who could ticket him then, right?) "I was so thankful he didn't give me a ticket," he said.

If our kids mature into courteous and grateful adults, not only will their homes and communities benefit, but they'll reap rewards as well.

What are some of the personal rewards we reap when we are grateful?

Seasons of Gratitude

*People don't notice whether it's winter or summer when
they're happy.*
—Anton Chekhov

There are many benefits to living a life marked by gratitude. Grateful people, doctors and therapists assert, have stronger immune systems and lower blood pressure, and they enjoy more restful sleep than their unappreciative peers. Of course, it's more agreeable for others to spend time with a thankful person than with a curmudgeon, so grateful people enjoy social benefits, too.

Don't despair, however, if you are in a season that makes it hard to be thankful. Everyone—even the most optimistic among us—go through honeymoons and high points as well as dreary, dark nights of the soul.

During some moments in life, the best we can do is trudge through, trying to hold tight to the fact that now isn't forever. And don't worry, your immune system won't suddenly fail and your blood pressure isn't going to skyrocket just because you're struggling.

In grimmer times, maybe the best you can do in terms of thankful living is to summon a polite "thank you" to the mail carrier or the playground supervisor. And, for now, that will be enough.

*What kind of season are you currently in? Is it easier, or harder, for
you to be thankful?*

November 16

Scars

Cultivate the habit of being grateful for every good thing that comes to you, and . . . give thanks continuously. And because all things have contributed to your advancement, you should include all things in your gratitude.

—Wallace D. Wattles, *The Science of Getting Rich*

After his resurrection, Christ's appearance was somehow changed. (It makes sense that being killed, visiting the depths of hell, and then coming to life again would do that to a person.)

Or maybe it was just that his friends were so brokenhearted and bleary eyed that they didn't recognize him at first, even after he moved through closed walls and locked doors to be with them. But, either way, he ended up having to prove his identity to them. To do it, he showed them his wounds.

His friend Thomas, though, remained skeptical: how could it really be Jesus? Christ said to Thomas, "Take your finger and examine my hands. Take your hand and stick it in my side. Believe" (John 20:27, ESV).

When we've been badly hurt—physically, emotionally, or both—we can't imagine ever being grateful for the injuries that have altered us. Our wounds will take time to heal. Scabs will drop off, leaving shiny new scars in their places. In time, those scars will fade but will never disappear. They now are a part of our identity and tell an important part of our story.

Like Christ's, our wounds show others something about who we are.

Can you imagine ever being grateful for your visible, or invisible, scars—or for the wounds that caused them?

November 17

Lying Fallow

It is well to lie fallow for a while.
—Martin Farquhar Tupper

I've been trying to "lie fallow" this month, as much as life has allowed.

Remembering my love of being alone in nature as a child, I've taken my dog, Shiloh, on long walks in the park, sometimes in biting cold and snow. I've spent time staring out the kitchen window at the birds—red-headed woodpeckers, mostly—on the swaying feeder that hangs in my backyard. I've been watching the sky move from gray to pink to black in the afternoons and evenings.

I refrained from having company, making lunch dates, or doing projects such as taking apart the linen closet and reorganizing its shelves. I did those sorts of things a few months ago, and I'm done for now. My label maker lies fallow, too. Instead, I've been making fires; reading books that please me; and thinking about poetry, about friendship, about gratitude, and about loss.

It's been a long while since I've had this kind of concentrated quiet time. Soon I'll have to wave good-bye to it, as the noise and color of the holidays approach. Then I'll let it go.

Is this a time of lying fallow for you? When have you unplugged from some of your usual commitments and just taken time to rest?

Best Practices

It will be conjectured that I was of course glad to return to the bosom of my kindred. Well! The amiable conjecture does no harm, and may therefore be safely left uncontradicted.
—Charlotte Brontë, *Villette*

Some of us wait expectantly for Thanksgiving all year long, impatient to dive into festive decorations and preparing special meals and shopping for gifts and, most of all, spending focused time with family and friends.

Others are filled with what can be described only as trepidation. We dread having to go to the mall and cooking elaborate meals. Maybe most of all, we dread the time that we're obligated to spend during the holidays with difficult family members.

Most of us, myself included, fall somewhere between these two extremes. When I'm wise—and happily this is such a year—I start the season after having taken a few weeks off from meetings and entertaining and other endeavors that necessitate planning and rushing around.

My "lying fallow" time before the holidays is a best practice for an introvert like me. It helps me take a (figurative) deep breath and enter the season centered. After a few quiet weekends spent only with David and the kids, I'm eager to see family and friends; happy to make new connections; and most of all, ready to relax in the loving presence of dear friends.

What are your "best practices" for entering the holiday season with a grateful heart?

Express Yourself

Feeling gratitude and not expressing it is like wrapping a present and not giving it.
—William Arthur Ward

Thanksgiving Day, for most of us, is a communal affair. Even if you spend it with favorite relatives or friends, you might not get a chance to express how grateful you truly are for them. You might be too busy mashing potatoes or rolling out pie dough or playing Chutes and Ladders at the kids' table for an intimate conversation.

Although, ideally, holidays are times to feel lovingly caught up in the web of family, too many times we can feel misunderstood or isolated, regardless of how many people are sitting around the table.

This year, especially if you live far away and see these loved ones only rarely, consider calling or writing notes before you get together on Thanksgiving.

Tell a cousin your favorite memory of her. Remind a friend of the silliest thing you've ever done together. Ask your grandmother or aunt or friend if there's anything she can share with you—burdens you could help her bear, parts of the meal you could prepare, or anything else—so that you better know what's on her mind and heart right now. Share your thoughts, too.

⌒

Set the tone for this year by making an authentic connection with a trusted relative or friend. Write her a note or give her a call in the next few days.

Protecting Your Heart

Heirlooms we don't have in our family. But stories we've got.
—Rose Cherin, *Family Therapies*

I love Erma Bombeck's joke about the controversial subjects no one should ever talk about in public: "religion, politics, family planning, and cereal." (Obviously she had strong feelings about breakfast.)

Some of the people you'll spend time with over the next couple of months will likely push your buttons. Maybe they insist on arguing about these taboo subjects, or they treat you poorly. Give some thought to how you'll interact with them this year. After spending the month delving into gratitude, it would be a shame to be thrust into a situation where you feel distinctly frustrated and ungrateful.

Even if you cannot change the other person's behavior, you can resolve, ahead of time, to remain disengaged from the usual kinds of arguments or conversations you get pulled into at such events. Unless heated debate energizes and amuses you, my two pieces of advice for dealing with difficult people at the holidays are

1. Don't engage.
2. Don't engage.

You can be polite to dear Uncle Whatsit, ask him about the cousins or how he's spending his time these days. But if he tries to lure you into a potentially explosive conversation or another source of holiday drama, feel free to say you're needed in the kitchen or offer to bring him a cup of tea.

Who pushes your buttons at family gatherings? Can you think of a respectful way to keep from repeating old, hurtful patterns?

Those Who Serve

Thankfulness is the tune of angels.
—Edmund Spenser

My friend William is single and travels for work much of the year. While we were out to dinner with William and a few mutual friends last month, my husband, David, mentioned that he'd over-tipped the housekeeper at the last hotel he stayed in when he couldn't find change for a twenty.

"You tip housekeeping?" William asked. "That never occurred to me." Everyone at the table gave him a hard time. Given all the hotel stays he's made over the past few years, someone suggested that he owed thousands of dollars.

"But how could I have known?" William asked.

"My general rule of thumb," another friend said. "Is that if a person is doing a job for me that I wouldn't want to do for someone else, I leave a tip."

"You tip your proctologist?" David joked.

"No! I only tip people who likely aren't paid enough—or if theirs is work that usually goes unnoticed," he explained.

During the holidays, express your gratitude to the people who are providing services to you that you might not want to do for anyone else; give larger tips than usual, mention good service to their supervisors, or even send a note expressing your thanks for their good work.

Who are the people who serve you or make your life more pleasant? How can you give them special thanks this month?

November 22

Expressing Thanks

O Lord, that lends me life,
Lend me a heart replete with thankfulness!
—William Shakespeare, *King Henry VI*

This afternoon, as I tidied up the kitchen, my daughters played a game of chess at the kitchen table. I was pleased; I haven't seen the chessboard out for what seems like years. As we chatted and they played, I noticed that the light outside had changed.

The sun was setting, the sky a beautiful pink. "Oh, look, girls," I said. "Come look at this sunset."

They pushed back their chairs, hurried over, and took a cursory look. "Nice," one said, sitting back down.

"Yeah. Pretty," said the other.

"I'm grateful for it," I said. "I'm so grateful to see those gorgeous colors in the sky. The pinks and oranges are like sherbet. Do you think God's in a show-offy mood today?" They laughed and continued their game.

Developing a habit of frequently expressing thanks helps me deepen a sense of gratitude. Talking to my children about beautiful sunsets or delicious meals or our warm house on a cold autumn day are other ways to help set them on a path toward lifelong gratitude.

In what ways do you model gratitude for your children?

Noting Affirmations

Angry people are not always wise.
—Jane Austen, *Pride and Prejudice*

Several years ago, I admitted to my spiritual director that the trolls were getting to me. *Trolls*, if you're not familiar with the term, refers to people who post hostile, confrontational, and otherwise insulting comments in response to online articles on blogs and websites.

If I wrote about my faith, the trolls would accuse me of being too religious—or not religious enough. When I wrote about parenting, they denounced me as an inept mother.

"Hmmm," said my spiritual director. "So, on your last article, about how many negative comments did you receive?"

"One or two," I said. "But they were truly malicious."

"Were there any positive responses?"

"Oh, yeah, maybe a dozen."

She asked me what the people who had liked my article had said, but I couldn't remember. I had to stop "ruminating" about the nasty comments, she said, even though our brains are hardwired to focus on criticism over approval. My homework was to write down every word of encouragement and praise I received in the coming week.

What floored me, truly, was how many affirming things my husband, kids, friends, and even online readers were saying. Having to write them down, literally "note" them, helped me put the negative comments into proper perspective.

People are grateful for you; this week, write down all the good things people say to you.

Charming Gardeners

Let us be grateful to the people who make us happy; they are the charming gardeners who make our souls blossom.

—Marcel Proust

Our family first spent Thanksgiving with my friend Brie and her family six years ago. Since then, it's been an annual tradition. Brie is one of my best friends and had, that year, married an old college friend of ours, Jarod. Jarod has two sons from a previous marriage. That Thanksgiving was the first time his kids met mine.

We hoped they'd get along, but indeed there was nothing to fear. Justin, the four-year-old, immediately fell in love with my son Theo, the way younger kids idolize older ones. He followed him around, would only eat what twelve-year-old Theo ate, and was his constant companion. Theo, I think, was flattered.

Before Thanksgiving dinner, adults and children gathered to make "thankfulness trees" on which we attached leaves that listed all the things for which we were grateful.

Justin, of course, was sitting beside Theo, and as we all got to work, pencil in hand, he asked, "Theo? How do you spell 'Theo'?" It was one of the sweetest expressions of gratitude I think I'll ever hear.

How do you make expressing gratitude part of your Thanksgiving tradition?

Signs of Growth

If you stand in the meat section at the grocery store long enough,
you start to get mad at turkeys. There's turkey ham, turkey
bologna, turkey pastrami. Someone needs to tell the turkey, "Man,
just be yourself."
—Mitch Hedberg

In a month full of exercises intended to deepen our experience of gratitude, let's take time to list what we best like about ourselves.

Here are a few of mine to help you get started:

I like that I'm a good listener.

I like how quickly I can get tedious tasks done well. (I can fold a mountain of laundry faster than a speeding locomotive.)

I like my sense of humor, and I like that I can laugh at myself.

I like that I'm patient. (Most of the time.)

I like that as the years pass, I ruminate about my flaws less and less.

Now it's your turn. What signs of growth have you seen in your own life this past year? What kinds of compliments do you receive? Are you a good cook? Are you organized? Good at crafts? Quick to laugh? Hardworking? Trustworthy?

Be grateful for your good qualities; write at least five of them
down today.

November 26
Every Single Day

Gratitude . . . is proof that we are attributing to God alone all that we have.

—St. Catherine of Siena

This month, we've cataloged some of the favorable consequences of living grateful lives, such as positive effects on health and relationships.

We've established that gratitude is not a magic trick, and that we can't bully ourselves—or others—into feeling it. We understand that true thankfulness is often the result of some perspective-bringing life event or tragedy that we haven't, and never would have, chosen.

And we've agreed that sometimes when we're feeling numb, broken, or otherwise distressed, the best we can do is go through the motions and be diligent about frequently speaking the words "Thank you."

My friend Marion sums it up: "To get good at gratitude, we have to practice. It takes being intentional about it. Every single day."

Marion speaks from experience. A young mother of two, she has spent both of her pregnancies suffering from a condition called hyperemesis gravidarum, a severe, and rare, form of morning sickness. Untreated, it can cause dehydration and malnutrition. Although Marion takes medication that lessens her nausea, her pregnancies haven't been easy.

And yet she is truly one of the most grateful people I know—ever expressing thanks for God's gifts, including her beautiful children.

Who is a model of gratitude for you?

Celebrating Sacramentally

You are my God, and I will give thanks to you; you are my God; I will extol you. Oh give thanks to the Lord, for he is good; for his steadfast love endures forever!
—Psalm 118:28–29 ESV

On Thanksgiving Day, we gather around a table with the people we love, give voice to our gratitude, and share a special meal. The rituals we perform as well as the food we eat are layered with meaning. Using a recipe created by a grandmother who passed away years ago makes a pecan pie much more than dessert. It evokes her spirit, and you feel close to her again.

These elements—a congregation, a table, familiar rites, prayer, and even eating the food that has been presented to us—echo the Eucharist. The word itself comes from the Greek term *eukaristein*, which literally means "to give thanks." We reflect God's loving care as we embrace the friends and family we may rarely see. As we receive gifts of good food, companionship, love, and laughter; we illustrate God's grace to one another.

This Thanksgiving, observe how the sacraments resonate through your celebration and remember that all of us are cherished members of the family of God.

In what ways is God's grace revealed in your celebrations?

Real Treasures

We can only be said to be alive in those moments when our hearts are conscious of our treasure.
—Thornton Wilder, *Our Town*

Thanksgiving, the most significant family holiday of the year, has been turned into a shopping holiday. It seems truly sinister to me. Not only has a day that has been dedicated to appreciating what we have become distorted into one for buying more of what we don't need, but more people must now work that day, losing the opportunity to focus on their blessings. Instead of "We give thanks!" the new message is "I want more!"

Shopping on Thanksgiving Day reveals that we, as a culture, most treasure the stuff we own. And isn't that the antithesis of the Christian message?

If we are to love others as much as we love ourselves, how can we ask people who work (often minimum-wage) jobs to give up one of their only universal vacation days so we can buy things? If we are to love God above all things, why would we distort a day that's organized around gratitude into a day about chasing after more "stuff"?

As people of faith who seek to detach ourselves from material things and grow to be more like God, we can opt out. I will; I hope you will, too.

Consider writing a letter to executives at department stores or hypermarts, expressing your displeasure with their Thanksgiving hours.

Winter Blahs

One kind word can warm three winter months.
—Japanese proverb

As I mentioned a few months ago, the two seasons we enjoy in Chicagoland are winter and road construction.

Currently, we are entering the first of the two. Many of us will experience low-level irritability, we're told. As it does perennially, the local news broadcasts warn that the "winter blahs" can progress into SAD, seasonal affective disorder, and potentially full-on depression. Fun, right?

My friends and I deal with the challenges of the season variously. Some increase their exposure to light on the blue-green end of the spectrum by using home "light boxes." Others escape to warmer climates at least once in the wintertime. I tend to stock up on firewood and hot chocolate and hunker down for a few months.

My friend Jen cultivates gratitude and keeps her friends' spirits up by writing daily PWTs, or positive weather thoughts:

PWT: At least all this rain isn't snow!

PWT: Who cares about the temps outside? I'm going to the Lady Antebellum concert tonight.

PWT: Sunshine. Sunshine. Sunshine.

PWT: Today is glorious! The sun feels awesome. Who knew forty degrees could feel so fabulous?

~

Do cold weather and low light affect your mood? How can you express gratitude about elements of the weather where you are?

Family Gratitude

Why, who makes much of a miracle?
As to me I know of nothing else but miracles . . .
—Walt Whitman, *Leaves of Grass*

How was your gratitude journey this month?

You might be surprised by today's exercise, given the ambivalence I've expressed about gratitude journals, but I want you to start one. This one, however, will have a twist. Instead of privately recording notes about the people, events, answered prayers, or things for which we are most grateful, let's make it a family affair.

Invite everyone who lives in your home to contribute. Leave the journal (or notepad or clipboard) in a central place—perhaps on a kitchen counter or in a shared workspace. Model for your children what sorts of things you'd like them to record: new friendships, your dog's smile, the way the sun makes the top layer of snow shine like glitter, a candy cane.

As you move into a time of year that can stir up ingratitude in your children, help your kids stay focused on all the blessings they have, right now, right in front of them. And stay focused yourself, in the whirl of the next few weeks, on all the good gifts you receive every single day.

Start your family gratitude journal today. Every week or two, invite
children to share what they've written. Not only will your family
remain more thankful, but the book will also serve as a wonderful
reminder of this time in your lives.

December

Practice Waiting on God

During Advent, Be Awake to Divine Mysteries

Advent

advent

an arrival or coming, esp. one which is awaited, the liturgical
season including the four Sundays preceding Christmas
—Merriam-Webster Dictionary

The word *advent* comes from the Latin *adventus,* meaning
"arrival." Advent is the liturgical season in which we await the coming of Christ. You might not have noticed it much before; it com-
petes with school concerts, holiday parties, and cookie swaps.

When Advent is over on December 25, we are markedly freer to
nestle in and enjoy celebrating with family and close friends. But
by then, we most likely feel wrung out by all that's come before.
(But that's not Advent's fault.)

Many of us swear, every single year, that we'll "do" Christmas
differently. We'll spend less money. We'll create new traditions
with our families. Maybe we'll even take time to reflect on the mysterious gift of the Incarnation.

It's a challenge, though. The minute we turn the calendar page
to December, it's as though a starting pistol has been fired and we
are racing toward December 25. We feel obligated to do a hundred
things: decorate the tree, shop for presents, send cards, bake cookies. Even when our very best intentions are to celebrate more simply, we find ourselves submerged in details and receipts.

What are your hopes for this Advent and Christmas season? Name
three adjectives that best describe those hopes.

December 2

Go for It

Maybe Christmas, [the Grinch] thought, doesn't come from a store.
—Dr. Seuss, *How the Grinch Stole Christmas*

I hope you weren't expecting that I'd share a secret plan that would—*poof!*—vanquish your stress and provide instant serenity to your household. (Perhaps with the snap of your fingers, you could even get Bing Crosby softly crooning "White Christmas" in the background.) Sorry, that's not one of my superpowers.

What we do have ahead of us in this month's reflections are opportunities to

Discern which traditions mean the most to us and to our kids (and purge the rest)

Reflect on what it means to wait

Prepare spiritually for a more wholehearted celebration of Christ's birth

Let's start by thinking about which traditions are most meaningful to you. Do you love choosing—or, if you're crafty, producing—a Christmas card, writing notes, and getting them addressed and stamped? If so, then go for it. If the thought of sending cards makes you want to crawl under the covers, skip it. The same goes for baking cookies, hosting a party, making gingerbread houses, and so on.

This year, opt out of what you and your family don't truly enjoy.

Ask your kids to identify their favorite Christmas traditions. Jot them down, along with your own. If you're invited to participate in something that's not on the list, then politely decline.

O Christmas Tree

I will honor Christmas in my heart, and try to keep it all the year.
—Charles Dickens, *A Christmas Carol*

One of my favorite traditions is heading out to the country with my family and chopping down our Christmas tree.

Yes, better waiters than me—Advent aficionados—postpone buying and decorating their trees until Christmas Eve. ("It's a Christmas tree, not an Advent tree," I was once told, with no small measure of reproach.)

But I like driving out in early December to one of the Christmas-tree farms in northern Illinois. Their cheery flyers promise hot chocolate and Christmas carols. Some even have horse-drawn carriages. Festive!

The reality, however, can be grimmer. Our ninety-minute journey west has often taken twice that long because of winter storms. One year we arrived after dark to find all the farms closed. We turned around and bought a precut tree two minutes from home.

This past Christmas may go down as my favorite tree misadventure. After navigating a bad storm, we arrived almost at closing to find that the only trees left were twenty-five feet high or taller. (The owners were transitioning out of the business.) Thanks to a helpful college student, we were able to stand on a vehicle and cut one down. The stump was much taller than any one of us.

But, oh, it made a lovely Christmas tree.

What are your favorite Christmas traditions and misadventures?

December 4

Christ before Me

Christ be with me, Christ within me,
Christ behind me, Christ before me,
Christ beside me, Christ to win me,
Christ to comfort and restore me.
Christ beneath me, Christ above me,
Christ in quiet, Christ in danger,
Christ in hearts of all that love me,
Christ in mouth of friend and stranger.

—St. Patrick

Advent invites us to take a break from twinkly lights and sugar cookies and contemplate the coming of Immanuel, which means "God with us."

The author of Hebrews wrote, "In the past God spoke to our ancestors through the prophets at many times and in various ways, but in these last days he has spoken to us by his Son, whom he appointed heir of all things, and through whom also he made the universe."

Through whom he made the universe. What?

"The Son is the radiance of God's glory and the exact representation of his being. . . . After he had provided purification for sins, he sat down at the right hand of the Majesty in heaven" (Hebrews 1:1–3, NIV).

So, before Christ, God was revealed in miracles; but in the Incarnation, God was revealed in a person, Jesus Christ. And they made the universe together?

What does the Incarnation mean to you? How would you explain it to a child?

December 5

Advent Traditions

Tradition is a guide and not a jailer.
—W. Somerset Maugham, *The Summing Up*

Although we can't expect our kids suddenly to become captivated by Messianic prophecy, we can test-drive a few traditions to introduce Advent to them in an appealing way.

Consider purchasing *The Advent Book*, by Jack and Kathy Stockman. We've used it with our family since the kids were tiny. It is similar to an Advent calendar, but in book format. Twenty-five doors (for use from the beginning of December through Christmas) open to pictures and text of the nativity story.

Another option is to allow your children to play with your nativity set, or buy an indestructible one. Yes, you might find Lego figures in the manger or Batman riding a camel, but the easy familiarity they'll enjoy will help make the story of the Incarnation feel more accessible to them.

You could also create a weekly Advent dinner. Because our regular family nights are on Sundays, that day works for us. Try to find an evening when everyone's home, and begin early enough that you won't be rushed. During these dinners, you can light Advent wreaths, read about the nativity story, or—as your children get older—discuss what the Incarnation means to them.

How else might you more deliberately observe Advent in the weeks leading up to Christmas?

December 6

On Tenterhooks

As selfishness and complaint pervert the mind, so love with its joy clears and sharpens the vision.
—Helen Keller

I have a dear friend whose preferred mode of correspondence is the postcard. He attaches images to blank cards: vintage photos of celebrities, landmarks, and other curiosities. On the back, he adds the date and the city from which it's been sent.

A few years ago, he sent my daughter a card from London. On one side, a picture of punk rockers. On the other, a note that read: "Jesus, Mary, and Joseph, this city is glorious! Just like you!"

Often, he sends the card from his home in Chicago: "Long weekend approaches. Our place? Must see you and family soon. On tenterhooks." Receiving such an invitation, I mail back a postcard with proposed dates. He replies again, and back and forth we go until the plan is set.

Waiting for his response truly puts me "on tenterhooks"; I look forward to receiving his cards and getting the event squared away on the calendar. Normally, I get antsy when someone takes a day to respond to texts or an email, but I enjoy these exchanges and know that anticipation can result in making our times together all the sweeter.

In Advent, we wait on tenterhooks for the joy—"Jesus, Mary, and Joseph!"—that is to come.

Are you comfortable being made to wait? What does waiting show you about yourself or your expectations?

Bustle-Free Christmas

"Bah!" said Scrooge, "Humbug."
—Charles Dickens

A friend of mine laughingly describes herself as a Scrooge who doesn't enjoy the fuss and frills of Christmas. She says she's relieved that her kids are older now because the only Christmas presents they want are gift cards. "I can stop by a drugstore and boom, boom, boom," she said. "And then I'm pretty much done."

The same friend puts in an order for twenty identical boxes of toffee from a neighbor's business in late November, and when the candy is delivered—each box tied with a festive red ribbon—she stacks it in the pantry and gives it to teachers, crossing guards, and as secret-Santa presents all season long.

"Oh, and I absolutely refuse to host anything in November or December," she said. "But if I really want to see friends, I tell them to come over and we'll order Thai food."

You can bet she doesn't do Christmas cards, feels no compulsion to decorate gingerbread houses, and even decides—before invitations start coming in—how many holiday parties she'll attend. Once her quota is met, she starts saying no.

Don't you love her practicality?

⌒

Is there anything you could cut from your usual list of Christmas preparations?

What Kids Want

Our hearts grow tender with childhood memories and love of kindred, and we are better throughout the year for having, in spirit, become a child again at Christmas-time.

—Laura Ingalls Wilder

I admire my friend who maintains such well-defined boundaries at Christmastime. She dislikes baking, so she doesn't do it. Too many nights out deplete her, so she attends only one or two holiday parties a year.

She's free, then, to stay home, spend time with her children, and relax. It's nice to see; they clearly savor one another's company.

In their book *Unplug the Christmas Machine*, Jo Robinson and Jean Coppock Staeheli say that the four things kids really want for Christmas are

1. Relaxed and loving time with their families

2. Realistic expectations about gifts

3. An evenly paced holiday season

4. Reliable family traditions

Somehow, if you're like me, you think kids must want much more than that. Electronics, maybe? To travel someplace great? A car when they turn sixteen? We can get in a trap, fearing that somehow we haven't given our children enough when, all along, the things they most want are right in front of us.

And they don't have to cost a dime.

Of the list here, which of the four things kids "really want" might be most important to your own children?

Christmas Letters

I don't like green Christmases. They're not green—they're just nasty faded browns and grays.
—L. M. Montgomery, *Anne of Green Gables*

Insomnia, cracked heels, the fifteen pounds we can't seem to lose, marital troubles, that colonoscopy we had last month, our child's bad grades or bed-wetting problem, the list of goals we fail to meet, year after year after year.

As much as these might define certain moments in our lives, they are never mentioned in our Christmas letters. They don't fit into the compressed, relentlessly chipper versions of our lives that we put forward.

Although it's a pleasure to recount one's blessings—to describe, for instance, our children's particular charms or talents, or the satisfaction we get from our work, or stories about that trip we took last summer—it's a shame we can't come clean about what hurts, what embarrasses us, or where we could use someone's help.

But still, newsletters serve a different purpose; if nothing else, they can function as a sort of annual journal entry. Their contents may be limited in scope and depth, but they remind us of the big events and small details we otherwise may have forgotten.

Looking back over the year, what are three of the high points you'd share if you were sending a family newsletter?

Snow

*Advice is like snow—the softer it falls, the longer it dwells upon,
and the deeper it sinks into, the mind.*
—Samuel Taylor Coleridge

It snowed last night, and this morning the world is changed. Snow covers everything, whitewashes the trunk of the birch tree outside, and carefully dusts each of its tiniest branches. I can't wait for the children to wake up and discover it.

As a snowplow scrapes by outside, I realize I'm eager for my kids to awaken to Advent as well, to the idea of holy waiting and that, in the birth of Christ, God's ancient promises are fulfilled.

"I will walk among you and be your God, and you will be my people," God says in the Hebrew Scriptures (Leviticus 26:12, NIV).

Then, hundreds and hundreds of years later, he does.

My kids bristle—I bristle—at being made to wait in ten-minute lines at the movie theater or grocery store. But a thousand years? How do we cling to faith when God has been silent for a long time, when we're waiting? How can I expect my children to grab hold of all the meaning in this quiet season when I am just waking up to it myself?

What do you do when you are waiting on God?

December 11

Approaching the Mystery

Carrying my babies was a marvelous mystery, lives growing unseen
except by the slow swelling of my belly. Death is an even greater
mystery. . . . The God I cry out to in anguish or joy can neither be
proved nor disapproved. The hope I have that death is not the
end . . . can neither be proved nor disproved.
—Madeleine L'Engle

Some years, during Advent, the concreteness of the nativity story—how normal, how tangible it is—draws me in. The awkward unease of late pregnancy. The human need for shelter and rest. Straw, wood, pieces of cloth. The scent of barn animals. A newborn baby's cry.

But this year, it's the swirl of mystery that hovers above and through the narrative that most captures my imagination. In an Advent homily, my priest quoted a theologian who said that thinking about God is like trying to draw a picture of a bird in flight.

"You end up with details of its wings caught in a certain position, feathers, eyes, claws frozen in place for careful scrutiny," he explained. "Or you end up with a blur that loses all detail, but captures speed and movement."

We're all theologians, he said, and we all envision various concepts of God in detail and others in motion. Do we choose one picture over another, or somehow hold both in tension?

I realize sometimes the "bird" I picture when I think of God is a faraway dot, flying high in the sky. At other times, it's just outside my window, allowing me to appreciate the details of its feathers and the angles of its tiny beak before it flies away.

⌒

Do either of these ways of describing the study of God mean more to
you than the other? A bird in motion? A high-definition photograph?

Know It All

Every sentence I utter must be understood not as an affirmation,
but as a question.
—Niels Bohr

Many years ago as we cleaned up after a dinner party, a college friend and I debriefed about the evening. She's a fluent Spanish speaker and referred to one of the people who had been there as a *sabelotodo*, a know-it-all.

It was true; one guest had monopolized the conversation, interrupted others when they tried to contribute, and seemed to think himself the most knowledgeable person in the room on everything from the best way to get to the airport to international relations to the correct way to pronounce the word *bruschetta*.

I never want to behave like a *sabelotodo*, blindly certain about my expertise, failing to listen to the ideas or opinions of others. I want to remain open and accept that part of being a person of faith is to reside in "in-between" places where there are often more questions than answers.

I want to remember that the conversation is much, much bigger than I am.

Are you comfortable living with questions about what you know to be true, about your faith, or about who you are? Do you find yourself wishing it all was easier to discern?

December 13

Doing Good

*Now you, my brothers and sisters, are the eyes through which
Christ's compassion is to look out upon this world, and yours are
the lips through which His love is to speak; yours are the hands
with which He is to bless men, and yours the feet with which He is
to go about doing good.*
—Mark Guy Pearse

The tree is lit, festive music plays. We bring in the mail and, ten minutes later, find ourselves still standing in the doorway in our coats and boots, grinning stupidly at pictures and news of faraway friends.

Of course, some years it's easier for us to be merry than others, but we know that having our basic needs met situates us among the most fortunate people in the world. And all around us are reminders that it's not all jingle bells and sugar cookies for people in our own communities. Schools collect coats and gloves for those who cannot afford them. Boxes wait at the entrances and exits of grocery stores, inviting us to drop something in for those who are hungry and cannot buy food.

The Bible passage that challenges (and inspires) me most is known as the parable of the sheep and the goats. Christ says, "I was hungry and you gave me food, I was thirsty and you gave me drink, I was a stranger and you welcomed me" (Matthew 25:35–36, ESV). He said that if we feed or clothe or console someone else, we truly comfort him and meet his needs.

*Are you more motivated to reach out to others when you know that
the hungry or lonely or shivering person you serve is Christ?*

Bleak Midwinter

In the bleak midwinter, frosty wind made moan,
Earth stood hard as iron, water like a stone;
Snow had fallen, snow on snow, snow on snow,
In the bleak midwinter, long ago.

—Christina Rossetti

Very close to Christmas, my family and I go to a funeral to offer our prayers and to stand in solidarity with a family who has lost a treasured husband and father. At church, every pew is packed. Some of us sit in Our Lady's Chapel, facing the wrong direction, our eyes fixed on the crucifix.

The service includes recollections from friends of the deceased who say his signature refrain was "We're lucky men." Our priest reminds us that someday the Scriptures we've read this morning will make more sense to us, but for now many of us will simply feel numb.

Afterward, there is a reception in the parish hall. We watch slides from this man's life. We pick at cheese cubes, sandwich triangles, and clusters of grapes. We embrace the widow. These rituals give us something to do; nothing could mitigate the family's grief today.

Before leaving for home, my daughters and I return to the chapel and light candles for the man who is now absent from our church community, from his friends, from his family.

We are in Advent. We grieve, and we wait.

How can Christ's coming be a comfort to us when we grieve?

Nostalgia

Remembrance of things past is not necessarily the remembrance of things as they were.
—Marcel Proust

In my late twenties, it seemed that every time I turned around, another friend was getting married. There were gift registries to navigate and parties to plan. Baby shower invitations arrived next, and before I knew it, I was chipping in for strollers and had a stack of birth announcements in my desk drawer.

Sadly, a decade or so later, news of separations and divorces began to arrive.

I'm in that season right now—no, not getting divorced, thankfully—but journeying with others through divorce and second marriages. I witness the heartache. I see what it takes to create child custody plans. And then, often, I watch as happiness envelops my friends when they risk and fall in love again.

But even in happy second marriages—full of romance, relief, and solid partnership—many spouses still sometimes long for what life was like before. It's not that they want to go back to being unhappy or taken for granted, but they long for what seems, in retrospect, a less complicated time.

They say there was just something about that original family unit: mom, dad, kids all together. They miss it from time to time.

Have you witnessed an intersection of hope, healing, and loss in your own life, or in the lives of friends?

Good Shepherd

I am the good shepherd. I know my own and my own know
me. . . . And I have other sheep that are not of this fold. I must
bring them also, and they will listen to my voice. So there will be
one flock, one shepherd.
—John 10:14–16 ESV

As a child, I knew just what Christ looked like: his picture was on my *Children's Living Bible*. The illustration showed Jesus the shepherd gently holding a little lamb as he navigated a rocky cliff. I knew that I was that lamb; he, my shepherd.

Later, the idea of shepherds seemed strange to me. I went through periods, and still do, when I wasn't quite sure whether I was more like a protected member of the flock or just forgotten and lost somewhere. "How could Christ be my shepherd when I feel like this? I don't see any 'pastures green' where he's led me. I just feel tired and alone. Maybe especially spiritually."

I've felt like giving up, but I've become less likely to have that kind of spiritual crisis as I grow older. I am much more mistrustful of my feelings, aware of the way they can trick and mislead me. And I have more faith in a good God.

I suppose I've learned, in tiny increments, something about trust.

What's your experience of trusting God right now? Does being in a difficult place make you rely on God more, or feel less trust in God?

Figuring It Out on Their Own

Some day you will be old enough to start reading fairy tales again.
—C. S. Lewis

One snowy morning recently, I felt a longing for my children to wake up—and not just so they'd get to appreciate that new, deep blanket of white. I yearned for them to somehow awaken to Advent itself and to breathe in its richness and mystery.

This, by the way, is a mistake I make again and again as a mother. I think I can talk my kids into understanding truths that, for better or worse, they have to learn on their own and by means of firsthand experiences.

I'm not quite this bad, but picture my twelve-year old daughter asking to walk to the library. Before she knows it, I'm lecturing her about a cross-country road trip she might make someday. I tell her that it's efficient to purchase an electronic pass so that she won't need to stop for tolls. I remind her to drive defensively. She has no idea what I'm talking about—all she wanted was to walk to the library. But my brain jumps ahead, trying to prepare her for the future and save her trouble later.

I know I can't prepare my kids for everything, can't get them to skip over their own trial-and-error journeys. They won't give serious thought to this broody season of Advent until they're ready, and they do.

⌒

When are you tempted to try to impart knowledge or insights to your children that they need to figure out on their own?

Happiness and Joy

I sometimes wonder whether all pleasures are not
substitutes for Joy.
—C. S. Lewis

We often use the words *happy* and *joy* as though they were indistin-guishable from each other, but that doesn't feel right, does it? You can certainly see the family resemblance, and both can really make us smile, but identical twins, they are not.

Happy's the younger, flightier sister. Joy has excellent posture and plays piano; she can be a bit intimidating. Happy, meanwhile, messes around on a kazoo and is very fond of stickers and the color yellow. *Joy* is embroidered on wall hangings; *Happy* is written in frosting on birthday cakes. Joy is Handel's *Messiah* (her best friend, of course, is Gloria), and Happy is the birthday song or a warm puppy. You get the point.

I'm happy when I'm experiencing something delicious or fun or lucky. But my happiness evaporates when that thing goes away. Joy, however, is what I grow into, the more unattached I become to all the things that can make me happy. Joy is a strength, and if I possess it, it doesn't go away in difficult times.

Happy is conditional and has a codependent relationship with expectation; Joy is more independent; she smiles and says, "Nevertheless."

(And let's leave Merry out of this, okay?)

How do you describe the difference between happiness and joy?

Hate and Indifference

It takes courage to grow up and become who you really are.
—e.e. cummings

This winter, my daughters have been playing board games at the kitchen table, begging to go out for hot chocolate and soy lattes, and snuggling up next to each other under a blanket to watch movies. For the past few years, they've said they're best friends.

It makes me happy to see them get along so well. And yes, I mean "happy"; when they bicker, that good feeling goes *poof.*

When they were younger, they fought more. After a shouting match, sometimes one of them would come to me and say, "She hates me." I always had the same response—and always hoped that what I was saying was true: "No, she doesn't. Remember what I told you?" I'd ask. "What's the opposite of love?"

"Indifference?"

"Right, which means a person doesn't care. So if you two are fighting like that, it shows you both care. You're connected. You're not indifferent."

I think I was right after all. I just had to wait until they grew up a bit.

For what or whom do you have indifference?

God's Time

To you, a thousand years is like the passing of a day, or like a few hours in the night.
—Psalm 90:4 NCV

The psalmist says that in God's experience a thousand years feels like a day.

A three-day cold, for me, feels like a month of misery. Or, for my youngest, hearing that it's still five days until Christmas is like saying she can't open presents until she's forty. When my oldest was waiting to hear which colleges had accepted him, three months felt like a year to him. But of course, those chunks of time can't be compared to a thousand years. (The High Middle Ages were a thousand years ago! Leif Eriksson was still around!)

Truth is, we can't imagine what experiencing a thousand years would feel like. We don't really have words to describe what a decade "feels like." Those units are too big for us to wrap our minds around, and we all experience the passage of time differently.

The older we get, the faster time seems to pass. The Creator is eternal, so it's no wonder that God's experience of time is that it goes by so quickly.

How are you and your children doing this Advent in terms of waiting for Christmas? Is December's passing "like a thousand years" for your kids?

December 21

Waiting on God

Waiting on God requires the willingness to bear uncertainty, to carry within oneself the unanswered question, lifting the heart to God about it whenever it intrudes upon one's thoughts.
—Elisabeth Elliot

Although it happened more than ten years ago, waiting for my daughter Mia's adoption to be finalized still reigns supreme as the most agonizing "felt like a thousand years" waiting period in my life. It wasn't so obscenely long, actually; she came home about nine months after we began the adoption process.

But it felt long. I think, mostly, it was the uncertainty of the situation. I worried about whether Guatemala's international adoption program would end, putting our case on permanent hold. (Sadly, this did happen for some families who were in the process at the same time we were.)

I worried that she might become sick and not have adequate care. I worried that, the older she got, the harder it would be for her to transition into her new life with us—the longer it would be for us to become truly family.

I went in cycles in terms of my ability or inability to trust God. Sometimes I knew he was with us like I know my own name; at other times I wondered if God was there at all.

And had I reflected on the "to God, a thousand years is like a day" idea, I would have resented that God could be so cavalier about time when I was going through that excruciating wait.

Think of the hardest waiting period in your life. What were you waiting for?

With Child

*Instead of wishing away nine months of pregnancy and
complaining about the shadow over my feet, I'd have cherished
every minute of it and realized that the wonderment growing
inside me was the only chance in life to assist God in a miracle.*

—Erma Bombeck

"What are you working on?" I ask my daughter. She's bent over a drawing, working carefully, methodically.

"It's for a book for Mrs. W.," she says. "She's having a baby. My class is making a book. We're supposed to give her advice about what to do with the baby."

"What's your advice?"

"To laugh together every day," she answers, continuing to color.

"Like we do," I say.

"Yep. Like we do."

"What's Mrs. W. going to have? Do you know?"

"A girl."

Suddenly I feel a pang of regret for how quickly my daughter's childhood is zooming past me. We do laugh together every day. Since she was a baby, I've prided myself on knowing exactly where to tickle her, exactly what face to make or what silly little phrase to speak to get her to giggle.

When the pang passes, I know that, moment by moment, I'm doing what I'm supposed to do: being present in the present.

*You may already miss your child's babyhood. Is there a way you can
enjoy him or her today?*

Gift of God

God is a God of the present. God is always in the moment, be that moment hard or easy, joyful or painful.
—Henri Nouwen

After my son Theo was born, I felt what can best be described as elation.

I was flooded with gratitude and chose his name, Theodore ("gift of God"), deliberately, so that every day I would be expressing thanks. Leaving the hospital a few days after his birth, I half expected the streets to be lined with well-wishers. Human history had changed: this beautiful child was here!

During my first few weeks of motherhood, I found myself smitten also with all the other mothers I would see. Even the most cranky, ungrateful, "yank your toddler by the elbow through the grocery store while barking unpleasantly at your kids" mom made me swoon. I didn't mind her faults—she was a mom, just like me. Aren't mothers awesome?

Soon this infatuation passed—maybe my new sleep-deprived state had taken the wind out of those sails—but it surged again during Advent when Theo was about eight months old. Sitting in church that December, hearing the nativity story, it was as though I'd never before comprehended it. She gave birth where?

I wondered what Mary felt after her son was born. Tired, yes. Homesick, probably.

But human history had changed! This precious child was here.

How did becoming a mother affect the way you hear and understand the nativity story?

Just You Wait

The universe is full of magical things patiently waiting for our wits to grow sharper.
—Eden Phillpotts

Maybe Mary felt the way we do when we've bought our child a wonderful surprise and we're waiting for the right time, his birthday maybe, to give it to him. Every time you see him sitting at the table doing homework or absently looking out the window, your heart skips. You know how happy he'll be when it's finally time to give him the gift.

Maybe Mary felt that way about all of us. She had just brought the most wonderful gift to everyone in the whole wide world—everyone who ever lived, or would. When she saw people passing by behind the stable's open doors, maybe she shivered or let out a giddy laugh.

Maybe Joseph heard it. Maybe he dismissed it as the giggle of a teenager. "Oh, Mary. Geez," he may have said with a sigh. "Can you keep it down? I'm trying to get a little sleep here. Not everyone got to ride the donkey all the way out here."

But Mary was smiling. *Just you wait*, she thought. *Just you wait.*

Can you imagine what Mary and Joseph's conversations were after Christ's birth?

Truth Is a Relationship

Truth, according to the Christian faith, is God's love for us in Jesus Christ. Therefore, truth is a relationship.
—Pope Francis

Every year, right around Thanksgiving, utility trucks appear on the streets of our downtown. Workers string white lights—thousands and thousands of them—in the trees in preparation for Christmas.

I've always wished that they'd leave them up all year, or all winter, anyway. Ever since my children were very little, whenever we would drive through town this time of year, we have broken into a chant, celebrating the effect that the lights have on dark winter nights. *Such pretty lights! Such pretty lights! Such pretty lights!*

Tonight the sidewalks around town will be nearly empty when we drive past on our way home from a family dinner. The lights will sparkle, reminding us of the one who called himself the Light of the World and who asked us, too, to "let our lights shine."

May yours be a most happy—and joyful—Christmas as you carry the gift of Christ's light out into the world.

Wishing you joy on Christmas!

Child of the Light

To love beauty is to see light.
—Victor Hugo

One of my favorite hymns is "I Want to Walk as a Child of the Light." I've heard it sung by a soloist (my husband sings it exquisitely) and by my own church congregation, and I have listened online to professional choirs performing it.

A few of my other favorite hymns include "Abide with Me" and "Good King Wenceslas" (yes, really!), but "I Want to Walk" has neither the gorgeous, angsty poetry of the former ("Abide with me; fast falls the eventide; / The darkness deepens; Lord, with me abide") nor the fairy-tale storytelling of the latter ("Page and monarch forth they went / Forth they went together / Through the rude wind's wild lament / And the bitter weather").

Nevertheless, "I Want to Walk" never fails to draw me in. I like the hymn's simplicity and unabashed focus on the "I" of the believer, who, singing it, admits to just taking reticent, hopeful steps toward Christ. Singing this hymn gives me permission to be a child of faith, excuses me from complex or controversial theological arguments, and lets me express what—at the very core of me—I desire.

Do you have a favorite hymn? Why does it affect you?

December 27
Advent Recap

Peace begins with a smile.
—Mother Teresa

As the tissue paper starts to settle, let's take a good, long look at what we'd like to repeat next December and what we might like to do differently. How would you answer the following questions? You can answer them here or in your journal.

In what ways did more fully participating in the season of Advent shift your focus this December?

Did a more intentional observation of Advent keep you "on tenterhooks" for Christmas?

What did you learn about waiting?

Did you have any new spiritual insights?

Did the recommendations from the authors of *Unplug the Christmas Machine* affect the way you interacted with your children?

What did you learn, if anything, about the difference between happiness and joy?

As you think about next year, the good news is that you don't have to do everything. You're simply invited to do what makes the most sense for you.

What would you name as the single practice that made the most sense for you and your family this Advent?

Taking Inventory

While you are proclaiming peace with your lips, be careful to have it even more fully in your heart.
—St. Francis of Assisi

You might feel as if you're in a kind of quiet twilight zone now that Christmas Day has come and gone.

Over the next few days, rest, if rest is what you need, or use days off to prepare for the new year. Listen to your body; if the thought of lying around in your pajamas makes your heart sing, do it! Or you might be in the mood to take inventory of the year and get a few projects done. If you are, then go for it.

Although the school year isn't really half over, we often think of Christmas break as the midway point of the academic year. Either way, between Christmas and New Year's Eve, take a little time with your family to reflect on the school year thus far.

Which morning routines work? Which don't? Are backpacks and coat closets cleaned out and straightened up? Are chores getting done? What meals haven't you prepared for a while that your family enjoys?

Talk it all out and consider how, for the second half of the school year, you and your kids can make your mornings and evenings run more smoothly. When school starts again, implement changes you've discussed together and enjoy that second half of the year.

Don't try to do everything at once. For starters, identify the one thing that has your name on it.

Hope Splashing

"Hope" is the thing with feathers—
That perches in the soul—
And sings the tune without the words—
And never stops—at all—
—Emily Dickinson

I was staring at the snowy slant of roof outside my window, day-dreaming at my desk when it arrived. It was sort of a waking dream; I felt as if a poem had gently landed in my mind. But it wasn't a poem; it was more like an explanation. I wrote it down, unaware of what, if anything, it would tell me.

"When we arrive, we're given a cup, a chalice," I wrote. "When we receive it, it's already filled with hope. We have to carry this cup wherever we go. We must keep it steady so it won't slosh and spill."

I continued writing: "Sometimes we walk paths that take us over green, mossy hills, dotted with red flowers. Boulders are scattered along these paths. When our feet knock against them, or when we step down awkwardly on uneven gravel, we spill a little hope."

And: "We stumble, and more hope splashes out of the cup; some people even fall down to their knees, and the cup empties entirely. But, every so often, we meet someone on the path whose cup is full, and they fill ours. We do the same for others. And so we go, splashing and emptying and filling and getting refilled."

At the top of the page, I wrote "Friendship."

What, or who, fills your cup of hope when you stumble or fall down?

December 30

Come See

The two disciples heard him and went after Jesus.
Jesus looked over his shoulder and said to them, "What are you
after?" They said, "Rabbi" (which means "Teacher"), "where are
you staying?"
He replied, "Come along and see for yourself."
—John 1:37–39 MSG

I guess when you are the Son of God, you don't panic when you think you're being followed. In this story from John, two men silently follow Jesus, until he turns around and says, "What are you after?" In other translations, Jesus says, "What do you want?" or "What do you wish?" or "What seek ye?"

When I first read the way the two men answered Jesus, I was confused. Jesus asks them what they are wishing for and, they respond, "Teacher, where are you staying?" Don't you think that's odd? I can think of some better answers. "I wish for peace." Or "I want to serve you." Or "I want to let go of this grief." Or "I want you to give me strength."

But "Where are you staying?" It's like if someone asked you about your dreams and you answered, "What did you have for lunch?"

In response, Jesus says, "Come see for yourself," and they do.

Now, I wonder whether "Where are you staying?" might have meant something like, "How much time have you got? I can't begin to tell you, in passing, what I wish for. Let's go talk at your place." Maybe their hearts were full of questions, as mine is, and they knew it would take a long time to untangle and express it all.

But Jesus is unperturbed and says, "Come along with me," and they walk alongside him and stay with him.

⌒

Today, what's the burden on your heart that you'd most like to unload on Jesus?

Beginning Again

Isn't it nice to think that tomorrow is a new day with no mistakes
in it yet?

—L. M. Montgomery, *Anne of Green Gables*

Thank you for making this journey with me this year through reflection, risk, and rest. I hope you feel more wholeheartedly yourself than when we began.

Take some time today to reflect on where you started and where you are today.

Say a prayer and ask God's forgiveness for the ways you've hurt others this year. You have. So have I. So has everyone we know.

Let go of the unforgiveness you hold toward others. Open your hands, let it go.

Let go of resentment for the ways life let you down this year. Maybe, after all, it was trying to do you a favor.

By making that fickle friend Happy disappear, maybe you'll get to know her big sister, Joy. I guarantee she'll be a better companion.

Forgive yourself for the times you let yourself down, were inauthentic, and clutched on to fear. You did the best you could. So did I. So did everyone we know.

Thank God for the good gifts of your life, even if your heart is strained right now and all you can do is say, "Thank you."

That's good enough.

Now, let's begin again—from scratch—tomorrow.

Acknowledgments

I'm grateful to the throng of friends, colleagues, and online connections with whom I spoke while writing this book. Your candid thoughts on body image, faith, parenting, forgiveness, and much more have brought richness to this book.

I'm grateful, too, for the support and companionship I receive as a member of a few superbly creative and life-giving groups of women: her.meneutics, INK: A Creative Collective, the OKJFC, and the Hive. You know who you are, and I hope you know what you mean to me.

Special thanks to Kelly Allison, Melinda Alston, Beth Andersen, Amy Julia Becker, Tricia Benich, Dale Hanson Bourke, Eileen Button, Robin Currie, Amy Hilbrich Davis, Ellen Painter Dollar, Becky Blue Dorf, Carolyn Ebner, Suzanne Ecklund, Tim Fall, Amy Hansfield, Rachel Klooster, Katy Low-Mangin, Angie Mabry-Nauta, Andrea McNaughton, Jennifer Merck, Andrea Nelson Le Roy, Jennifer Ochs, Rowena Palackdharry Rea, Sharon Parker Jackson, Catharine Phillips, Marlena Proper-Graves, Anthony Platipodis, Angela Raske, Susan Shorney, Vallari Talapatra, George Smith, Thaddaeus V. Smith, Karen Swallow Prior, Sarah Vanderveen, Michelle Van Loon, and Cara Whiting for the ways they contributed to this book and, always, for their generosity, wisdom, and good humor.

Thank you to my agent, Christopher Ferebee, and to Joe Durepos and team at Loyola Press.

Thank you to those who sustain me:

Sara Hendren, for being a genius sister-in-law and friend.

Kathy Treat, for being my heart friend, providing me space—mental and otherwise—to think and to write.

Margot Starbuck, for your big-heartedness, for all you did to sharpen my ideas and fix things here, and for talking me down a number of times by telling me I just needed more sleep.

Jenny Sheffer-Stevens, for laughter, roasted kale, and decades of friendship.

James Saba, for choosing my family as part of yours—can't imagine mine without you in it.

Caryn Rivadeneira for advocating for all things creepy, making me laugh, and patience.

Brilliant Susan Maynor, for brainstorming with me and for sharing her exquisite wisdom.

Keiko Feldman, for teaching me "Not My Dog"; being an early, reassuring reader of this material; and—even more than for caramel corn—for her friendship.

Thank you to Cathleen Falsani, for calming me when I'm in transition during the birth of my books and for her loyalty.

Oh, Mark and Mary Lewis—and the strong- and beautiful-hearted Olivia, Ruby, Leah, Sena, and Sadie—I truly could not do without you. (But I think you know that.)

Most of all, I thank my husband, David, and my children Theo, Ian, Isabel, and Mia for making my life so delicious that it's weep-worthy. I love you more.